Foundations in Accountancy

FFM

FOUNDATIONS IN FINANCIAL MANAGEMENT

Welcome to BPP Learning Media's Exam Practice Kit for FFM. In this Exam Practice Kit, which has been reviewed by the **ACCA examining team,** we:

- Include **Do you know?** Checklists to test your knowledge and understanding of topics
- Provide you with **two** mock exams including the Specimen exam
- Provide the **ACCA's exam answers** to the Specimen exam and our explanations as an additional revision aid

FFM PRACTICE KIT

FOR EXAMS IN DECEMBER 2025 AND JUNE 2026

BPP LEARNING MEDIA

Fourteenth edition March 2025

ISBN 9781 5097 4833 4
Previous ISBN 9781 0355 1486 1

e-ISBN 9781 5097 4839 6

British Library Cataloguing-in-Publication Data
A catalogue record for this book
is available from the British Library

Published by

BPP Learning Media Ltd
BPP House, Aldine Place
London W12 8AA

learningmedia.bpp.com

Your learning materials, published by BPP Learning Media Ltd, are printed on paper obtained from traceable sustainable sources.

All our rights reserved. No part of this publication may be reproduced, stored in a retrieval system or transmitted, in any form or by any means, electronic, mechanical, photocopying, recording or otherwise, without the prior written permission of BPP Learning Media.

Contains public sector information licensed under the Open Government licence v3.0.

We are grateful to the Association of Chartered Certified Accountants for permission to reproduce past examination questions.

©
BPP Learning Media Ltd
2025

A note about copyright

Breach of copyright is a form of theft. Without the express permission of BPP you are breaching copyright if you:

- Photocopy our materials

- Print our digital materials in order to share them with or forward them to a third party or use them in any way other than in connection with your BPP studies

- Distribute our digital materials online (including sharing them with third parties and uploading them to websites)

Please note that eBooks are sold on a single user licence basis.

NO AI TRAINING. Unless otherwise agreed in writing, the use of BPP material for the purpose of AI training is not permitted. Any use of this material to "train" generative artificial intelligence (AI) technologies is prohibited, as is providing archived or cached data sets containing such material to another person or entity.

Contents

Page

Finding questions
Question index v

Helping you with your revision ix
Using your BPP Practice and Revision Kit x
Passing the FFM exam xi
Approach to examining the syllabus xii
Tackling multiple choice questions xiii
Tips for using spreadsheets xiv
Using your BPP products xvi

Questions and answers
Questions 5
Answers 117

Appendix: Mathematical tables 235

Exam practice
Mock exam 1 – Specimen Exam
- Questions 239
- Answers 249

Mock exam 2
- Questions 257
- Answers 267

Review form

Question index

	Marks	Time allocation Mins	Page Questions	Answer
Part A: Working capital management				
1 MCQ Question Bank 1	20	24	5	117
2 Question with help: Seats Co	20	24	7	118
3 Pooch Co	20	24	8	119
4 Shoes for You Co	15	18	8	120
5 Victory Co	20	24	9	121
6 Rant Co	20	24	10	122
7 Fleet Co (December 2019 exam)	15	18	10	123
8 Overtrading (June 2020 exam)	5	6	11	124
9 The Kitchen Co	20	24	11	125
10 Brush Co	20	24	12	126
11 Choc Co	15	18	13	127
12 Bulb Co	20	24	14	128
13 All Weather Windows Co	15	18	14	129
14 Z Company	15	18	15	130
15 Drab Company	15	18	16	132
Part B: Cash flows and cash budgeting				
16 MCQ Question Bank 2	20	24	19	133
17 MCQ Question Bank 3	20	24	21	134
18 Question with help: Coolshades Co	20	24	22	135
19 Chocoholics Co	20	24	24	136
20 Health Foods Co	20	24	25	136
21 Tots Co	20	24	26	138
22 Risky Co	15	18	27	139
23 Sporty Co	5	6	27	139
24 Print Co	20	24	28	140
25 Rich Co	15	18	29	141
26 Porkys Co	15	18	30	142
27 Cleared funds	20	24	30	143
28 Larcher Co (December 2019 exam)	20	24	31	144
29 GES Co (June 2020 exam)	20	24	32	148

	Marks	Time allocation Mins	Page Questions	Page Answer
Part C: Managing cash balances				
30 MCQ Question Bank 4	20	24	37	151
31 MCQ Question Bank 5	20	24	38	152
32 MCQ Question Bank 6	20	24	40	153
33 Treasury function	5	6	41	154
34 Cleanly Co	20	24	41	154
35 Waslet Co	5	6	42	155
36 KM Co	15	18	43	155
37 Interest rates (1)	15	18	43	156
38 Interest rates (2)	5	6	43	157
39 Financial intermediaries (1)	5	6	43	157
40 Money market instruments	5	6	43	158
41 Banks and money markets	5	6	44	158
42 Banks and their customers (1)	5	6	44	159
43 Banks and their customers (2)	5	6	44	160
44 Treasury Management	5	6	44	160
45 Curtain Co (Specimen exam)	5	6	44	161
46 Trade credit	5	6	44	161
47 Bills and securities (December 2019 exam)	5	6	45	162
48 Surplus funds	5	6	45	162
49 Appropriate liquidity	5	6	45	163
Part D: Financing decisions				
50 MCQ Question Bank 7	20	24	49	164
51 MCQ Question Bank 8	20	24	50	165
52 MCQ Question Bank 9	20	24	52	165
53 Question with help: Money supply	5	6	54	166
54 Question with help: Commercial banks	5	6	54	166
55 Trob Co (June 2020 exam)	5	6	54	167
56 Retailer Co	20	24	55	168
57 Clean Lens Co	5	6	56	170
58 Caterer Co	20	24	57	170
59 Zimmer Co	15	18	58	172
60 Gym Jam Co	15	18	58	173
61 Sources of finance	15	18	58	173
62 Slim Jim Co	5	6	59	175
63 Convertible loan notes (June 2020 exam)	5	6	59	175
64 Educate Co	15	18	59	176
65 Venture capital (December 2019 exam)	5	6	60	177

QUESTION INDEX

	Marks	Time allocation Mins	Page Questions	Answer
66 Skint Co	5	6	60	177
67 Lease and hire purchase (June 2020 exam)	5	6	60	178
68 Leasing and hire purchase	5	6	60	179
69 Gearing and EPS	15	18	61	180
70 Blimp Company	15	18	61	181
71 Internally generated funds	5	6	62	181
72 New company	15	18	62	182
Part E: Investment decisions				
73 MCQ Question Bank 10	10	12	65	183
74 MCQ Question Bank 11	20	24	66	184
75 Financing concepts	5	6	68	186
76 Question with help: Two capital projects	20	24	69	186
77 Taxi Co	20	24	70	188
78 Quick Freeze Foods Co	20	24	71	189
79 Weavers Co	20	24	71	190
80 Rainbow Co	20	24	72	192
81 Pills Co	20	24	73	192
82 Soke Co	15	18	74	193
83 Silly Filly Co	20	24	74	195
84 Mr Food	20	24	75	195
85 Nippers	20	24	76	197
86 Robo Clean Co	20	24	77	198
87 Go Green Co	20	24	78	199
88 Wicker Co	20	24	79	199
89 Painless Co	20	24	80	201
90 Discounted payback period (December 2019 exam)	5	6	81	202
91 Edgely Co (December 2019 exam)	15	18	81	203
92 Mem Co (June 2020 exam)	15	18	82	206
Part F: Credit management				
93 MCQ Question Bank 12	20	24	87	208
94 Collecting debts	15	18	88	209
95 Doha Co	5	6	89	210
96 Receivables analysis	15	18	89	210
97 Monitoring accounts receivable	5	6	90	211
98 VDO Co	20	24	90	212
99 Noise Co	5	6	91	214
100 Credit control	5	6	91	215

FFM FOUNDATIONS IN FINANCIAL MANAGEMENT

	Marks	Time allocation Mins	Page Questions	Page Answer
101 Trade references (December 2019 exam)	5	6	91	215
102 Expander Co	20	24	92	216
103 Beff Co (June 2020 exam)	15	18	92	217
104 Waste Co	20	24	93	220
105 Jay Co	15	18	94	221
106 Light Co	20	24	94	221
107 Waste Co	5	6	95	222
108 Mr Allan	5	6	95	223
Mixed bank questions				
109 Mixed bank 1	20	24	96	223
110 Mixed bank 2	20	24	97	224
111 Mixed bank 3	20	24	99	225
112 Mixed bank 4	20	24	101	226
113 Mixed bank 5	20	24	103	227
114 Mixed bank 6	20	24	105	228
115 Mixed bank 7	20	24	107	229
116 Mixed bank 8 (December 2019 real exam)	30	36	109	230
117 Mixed bank 9 (June 2020 real exam)	30	36	111	231
Mock exams				
Mock exam 1 (Specimen Exam)	100	120	239	249
Mock exam 2	100	120	257	267

BPP LEARNING MEDIA

Helping you with your revision

BPP Learning Media – ACCA Approved Content Provider

As an ACCA **Approved Content Provider**, BPP Learning Media gives you the **opportunity** to use revision materials reviewed by the ACCA examining team. By incorporating the ACCA examining team's comments and suggestions regarding the depth and breadth of syllabus coverage, the BPP Learning Media Exam Practice Kit provides excellent, **ACCA-approved** support for your revision.

These materials are reviewed by the ACCA examining team. The objective of the review is to ensure that the material properly covers the syllabus and study guide outcomes, used by the examining team in setting the exams, in the appropriate breadth and depth. The review does not ensure that every eventuality, combination or application of examinable topics is addressed by the ACCA Approved Content. Nor does the review comprise a detailed technical check of the content as the Approved Content Provider has its own quality assurance processes in place in this respect.

BPP Learning Media do everything possible to ensure the material is accurate and up to date when sending to print. In the event that any errors are found after the print date, they are uploaded to the following website: www.bpp.com/learningmedia/Errata.

Selecting questions

We provide signposts to help you plan your revision.

- A full **question index**

Attempting mock exams

There are two mock exams that provide practice at coping with the pressures of the exam day. We strongly recommend that you attempt them under exam conditions. **Mock exam 1** is the Specimen Exam. **Mock exam 2** reflects the question styles and syllabus coverage of the exam.

Using your BPP Exam Practice Kit

Aim of this Exam Practice Kit

To provide the practice to help you succeed in the examination for FFM *Foundations in Financial Management*.

To pass the examination you need a thorough understanding in all areas covered by the syllabus and teaching guide.

Recommended approach

- Make sure you are able to answer questions on **everything** specified by the syllabus and teaching guide. You cannot make any assumptions about what questions may come up in your exam. The examining team aims to discourage 'question spotting'.

- Learning is an **active** process. Use the **DO YOU KNOW?** Checklists to test your knowledge and understanding of the topics covered in FFM *Foundations in Financial Management* by filling in the blank spaces. Then check your answers against the **DID YOU KNOW?** Checklists. Do not attempt any questions if you are unable to fill in any of the blanks – go back to your **BPP Interactive Text** and revise first.

- When you are revising a topic, think about the mistakes that you know that you should avoid by writing down **POSSIBLE PITFALLS** at the end of each **DO YOU KNOW?** Checklist.

- Once you have completed the checklists successfully, you should attempt the questions on that topic. Each section has a selection of **MULTIPLE CHOICE QUESTIONS** and **COMPULSORY WRITTEN QUESTIONS**. Make good use of the **HELPING HANDS** provided to help you answer the questions.

- There is a mark allocation for each written question. Each mark carries with it a time allocation of 1.2 minutes (including time for selecting and reading questions). A 15-mark question should therefore be completed in 18 minutes.

- Twenty percent of the exam consists of **multiple choice questions**. You should attempt each bank of MCQs to ensure that you are familiar with their styles and to practise your technique. Ensure you read **Tackling multiple choice questions** on page xiii to get advice on how best to approach them.

- Once you have completed all of the questions in the body of this Exam Practice Kit, you should attempt the **MOCK EXAMS** under examination conditions. Check your answers against our answers to find out how well you did.

Passing the FFM exam

Foundations in Financial Management (FFM) is the only financial management exam in the Foundations in Accountancy suite of qualifications. However, it builds on knowledge you have acquired in earlier exams and some of the terminology may be familiar. Some of the topics are quite challenging but if you take your time and attempt as many questions as you can, you will be prepared for the exam. If you find you are struggling with some of the questions, go back to your BPP Learning Media Interactive Text and revise the topics again before moving on.

Employability and technology

The FFM syllabus considers digital and employability skills to be important when preparing for and taking the FFM exam. Therefore, in FFM, syllabus area G: Employability and technology test the following skills during the exam:

- Using computer technology to efficiently access and manipulate relevant information
- Working on relevant response options, using available functions and technology
- Navigating windows and computer screens to create and amend responses to exam requirements using the appropriate tools
- Presenting data and information effectively using the appropriate tools

These skills can be developed by practising and preparing for the FFM examination, using the learning support content for computer-based examinations available via the practice platform and the ACCA website.

The exam

This is a two-hour computer-based exam. All questions in the exam are compulsory. This means you cannot avoid any topic, but also means that you do not need to waste time in the exam deciding which questions to attempt. There are fifteen MCQs with varying mark allocations and seven long-form questions, again with different marks. This means that the examining team is able to test most of the syllabus at each sitting, and that is what they aim to do. So, you need to have revised right across the syllabus for this exam.

Employability and technology skills will need to be demonstrated during the live examinations.

Revision

This Exam Practice Kit has been reviewed by the FFM examining team and contains questions from the Specimen Exam as mock exam 1, so if you just worked through it to the end you would be very well prepared for the exam. It is important to tackle questions under exam conditions. Allow yourself just the number of minutes shown next to the questions in the index and don't look at the answers until you have finished. Then correct your answer and go back to the Interactive Text for any topic you are really having trouble with. Try the same question again a week later – you will be surprised how much better you are getting. Doing the questions like this will really show you what you know and will make the exam experience less worrying.

Doing the exam

If you have completed your revision you can pass this exam. There are certain points which you must bear in mind:

- Read the question properly, particularly the longer questions. You don't want to waste time doing something that has not been asked for. It is worth reading a longer question through twice.
- Make sure you answer the question actually set, rather than the question you might wish had been set.
- Make sure you present your answer well to give it structure and to make it easier for the marker to identify where marks can be awarded. You can do this by using headings, short paragraphs, spaces between paragraphs and bullet points.
- Don't spend more than the allotted time on each question. If you are having trouble with a question leave it and carry on. You can come back to it at the end. If there is part of a question that you can't do, leave it and do the rest.

Approach to examining the syllabus

FFM is a two-hour computer-based exam. All questions are compulsory. The exam is structured as follows:

The two-hour time allocation **does not** provide for any reading time.

The exam is structured as follows:

	No of marks
Section A	
15 multiple choice questions of 2 marks each	30
Section B	
One 20-mark question	20
Four 5-mark questions	20
Two 15-mark questions	30
	100

CBE Question Practice

Practising as many exam-style questions as possible in the ACCA CBE practice platform will be the key to passing this exam. You must do questions under timed conditions and ensure you produce full answers to the discussion parts as well as doing the calculations.

Also ensure that you attempt all mock exams under exam conditions.

The ACCA have launched a free on-demand resource designed to mirror the live exam experience helping you to become more familiar with the exam format. You can access the platform via the Study Support Resources section of the ACCA website navigating to the CBE question practice section and logging in with your myACCA credentials.

Review Examining Team guidance

On the ACCA website, the study support resources for this exam also include guidance from the examining team for a number of past exams. These examiner reports are useful to review as they highlight some important areas of exam technique.

Tackling multiple choice questions

MCQs are part of all Foundations in Accountancy exams.

The 2-mark MCQs in your exam contain four possible answers. You have to **choose the option that best answers the question**. The incorrect options are called distracters. There is a skill in answering MCQs quickly and correctly. By practising MCQs you can develop this skill, giving you a better chance of passing the exam.

You may wish to follow the approach outlined below, or you may prefer to adapt it.

Step 1	Answer the questions you know first. If you're having difficulty answering a question, move on and come back to tackle it once you've answered all the questions you know. It is often quicker to answer discursive style OT questions first, leaving more time for calculations.
Step 2	Answer all questions. There is no penalty for an incorrect answer in ACCA exams; there is nothing to be gained by leaving an OT question unanswered. If you are stuck on a question, as a last resort, it is worth selecting the option you consider most likely to be correct and moving on. Make a note of the question, so if you have time after you've answered the rest of the questions, you can revisit it.
Step 3	Read the options and see if one matches your own answer. Be careful with numerical questions as the distracters are designed to match answers that incorporate common errors. Check that your calculation is correct. Have you followed the requirement exactly? Have you included every stage of the calculation?
Step 4	You may find that none of the options matches your answer. • Re-read the question to ensure that you understand it and are answering the requirement • Eliminate any obviously wrong answers • Consider which of the remaining answers is the most likely to be correct and select the option
Step 5	If you are still unsure, flag it, and continue to the next question.
Step 6	Revisit unanswered questions. When you come back to a question after a break you often find you are able to answer it correctly straight away. If you are still unsure have a guess. You are not penalised for incorrect answers, so **never leave a question unanswered!**

After extensive practice and revision of MCQs, you may find that you recognise a question when you sit the exam. Be aware that the detail and/or requirement may be different. If the question seems familiar read the requirement and options carefully – do not assume that it is identical.

Tips for using spreadsheets (in a Section B exam question)

1. **Show the marker the logic of the calculations**

   In a **computer-based exam** (CBE) it is important to show the marker where numbers have come from ie it is not sensible to perform the calculations on a calculator and then manually transfer them to the spreadsheet.

   For example, in the following spreadsheet the marker can see that the highlighted calculation in cell G10 is calculated as 1.5% of sales recorded in cell G18 of $1,100,000 because this is what is recorded in the spreadsheet cell (as shown in the first row). This helps the marker follow the logic of calculations and reduces the risk of error.

   [Note that any rounding issues in the calculations can be ignored eg the subtotal in cell G13 is correct because the calculations in cells G9 to G12 are only displayed to the nearest whole number].

G10				fx	=0.015*G18					
	A	B	C	D	E	F	G	H	I	J	K
1		Current situation									
2							$		Workings		
3		Irrecoverable debts					11055		0.01 x $1,105,528		
4		Financing receivables					7421		0.07 x $106,010		
5		Credit controller					11000				
6							29476				
7		With the factor									
8											
9		Financing remaining receivables					1055		0.20 x $75,342 x 0.07 (see workings)		
10		Credit insurance					16500		0.015 x $1,100,000 (see workings)		
11		Cost of advance					3014		0.80 x $75,342 x 0.05		
12		Lost profit					4146		$5,528 x 0.75		
13							24714				
14											
15		Drab Co should employ the services of the factor as the costs are lower by $29,476 - $24,714 = $4,761.									
16											
17		Workings									
18		New sales					1100000		0.995 x $1,105,528		
19		New receivables					75342		25/365 x $1,100,000		
20											

   If the workings are visible in the cell as shown here, then there is **less need to show detailed workings**.

   For example in cell I10, in the previous spreadsheet extract, workings are not needed because the marker will be able to follow the logic by looking at the basis for the calculation in F16.

   It will be **helpful to produce workings where they reduce the likelihood of errors being made if calculations are complex**.

   For example in cell G18, in the previous spreadsheet extract, workings are helpful for new sales and new receivables (G18 and G19), although there is no real need for the narrative in cells I18 and I19 as the marker will be able to follow the logic by looking at the basis for the calculation in cells G18 and G19.

2. **Use spreadsheet short-cuts**

   In a **computer-based exam** (CBE) you can also use useful spreadsheet short-cuts to improve the efficiency of numerical analysis. For FFM useful short-cuts include the ability to calculate totals and also to apply techniques such as Net Present Value (NPV) and Internal Rate of Return (IRR).

Further details are given in the following table.

Function	Guidance and examples
Sum	= SUM(A1:A10) adds all the numbers in spreadsheet cells A1 to A10.
NPV	Net present value is based on future cash flows, assuming that the first cash flow is in one year's time. For example, if the future cash flows from a project arise over 5 years and need to be discounted at 10% then the formula could be as follows: = NPV(0.1,B10:F10) This would give the present value of cash flows from time period 1-5 the cash outflow in time 0 would then need to be deducted to calculate the net present value.
IRR	Internal rate of return is based on future cash flows (looking at cash outflows and inflows) in each year of a project, from time 0 onwards. For example, to identify the internal rate of return of a project arising over 5 years (involving time periods 0-5) the formula could be as follows: = IRR(A10:F10)

Using your BPP products

This Kit gives you the question practice and guidance you need in the exam. Our other products can also help you pass:

- **Interactive Text** introduces and explains the knowledge required for your exam
- **Passcards** provide you with clear topic summaries and exam tips

You can purchase these products by visiting learningmedia.bpp.com

Questions

Do you know? – Working capital management

Check that you can fill in the blanks in the statements below before you attempt any questions. If in doubt, you should go back to your BPP Interactive Text and revise first.

- Working capital is the net difference between a firm's .... and its ....

- The operating cycle measures the period of time between .... and ....

- A situation of excessive working capital is referred to as ....

- A situation where a business tries to do too much with too little long-term capital is called ....

- The optimal quantity of order to minimise inventory costs is called the ....

- JIT stands for .... procurement and involves obtaining goods from suppliers at the latest possible time, thus avoiding the need to carry materials or components inventory.

- Management of trade payables involves seeking ...., ..., and ....

- Methods of paying suppliers include ...., ..., ..., ..., ..., and ....

- Suppliers should be paid just early enough so as to .... or ....

TRY QUESTIONS 1–15

- *Possible pitfalls*

    Write down the mistakes you know you should avoid.

Did you know? – Working capital management

Could you fill in the blanks? The answers are in bold. Use this page for revision purposes as you approach the exam.

- Working capital is the net difference between a firm's **current assets** and its **current liabilities**.
- The operating cycle measures the period of time between **cash outflows for materials etc** and **cash inflows from sales or receivables**.
- A situation of excessive working capital is referred to as **over-capitalisation**.
- A situation where a business tries to do too much with too little long-term capital is called **overtrading**.
- The optimal quantity of order to minimise inventory costs is called the **economic order quantity**.
- JIT stands for **Just-In-Time** procurement and involves obtaining goods from suppliers at the latest possible time, thus avoiding the need to carry materials or components inventory.
- Management of trade payables involves seeking **satisfactory credit from suppliers, extended credit during cash shortages,** and **good relations with key suppliers**.
- Methods of paying suppliers include **cash, cheque, banker's draft, standing order, direct debit,** and **electronic funds transfer**.
- Suppliers should be paid just early enough so as to **avoid costly penalties** or **to secure worthwhile discounts**.

TRY QUESTIONS 1–15

- *Possible pitfalls*
    - **Not looking at working capital as a whole: controlling working capital means controlling costs.**

1 MCQ Question Bank 1 — 24 mins

1.1 Which of the following is the Quick, or Acid Test, Ratio?

- ○ Current assets/Current liabilities
- ○ Current assets less inventories/Current liabilities
- ○ Profit/Revenue
- ○ Debt/Equity

(2 marks)

1.2 If a business has excessive current assets compared to current liabilities it is said to be:

- ○ Overtrading
- ○ Overvalued
- ○ Overstated
- ○ Over-capitalised

(2 marks)

1.3 The following information is available for Product 7TY which is sold in packs of 125 kg.

	Maximum	Minimum
Usage levels	250 kg per day	25 kg per day
Lead times	7 days	3 days

Calculate the maximum inventory level for Product 7TY.

- ○ 175 kg
- ○ 750 kg
- ○ 1,750 kg
- ○ 1,800 kg

(2 marks)

1.4 Getting things done right first time is the key principle of:

- ○ Lean production
- ○ Just-in-time procurement
- ○ Total quality management
- ○ Quality circles

(2 marks)

1.5 The following extracts are available from Peter Co's statement of financial position.

	$
Non-current assets	100,000
Inventory	12,000
Receivables	8,000
Payables	2,500
Overdraft	17,500
Long-term bank loan	75,000

Calculate Peter Co's working capital.

- ○ Zero
- ○ $25,000
- ○ $40,000
- ○ $100,000

(2 marks)

1.6 The following ratios are available from the accounts of Pop Co.

Receivables payment period = 34 days
Finished goods inventory turnover period = 23 days
Raw materials inventory turnover period = 3 days
Payables payment period = 28 days

Calculate the length of Pop Co's cash cycle.

○ 6 days
○ 26 days
○ 32 days
○ 88 days

(2 marks)

1.7 The following ratios are available for Loopy Co.

Inventory turnover period 170 days
Payables payment period 35 days
Receivables collection period 22 days

Calculate the length of Loopy Co's working capital cycle.

○ 157 days
○ 183 days
○ 165 days
○ 227 days

(2 marks)

1.8 The following data has been extracted from Blind Co's accounting system.

Average inventory (finished goods) $275,500
Average inventory (60% complete) $85,000
Sales $2,750,000
Cost of sales $2,250,000

Calculate Blind Co's average production period.

○ 14 days
○ 23 days
○ 45 days
○ 75 days

(2 marks)

1.9 Annual demand for Product QI is 65 units. Administration costs of placing each order is $1,000 regardless of the number of units purchased. The cost of holding each unit in inventory for a year is $10.

What is the Economic Order Quantity (EOQ) of Product QI?

○ 5 units
○ 18 units
○ 76 units
○ 114 units

(2 marks)

1.10 Which of the following shows the correct way to calculate a company's working capital cycle?

○ Inventory turnover period + receivables collection period + payables payment period
○ Inventory turnover period − receivables collection period − payables payment period
○ Inventory turnover period − receivables collection period + payables payment period
○ Inventory turnover period + receivables collection period − payables payment period

(2 marks)

(Total = 20 marks)

2 Question with help: Seats Co — 24 mins

Seats Co manufactures and sells two types of chair, the Comfyseat and the Bigseat. The Comfyseat uses less expensive materials, but has a lower profit margin than the Bigseat.

	Comfyseat	Bigseat
Projected annual sales volume	25,000	25,000
Selling price per unit	$100	$245
Contribution as a % mark up on variable costs	25%	40%
Variable cost elements breakdown in %		
Raw material	40%	50%
Direct labour	30%	25%
Variable overheads	30%	25%
	100%	100%
Working capital statistics		
Average receivables collection period	6 weeks	8 weeks
Average raw material inventory holding period	4 weeks	6 weeks
Average work-in-progress holding period (See Notes 1 and 2)	4 weeks	4 weeks
Average finished goods inventory holding period	3 weeks	3 weeks
Average raw material supplier credit received	5 weeks	5 weeks
Average period of credit on overhead expenses	6 weeks	3 weeks
Average period of credit on direct labour	1 week	1 week

Notes

1. All raw materials are input at the start of the production process.
2. Work-in-progress is valued at the entire raw material content and 40% of the labour and variable overhead elements.
3. During the year, production volume is expected to equal sales volume, which is anticipated to be spread evenly over the year.

Required

Calculate the estimated working capital finance required to the nearest $'000, assuming a 52 week year.

(20 marks)

Approaching the answer

Use this answer plan to construct your answer if you are stuck.

For both Comfyseat and Bigseat:

- Work out sales
- Work out costs, bearing margins in mind
- Work out current assets

Then carry out main calculation which should contain the following elements

- Raw materials
- Work in progress, calculating material, labour and overheads separately
- Finished goods, calculating material, labour and overheads separately
- Receivables
- Current liabilities, calculating material, labour and overheads separately

FFM FOUNDATIONS IN FINANCIAL MANAGEMENT

3 Pooch Co — 24 mins

Pooch Co makes and sells pet care products. The following projected data for the next year is available.

Sales	$2,200,000

Cost as percentage of sales

Raw materials	15%
Direct labour	20%
Variable production overheads	11%
Fixed production overheads	10%
Other costs	12%

Working capital statistics

Average raw material holding period	4 weeks
Average work-in-progress (WIP) holding period	2 weeks
Average finished goods holding period	4 weeks
Average receivables collection period	6 weeks
Average payables payment period on:	
Raw materials	4 weeks
Direct labour	1 week
Variable production overheads	8 weeks
Fixed production overheads	5 weeks
Other costs	12 weeks

Other relevant information

- All finished goods, inventory and WIP values include raw materials, direct labour, variable production overheads and apportioned fixed production overhead costs.
- Assume WIP is 75% complete as to materials and 50% complete as to direct labour, variable production overheads and fixed production overheads.
- Assume there are 52 weeks in one year.
- Assume that production and sales volumes are the same.

Required

Calculate the estimated average working capital required by Pooch Co for the year, showing clearly all necessary workings.

Note. All workings should be in $'000. **(20 marks)**

4 Shoes for You Co — 18 mins

You are an accounting technician working at Shoes for You Co, a company that manufactures and distributes a range of fashion shoes. All shoes are made at the company's factory in the country of Bushai, where materials and labour have historically been very cheap. The shoes are then exported to the UK where they are sold to a number of retail outlets.

All costs are incurred in Bushai's unit of currency. All materials are paid for in cash at the time of purchase. Production staff are paid their wages daily in cash. They have not had a pay increase in the last year. All other overheads, production and sales, are on credit.

All sales are to UK customers and are on credit. They are, therefore, invoiced (and amounts are received) in £ sterling. Any finance needed for the business is also obtained from the UK.

You have estimated the figures below for the coming year. Sterling has been used for all figures so as to avoid any distortion caused by high inflation in Bushai.

	$
Revenue	2,500,000
Average receivables	410,000
Materials purchases	630,000
Production staff wages	450,000
Other production overheads	350,000
Sales overheads	320,000
Net profit margin	30%
Average inventory	
Finished goods	325,000
Work in progress (65% complete)	195,000
Raw materials	133,000
Average payables	73,000

The economy in Bushai has recently become unstable. This has led to a rapid increase in inflation levels over the last year, from 10% at the beginning of the year to 25% at the end of the year. Interest rates are controlled by Bushai's central bank. Inflation in the UK has remained stable at about 4% per annum.

Required

Calculate the cash operating cycle. **(15 marks)**

5 Victory Co — 24 mins

Victory Co is a retailer, specialising in vitamin supplements and health foods claimed to enhance performance. One of the products purchased by Victory Co for resale is a performance enhancing vitamin drink called 'Buzz'.

Victory Co sells a fixed quantity of 200 bottles of Buzz per week. The estimated storage costs for a bottle of Buzz are $2.00 per annum per bottle.

Delivery from Victory Co's existing supplier takes two weeks and the purchase price per bottle delivered is $20. The current supplier charges a fixed $75 order processing charge for each order, regardless of the order size.

Victory Co has recently been approached by another supplier of Buzz with the following offer:

(1) The cost to Victory Co per bottle will be $19 each.

(2) There will be a fixed order processing charge of $250 regardless of order size.

(3) Delivery time will be one week.

(4) Victory Co estimates that due to packaging differences, the storage cost per bottle will be $1.80 per annum per bottle.

Required

(a) Assuming Victory Co continues to purchase from the existing supplier, calculate:

    (i) Economic order quantity
    (ii) Reorder level
    (iii) Total cost of stocking Buzz for one year to the nearest $ **(13 marks)**

(b) Calculate the economic order quantity if Victory Co changes to the new supplier and determine if it would be financially viable to change to this new supplier. **(7 marks)**

(Total = 20 marks)

6 Rant Co   24 mins

Rant Co manufactures and distributes plasma screen televisions to a number of electric retailers. Due to the increased popularity of these products, growth has been rapid and the Financial Director (FD) of the company is concerned that the company is overtrading. Revenue has increased by 250% over the last year, and non-current assets have increased by 75%. The bank overdraft limit of $3 million has been exceeded on five occasions in the last year, culminating in a recent threat by the bank to withdraw the facility altogether.

Rant Co is a largely family-owned company, with twelve shareholders in total. Whilst the long-term plan involves making a rights issue in two years' time, none of the current shareholders are in a position to inject new capital into the company at present. Neither do they wish to issue new shares outside the current group of shareholders, as they do not want to lose their collective control of the company.

Some preliminary analysis has revealed that receivables are increasing rapidly and raw material inventory days have gone from 30 days to 55 days. The FD is concerned that these inventory levels are so high. They have asked you, an accounting technician, to assist in reviewing them.

One of the key costs of making a plasma television is the screen. These screens are bought in ready-made at a cost of $250 per unit. It costs $150 to place an order for these screens, irrespective of the number of units ordered. At current sales levels, which are expected to stabilise now, 150,000 screens are needed per annum. The cost of holding one screen in stock for one year is $15.

Required

(a) Briefly describe the symptoms of overtrading. Conclude whether Rant Co is overtrading, giving reasons for your conclusion. **(10 marks)**

(b) Explain how the economic order quantity (EOQ) model can assist in reducing inventory costs AND the assumptions it is based on. **(6 marks)**

(c) Calculate the EOQ for screens using the data contained in the question. **(4 marks)**

(Total = 20 marks)

7 Fleet Co (December 2019 exam)   18 mins

This scenario relates to three requirements.

Fleet Co is a wholesaler. It purchases shoes from an overseas supplier on 90 days credit and sells them to retailers in its home market.

Fleet Co sells 800,000 pairs of shoes each year to retailers and these sales are spread evenly over the year. All retailers are given 30 days credit.

The overseas supplier loads the shoes into a shipping container and the shoes are transported by sea to Fleet Co's warehouse. Fleet Co's cost of storing a pair of shoes for one year is $0.125. Fleet Co's cost of providing and transporting the shipping container is $500 per order.

Fleet Co currently uses the economic order quantity (EOQ) model to calculate its optimal order size.

The overseas supplier has offered to reduce the price of shoes by 2.5% to $4.875 a pair if Fleet Co orders a minimum of 100,000 pairs of shoes per order. There is enough room in the shipping containers to accommodate this order size and shipping cost per container will be unchanged.

Fleet Co's chief executive officer (CEO) has been advised that increasing the order size for shoes will lengthen its working capital cycle and affect its liquidity. The CEO is not financially qualified and does not understand what this means.

(a) Calculate the economic order quantity for Fleet Co. **(2 marks)**

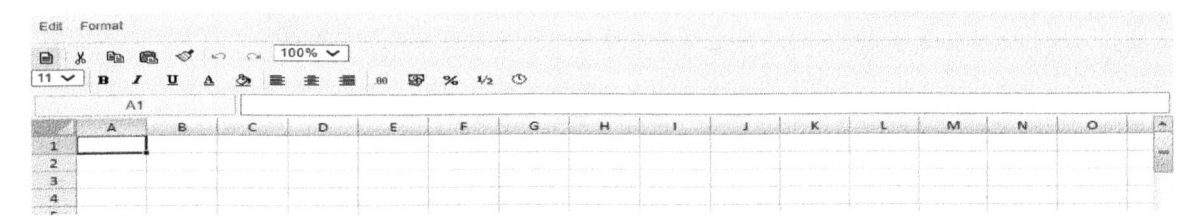

(b) Calculate and conclude whether Fleet Co should except the offer to purchase 100,000 pairs of shoes per order. **(7 marks)**

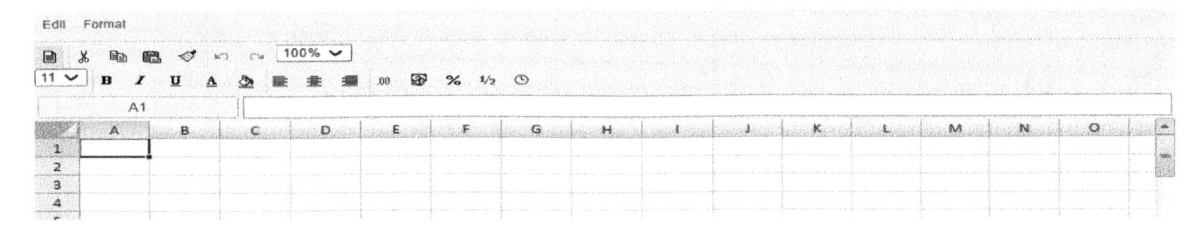

(c) Explain the working capital cycle and discuss the effect of increased order size on Fleet Co's working capital cycle and liquidity. **(6 marks)**

(Total = 15 marks)

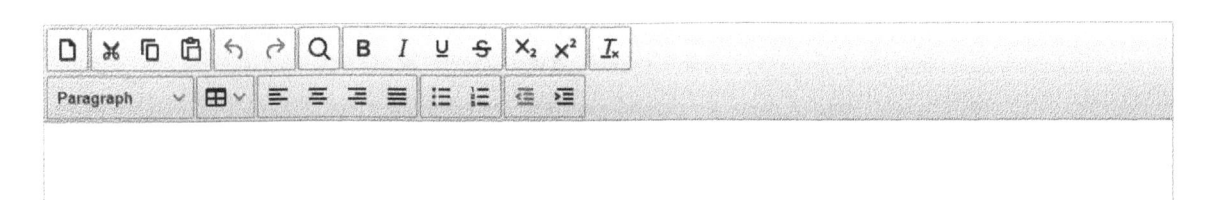

8 Overtrading (June 2020 exam) — 6 mins

Define overtrading and explain the symptoms associated with overtrading. **(5 marks)**

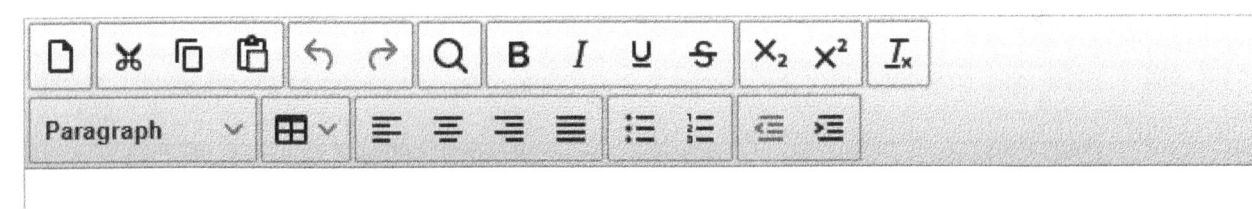

9 The Kitchen Co — 24 mins

The Kitchen Co is an innovation company set up two years ago by its key shareholder and director, Brian Geek. It currently has a range of about two thousand kitchen products on the market, the most successful of which is a gadget called the 'Fish Eye'. This is a revolutionary utensil, the size of a kitchen knife, which plugs into the power supply and is used on cooked fish to identify any fish bones that need to be removed prior to serving. The 'Fish Eye' exploded on to the market two years ago, as the company's introductory product, and sales have continued to grow rapidly ever since.

One of Brian Geek's friends has warned him about the high incidence of overtrading for new businesses selling high demand, innovative products. Brian Geek is therefore concerned that The Kitchen Co's financial position be carefully monitored. Its turnover has increased by 100% over the last year, and its trade receivables and inventories have doubled. The company's current ratio has fallen over the last year from a ratio of 3:1 to a ratio of 2.5:1. The industry norm is 2:1. The company has a $1 million overdraft facility on its current account from its bank. Whilst the company has never used even half of its limit, it often relies on the overdraft facility to finance its working capital.

Required

(a) Explain the term 'overtrading'. **(3 marks)**

(b) Briefly discuss whether The Kitchen Co is overtrading. **(6 marks)**

(c) One of the key components used to make the 'Fish Eye' is component X, which is imported from overseas. Brian Geek wants to manage his inventory levels of component X more efficiently. He wants to make sure that he can meet demand for production and sales whilst at the same time avoiding excessive inventory levels. The following information relates to component X:

Cost of component X	$24 per unit
Usage per day	1,000 units
Maximum lead time	20 days
Minimum lead time	10 days
Average lead time	15 days
Cost of ordering	$650 per order
Holding costs	$2 per unit per annum

Usage per day is always constant. The re-order level is set at the maximum expected requirement in lead time plus 25%.

Required

(i) Calculate the re-order level; **(4 marks)**

(ii) Calculate the Economic Order Quantity (EOQ).

Note. You should assume that there are 48 working weeks in the year and five working days in each of the weeks. **(3 marks)**

(iii) Calculate the maximum inventory level for component X using the information provided. **(4 marks)**

(Total = 20 marks)

10 Brush Co — 24 mins

Brush Co is a recently established company specialising in the manufacture of a range of drugs for the pharmaceutical industry. Two brothers, Thomas and Gerald Broom, formed the company and have just finished the first year of business. Sales are made to customers on 60-day payment terms and all suppliers offer 30 days' credit. All of the raw materials purchased by Brush Co only last for a limited time. Therefore, it is the company's policy that such chemicals are used within 75 days of purchase.

Whilst the brothers are experienced in the field of pharmaceuticals, they are finding it difficult to understand some of the financial matters associated with running a company.

You are employed in the company as an accounting technician and have collated the following information for the last year.

	$
Sales	1,500,000
Raw material purchases	378,000
Direct labour costs	240,000
Variable production overheads	215,000
Apportioned fixed production overheads	185,000
Average receivables	356,000
Average inventories:	
Finished goods	210,000
Work-in-progress (WIP)	58,000

	$
Raw materials	82,000
Average payables:	
Materials	45,000
Variable and fixed overheads	75,000
Direct labour	9,000

Other relevant information

- All finished goods inventory and WIP values include raw materials, direct labour, variable production overheads and apportioned fixed production overhead costs.
- Assume WIP is 70% complete.
- Assume there are 365 days in one year.
- Assume that production and sales volumes are the same.
- The length of the average working capital cycle in this type of business is 90 days.

Required

(a) Calculate Brush Co's working capital cycle (cash operating cycle) in days. All workings should be rounded to the nearest complete day. **(14 marks)**

(b) From your calculations in part (a), identify **two** possible concerns that Brush Co's chief accountant may have about the company's working capital cycle. **(6 marks)**

(Total = 20 marks)

11 Choc Co — 18 mins

Choc Co is a recently established company in the confectionery business. It has a keen and flexible workforce. It makes a range of organic chocolate bars. Its main customers are supermarkets, petrol stations and newsagents. The purchase patterns of Choc Co's customers vary slightly. The supermarkets tend to order large amounts at varying times throughout the year. The petrol stations make regular weekly orders for smaller amounts and the newsagents have no regular pattern for their order size or frequency at all. The company's chocolate bars are becoming increasingly popular, with demand peaking at 5,000,000 bars over the last year.

The two key ingredients for Choc Co's products are cocoa and sugar. Both of these ingredients are bought from different suppliers. Over the last year, the company has used 100,000 kg of sugar for its production. It currently orders 5,000 kg of sugar at a time, at regular intervals throughout the year. The cost of placing an order is $35 and the cost of storing 1 kg of sugar is $0.20 per annum. Choc Co does not hold any safety inventories of sugar since it has always found its supplier to be very quick and reliable when Choc Co places an order.

Cocoa is the more expensive of the two ingredients; therefore Choc Co's purchasing policy in relation to this has already been established. It is bought from a very reliable supplier with whom it has good relationships. The current ordering policy for cocoa (ie total ordering and holding costs) costs the company in the region of $10,000 per annum.

Required

(a) Calculate the annual cost of the current ordering policy for sugar. Ignore finance costs. **(5 marks)**

(b) Calculate the annual cost if the economic order quantity is used to determine the optimum order size for sugar. Ignore finance costs. **(5 marks)**

(c) Describe three costs associated with running out of sugar. **(5 marks)**

(Total = 15 marks)

12 Bulb Co — 24 mins

Bulb Co is a company specialising in the manufacture of a large range of light bulbs. Over the last six months, the business has begun to expand, with an increase in sales of 20% compared to the same six month period last year. This expansion has given rise to a need for increased working capital. The company has very little cash at present, and needs to accurately ascertain its working capital requirements for the next year. The following forecast figures are available.

Turnover for the year	$65,000,000
Costs as a percentage of sales:	
Direct materials	20%
Direct labour	25%
Variable overheads	15%
Fixed overheads and selling and distribution costs	23%

The following average time periods are expected:

(1) Inventories

Raw materials are held in inventory for eight weeks and finished goods are held for six weeks. All finished goods inventories and work-in-progress inventories include direct materials, direct labour and variable overhead costs. Assume that goods remain in work in progress for two weeks and are 75% complete as regards direct materials and 50% complete as regards direct labour and variable overheads.

(2) Accounts receivable

All customers are credit customers and take on average nine weeks to pay.

(3) Accounts payable

The credit taken is four weeks for all expense categories.

Required

(a) Calculate the working capital requirement of Bulb Co for the next year. Assume that there are 52 working weeks in the year. **(14 marks)**

(b) Bulb Co has decided that it should apply to the bank for an overdraft or short term loan to cover the increase in its working capital requirements over the next year. Having run its business with very little debt for many years now, it is unsure what factors the bank will take into account when deciding whether to lend to the company.

Describe **three** factors that the bank will consider when deciding whether to grant this loan or overdraft to Bulb Co. **(6 marks)**

(Total = 20 marks)

13 All Weather Windows Co — 18 mins

All Weather Windows Co manufactures and fits windows for domestic customers. The company needs to forecast its working capital requirements for the year ahead. The following figures are available:

Sales revenue	$7,600,000
Costs as percentage of sales revenue	
Raw materials	22%
Direct labour	18%
Variable production overheads	7%
Apportioned fixed production overheads	12%
Other costs	5%
Working capital statistics	
Average raw material holding period	6 weeks
Average work-in-progress (WIP) holding period	3 weeks

QUESTIONS

Average finished goods holding period	5 weeks
Average trade receivables' collection period	2.5 weeks
Average trade payables' payment period on:	
Raw materials	8 weeks
Direct labour	2 weeks
Variable production overheads	4 weeks
Fixed production overheads	6 weeks
Other costs	3 weeks

Other relevant information

(1) All finished goods inventory and WIP values include raw materials, direct labour, variable production overheads and apportioned fixed production overhead costs.

(2) Assume WIP is 80% complete as to materials; 75% complete as to direct labour; 50% complete as to variable production overheads and fixed production overheads.

(3) Assume there are 52 weeks in one year.

(4) Assume that production and sales volumes are the same.

(5) All workings should be in $'000, to the nearest $'000.

Required

Calculate the estimated average working capital required by All Weather Windows Co for the year, showing all necessary workings. **(15 marks)**

14 Z Company — 18 mins

Z Company is a courier company based in the centre of a large city. At the moment it pays all salaries, all suppliers and all other expenses by cheque, except for some items paid for out of petty cash.

The managing director has been advised that the company should consider other methods of making payments to suppliers, particularly in view of the fact that the company is growing and now employs more people than in the past.

The main expenditures of the company, except for dividends and taxation, are employees' salaries, accommodation rental costs, utility bills (such as electricity, gas and phone bills) and payments to suppliers. Rental costs are revised annually.

The methods of payment the company has been advised to consider are direct debit, standing order and BACS.

Required

(a) Briefly explain why Z Company should consider significantly reducing its use of cheques for payments. **(4 marks)**

(b) Suggest, with reasons, which method of payment would probably be appropriate for:

 (i) Payments of monthly salaries to employees
 (ii) Payments of utility bills
 (iii) Payments to other suppliers
 (iv) Payments of rent, which occur every six months. **(9 marks)**

(c) Explain briefly why the use of CHAPS is unlikely to be appropriate for Z Company as a regular method of making payments. **(2 marks)**

(Total = 15 marks)

15 Drab Company — 18 mins

The financial manager of Drab Company is worried about the company's cash position. There are occasions during the year when the company has had insufficient cash to pay its suppliers on time, so that payments are delayed – and suppliers complain and occasionally threaten to stop supplying the company.

The financial manager has been given two suggestions to improve the company's cash position.

Suggestions:

(1) The company should improve its management of accounts payables and accounts receivable, because better management will improve the working capital cycle and cash flow.

(2) The company should set up a company credit card arrangement with its bank, and issue credit cards to senior management and sales representatives.

Required

(a) Describe the relevance of trade payables and trade receivables to the working capital cycle, and suggest how better management of trade payables and trade receivables should help to improve this cycle and the company's cash position. **(9 marks)**

(b) Comment briefly on the advantages and problems with having a company credit card for expenditures by senior management and sales representatives. **(6 marks)**

(Total = 15 marks)

Do you know? – Cash flows and cash budgeting

Check that you can fill in the blanks in the statements below before you attempt any questions. If in doubt, you should go back to your BPP Interactive Text and revise first.

- There are four components of a time series: ...., ..., ... and ....

- One method of finding the trend is by the use of ....

- When finding the moving average of an even number of results, a second moving average has to be calculated so that trend values can relate to specific actual figures.

- Seasonal variations can be estimated using the .... (Y = T + S + R) or the .... (Y = T × S × R).

- Cash transactions take different forms. Capital items relate to .... Revenue items relate to ....

- Cash flow can be defined in many ways. Net cash flow is the .... Operational cash flow is the .... Priority cash flows do not relate to trade, but are vital to keep the company afloat. Operational flows can be improved by better management of ...., ... and .... (eg ...., ..., ...).

- Nearly all businesses' accounts are prepared not on a cash basis, but on an .... basis. Under the .... or .... concept, revenue and profits are matched with associated costs and expenses in the same account.

- Cash budgets are prepared on a .... basis.

- A cash budget is a detailed prediction of cash receipts, payments and balances over a planning period. It is formally adopted as part of the .... or .... for the period. The budget should indicate the highest and lowest .... in a period as well as the .... at the end of the period.

- A rolling cash budget is a budget that is ....

- There is more than one way of preparing a budget.

    – A forecast can be prepared of cash receipts and payments, and net cash flows (...............based forecasts). These include .... and .... forecasts. They can be used for control reporting.

    – Alternatively, a cash surplus or .... requirement can be prepared by constructing a forecasted .... These are used for long-term strategic analysis.

- Cleared funds forecasts are used for short-term planning. They take .... delays into account.

- If a shortage of cash is predicted, the following actions might be taken to deal with the problem

    – ....
    – ....
    – ....
    – ....
    – ....
    – ....

- A long-term business plan should show:

    – ....   – ....   – ....
    – ....   – ....

TRY QUESTIONS 16–29

Did you know? – Cash flows and cash budgeting

Could you fill in the blanks? The answers are in bold. Use this page for revision purposes as you approach the exam.

- There are four components of a time series: **trend, seasonal variations, cyclical variations** and **random variations**.
- One method of finding the trend is by the use of **moving averages**.
- When finding the moving average of an even number of results, a second moving average has to be calculated so that trend values can relate to specific actual figures.
- Seasonal variations can be estimated using the **additive model** (Y = T + S + R) or the **multiplicative model** (Y = T × S × R).
- Cash transactions take different forms. Capital items relate to **the long term functioning of the business**. Revenue items relate to **day-to-day operations**.
- Cash flow can be defined in many ways. Net cash flow is the **total change in a company's cash balances over a period of time**. Operational cash flow is the **net cash flow arising over a period from trading operations**. Priority cash flows do not relate to trade, but are vital to keep the company afloat. Operational flows can be improved by better management of **inventories, receivables,** and **payables** (eg **fewer inventories, collecting money earlier, paying later**).
- Nearly all businesses' accounts are prepared not on a cash basis, but on an **accruals** basis. Under the **accruals** or **matching** concept, revenue and profits are matched with associated costs and expenses in the same account.
- Cash budgets are prepared on a **cash** basis.
- A cash budget is a detailed prediction of cash receipts, payments and balances over a planning period. It is formally adopted as part of the **business plan** or **master budget** for the period. The budget should indicate the highest and lowest **cash balance** in a period as well as the **cash balance** at the end of the period.
- A rolling cash budget is a budget that is **continually updated**.
- There is more than one way of preparing a budget.
    - A forecast can be prepared of cash receipts and payments, and net cash flows (**cash flow** based forecasts). These include **cash budgets** and **short-term cleared funds** forecasts. They can be used for control reporting.
    - Alternatively, a cash surplus or **funding** requirement can be prepared by constructing a forecasted **statement of financial position**. These are used for long-term strategic analysis.
- Cleared funds forecasts are used for short-term planning. They take **clearance** delays into account.
- If a shortage of cash is predicted, the following actions might be taken to deal with the problem
    - **Overdraft facilities arranged**
    - **Short-term loans taken out**
    - **Non-current asset purchases postponed**
    - **Non-current asset sales brought forward**
    - **Collection from customers speeded up**
    - **Payments to suppliers delayed**
- A long-term business plan should show:
    - **Long-term objectives**
    - **Projected cash flows**
    - **Projected profits**
    - **Capital expenditure plans**
    - **Statement of financial position forecasts**

TRY QUESTIONS 16–29

16 MCQ Question Bank 2 — 24 mins

16.1 Which of the following statements correctly describes capital items?

- ○ Items which relate to the long-term running of the business.
- ○ Items which relate to the day-to-day running of the business.
- ○ Items which are part of the business' working capital.
- ○ Items which are unusual, for example costs of closing down part of the business. **(2 marks)**

16.2 The accounts technician of Good Co has prepared the following cash flow.

	$
Sales	325,000
Opening receivables	(23,500)
Closing receivables	17,500
Bank loan received	125,000
Cash in	444,000
Purchases	193,500
Opening payables	27,000
Closing payables	(12,500)
Depreciation	(26,000)
Cash out	182,000
Cash flow	262,000

Has the technician calculated the cash flow correctly?

- ○ Yes, the total of $262,000 is correct.
- ○ No, the total cash flow should be $137,000.
- ○ No, the total cash flow should be $248,000.
- ○ No, the total cash flow should be $277,000. **(2 marks)**

16.3 Which of the following budgets is **NOT** prepared using the accruals concept?

- ○ The production budget
- ○ The capital budget
- ○ The cash budget
- ○ The sales budget **(2 marks)**

16.4 Which of the following would be classed as a priority cash flow?

- ○ Payments to suppliers
- ○ Payments from customers
- ○ Bank charges
- ○ Tax payments **(2 marks)**

16.5 The accountant of Hot Co needs a short-term forecast that shows the amount of money available in the business bank account. Which type of forecast would you recommend?

- ○ Cash book forecast
- ○ Cleared funds forecast
- ○ Statement of financial position forecast
- ○ Statement of profit or loss forecast **(2 marks)**

16.6 Which of the following could cause differences between a company's cash flow forecast and its actual cash flows?

(i) Poor forecasting techniques
(ii) Inflation
(iii) Loss of a major customer
(iv) Changes in interest rates

○ All of them
○ (i), (ii) and (iv) only
○ (i), (iii) and (iv) only
○ (ii) and (iii) only (2 marks)

16.7 Which of the following indicates a weak forecasting system?

○ Sales figures which change from month to month
○ The use of modelling software such as spreadsheets
○ Receivables figures which are based on assumptions
○ Purchases figures which do not change over a number of months (2 marks)

16.8 Charlie Co manufactures a product known as a JigJog. Each JigJog sells for $150 and costs $95 to make. What is the margin Charlie Co makes on each JigJog sold?

○ 37%
○ 55%
○ 58%
○ 63% (2 marks)

16.9 Which of the following items will be excluded from a cash forecast?

○ A tax payment that relates to profits in a previous accounting period
○ A payment for a capital purchase
○ Interest received
○ Depreciation (2 marks)

16.10 As the accounts technician of LPG Co, you have been asked to help on the production of the company's forecasted cash flow for 20X8.

The following extracts from the financial statements are available.

STATEMENT OF FINANCIAL POSITION

	20X7 $	20X8 $
Non-current assets	7,500	10,275

STATEMENT OF PROFIT OR LOSS

	20X7 $	20X8 $
Depreciation	2,000	1,500

Using the information above, what is the cash outflow in respect of non-current assets?

○ $775
○ $1,275
○ $4,275
○ $4,775 (2 marks)

(Total = 20 marks)

17 MCQ Question Bank 3 — 24 mins

17.1 Which of the following items should be included on a cash flow report?

(i) Interest payments
(ii) Receipts from a share issue
(iii) Depreciation
(iv) Dividend payment

○ All of them
○ (i) and (ii) only
○ (i), (ii) and (iv) only
○ (ii) and (iv) only (2 marks)

17.2 A cash payment to purchase new machinery should be classed as a(n):

○ Operational cash flow
○ Discretionary cash flow
○ Priority cash flow
○ Unnecessary cash flow (2 marks)

17.3 Tosh Co manufactures a range of toys for children. On average, raw materials sit in the storeroom for five days once delivered before moving to the factory. The toys take a few hours to make and the finished goods are then moved to the warehouse prior to despatch to customers. The finished toys usually remain in the warehouse for ten days before being delivered to customer shops. The company has negotiated payment terms with its suppliers of 25 days and its customers pay within 20 days.

What is the length of Tosh Co's cash cycle?

○ 5 days
○ 10 days
○ 20 days
○ 60 days (2 marks)

17.4 Which of the following is **NOT** classed as working capital?

○ Overdraft
○ Trade payables
○ Interest payable
○ Bank loan (2 marks)

17.5 Which of the following correctly describes the accruals basis of accounting?

○ The effects of transactions and other events are recognised when they occur.
○ The effects of transactions and other events are recognised when the related cash payment is made or cash receipt is received.
○ Financial statements must take into account future transactions and events if they are likely to occur.
○ Financial statements must reflect all transactions and events in a manner which is true and fair. (2 marks)

17.6 Delaying payments to suppliers whilst speeding up payment collection from customers is known as:

○ Borrowing and lending
○ Lagging and shorting
○ Pulling and pushing
○ Leading and lagging (2 marks)

17.7 Product YTW costs $55 to make and is sold for $65. What is the mark up on Product YTW?

- ○ 10%
- ○ 15%
- ○ 18%
- ○ 85%

(2 marks)

17.8 Which of the following correctly describes float?

- ○ The amount of money left in a business' premises overnight.
- ○ The amount of money tied up between the time a payment is initiated and the cleared funds being available in a business's bank account.
- ○ The amount of money available to a business as cleared funds.
- ○ The amount of money held up in the banking system in the form of cheques deposited by a business.

(2 marks)

17.9 The following information is available for Desert Co.

Sales in January 20X9 are expected to be $10,000 and this will increase by $1,500 per month. 75% of customers pay cash in the month of sale with 25% paying the following month.

Purchases in January are expected to be $8,000 and this will increase by $500 per month. Desert Co pays its suppliers two months after purchase.

Wages and salaries are fixed at $1,000 per month and are paid a month in arrears.

Calculate Desert Co's forecasted cash flow for April 20X9.

- ○ $2,875
- ○ $3,625
- ○ $3,875
- ○ $4,625

(2 marks)

17.10 The forecasted Statement of Financial Position of Donn Co indicates a surplus of equity and liabilities over assets. This means the company should plan for:

- ○ A cash surplus
- ○ A cash deficit
- ○ A share issue
- ○ A sale of its assets

(2 marks)

(Total = 20 marks)

18 Question with help: Coolshades Co — 24 mins

Coolshades Co is a prosperous, private company whose five directors each own 20% of the share capital. The company is involved in the distribution of a range of branded sunglasses to various retail outlets. Since its foundation three years ago, the company has grown rapidly. To date, the critical success factors have been the ability to offer a quality product at a competitive price and to guarantee 24 hour delivery to customers.

To date, the company's records have been maintained by a bookkeeper, with the auditors preparing the half-yearly accounts for management review. The bookkeeper has recently retired and you have been recruited as the accounting technician. The role has been expanded to incorporate the preparation of monthly management accounts.

Although Coolshades Co is profitable, the company's bank is increasingly concerned about the current liquidity position and the management of working capital. Indications are that the profitability of the company is being significantly eroded, despite the growth in sales.

At a recent meeting with the board of directors, you have been given a series of notes in order to prepare a forecast cash flow for the next three months commencing 1 July 20X1.

Notes

1. Opening receivables are $590,000, of which $307,000 will be paid in July and the remainder in August.

2. Sales for the six months to 31 December are a total of $1,500,000.

3. 10% of sales revenue are for cash, the remainder are on credit. 4% of credit sales end up as bad debts. 50% of customers pay in the month following sale and the remainder pay in the subsequent month.

4. The gross profit percentage is 30%.

5. Purchases are obtained in the month prior to sale, and the related suppliers are paid in the subsequent month (ie July purchases are paid for in August).

6. Opening payables which will be paid in July are:

Trade payables	$210,000
Distribution expense payables	$35,000

7. Distribution expenses for this period will be $33,000 per month, including $7,000 depreciation. Distribution expenses are paid for in the month following the expense.

8. Administration expenses are a total of $120,000, for the half year. This includes a bonus of $12,000, payable in December. All other expenses accrue evenly over the period.

9. It is proposed that the company purchase new delivery vans from operating cash flows, costing $80,000, and directors cars costing $100,000. Both would be purchased in August and paid for in September.

10. Other payments are as follows:

Corporation tax for year ended 31.12.20X0	$75,000 (due in September)
Dividends for year ended 31.12.20X0	$125,000 (due in August)

11. Inventory levels currently at $825,000 are not expected to change.

12. Loan repayments totalling $25,000 are quarterly in arrears (September and December) and compromise $20,000 principal and $5,000 interest.

    Bank overdraft interest of $9,000 is charged at the end of each quarter in arrears.

13. The company intends to undertake a market research project costing $20,000 which is to be paid in October. This project is to investigate the viability of setting up distribution outlets in a neighbouring country.

14. Opening bank balance is $200,000 overdrawn.

Required

Prepare a budgeted cash flow for **EACH** of the three months to 30 September 20X1, (all figures to the nearest $'000), stating clearly any assumptions you make. **(20 marks)**

Approaching the answer

Use this answer plan to construct your answer if you are stuck.

Budget

- Receipts – show cash and credit sales receipts separately and distinguish between receipts from opening receivables, receipts in following month, and receipts in month after following month.

- Payments – show each category separately and show workings for trade payables, expense creditors payables and admin expenses.
- Net cash flow
- Opening balance, and then closing balance

19 Chocoholics Co — 24 mins

Chocoholics Co sells high quality Belgian chocolates that it buys in ready-made. Its main attraction to customers is that it gift wraps the items and delivers them to an address of the customer's choice. The company has just expanded its product range to include flowers.

You are an accounting technician and have been asked to prepare a cash budget for the next six months, incorporating the sales of the new products. You have been provided with the following table of estimated revenues and their relative costs. Other costs are also included in the notes below.

20X4	July $'000	August $'000	September $'000	October $'000	November $'000	December $'000
Revenue	250	266	282	306	320	330
Purchases of chocolates and flowers	125	133	141	153	160	165
Administration expenses	55	60	62	65	68	70
Packaging costs	2	3	3	3	4	4
Miscellaneous expenses	6	6	7	7	8	8
Loan repayments	50				50	

Notes

1. Opening inventory of chocolates and flowers will amount to $250,000 at 1 July 20X4. Closing inventory at 31 December 20X4 is estimated at $170,000.

2. Suppliers allow one month's credit. Purchases in June will total $60,000.

3. 30% of sales revenue is paid for by cash but the remaining 70% take advantage of the company's offer of 'Buy now, pay in one month'. June 20X4 sales are expected to be $140,000.

4. Delivery costs are 1% of sales revenue each month, and are paid in the month in which they are incurred. Administration and miscellaneous expenses are also paid as they are incurred.

5. Packaging expenses are paid two months after they are incurred. These costs were $1,000 in May and will be the same in June.

6. The bank charges interest of 1% per month for the overdraft, calculated on the closing bank balance each month, and payable the following month.

7. The bank overdraft at 1 July 20X4 is expected to be $155,000.

8. The loan repayments above refer to an interest free loan obtained by the company when it moved its business to a new bank.

9. The business has no depreciable non-current assets.

Required

Prepare a monthly cash budget for **EACH** of the three months to 30 September 20X4, showing the cash balance at the end of each month. **(20 marks)**

Note. All workings should be shown clearly in order to score maximum marks. Please show workings in $'000, to the nearest $'000.

20 Health Foods Co — 24 mins

You have been provided with the following financial information relating to Health Foods Co.

FORECAST STATEMENT OF PROFIT OR LOSS
FOR THE YEAR ENDING 30 JUNE 20X7

	$'000
Revenue	20,350
Cost of sales	(12,265)
Gross profit	8,085
Finance cost	(785)
Profit before tax	7,300
Income tax expense	(2,230)
Profit for the year	5,070

EXTRACT FROM HISTORICAL STATEMENT OF FINANCIAL POSITION
AS AT 30 JUNE 20X6 (ACTUAL FIGURES)

	$'000
Non-current assets	8,000
Current assets	
Inventory	2,167
Receivables	2,543
Bank	1,264
	5,974
Current liabilities	
Payables	1,737
Income tax payable	1,895
	3,632

EXTRACT FROM FORECAST STATEMENT OF FINANCIAL POSITION
AS AT JUNE 20X7

	$'000
Non-current assets	8,300
Current assets	
Inventory	3,245
Receivables	3,318
Bank	2,984
	9,547
Equity and liabilities	
Current liabilities	
Payables	1,723
Income tax payable	2,289
	4,012

Note. Health Foods Co is forecasting to pay dividends of $2,270,000 for the year to 30 June 20X7, had dividend liabilities at 30 June 20X6 of $1,542,000 and is forecasting to have $2,235,000 outstanding at 30 June 20X7.

Additional information

(1) Operating costs (costs of sales) include depreciation of $200,000.
(2) The company does not plan to sell any non-current assets over the next year.
(3) Non-current assets are all tangible (physical) assets.
(4) All finance costs are paid in the year in which they are incurred.

Required

Prepare a forecast cash flow statement for Health Foods Co for the year ending 30 June 20X7 identifying the net cash flow for the business. **Note.** Accounting standards format is not required. **(20 marks)**

21 Tots Co — 24 mins

Tots Co specialises in the importation and sale of equipment for children's indoor play centres. The company was set up two years ago by its joint shareholders, Mr and Mrs Brute.

The business has been very successful, expanding rapidly over the last year, and the cash balance in the company's current account has exceeded $1 million on several occasions recently.

Mr and Mrs Brute have asked you, an accounting technician for Tots Co, to assist them in managing their cash balances over the next three months.

You have been provided with the following information.

(1) The bank balance on 1 January 20X4 is forecast at $1.2 million in credit.

(2) Revenue for November and December 20X4 is $1.3 million per month. This is expected to rise to $1.5 million in January 20X5, $1.7 million in February and $1.9 million in March. It will then fall to $1.4 million for each of the following six months. This is due to a downturn in demand as the weather improves.

(3) All sales are made on credit: 2% of customers do not pay at all, 70% pay one month after sale and the remaining 28% pay two months after sale.

(4) Purchases are made one month prior to sales, and two months' credit is taken from suppliers.

(5) The company's gross profit margin is 50%.

(6) The cost of employing Tots Co's permanent staff is $150,000 per month. Tots Co also employs temporary staff during January, February and March at an additional cost equating to 3% of sales each month.

(7) Tots Co uses a courier to despatch the equipment to its customers. The cost of this service is 2% of sales value in January to March.

(8) Administration costs are forecast at $30,000 for January. These costs are directly proportional to sales each month.

(9) Mr and Mrs Brute will be attending a conference abroad in July 20X5 at a total cost of $5,000. They must complete the booking form and send it off, along with a deposit of $2,000, by the end of January 20X5. The final balance is due in June.

(10) The company charges deprecation of $45,000 each month.

(11) Tots Co also owns two indoor play centres that it rents out at the rate of $3,500 each per month from January to April, falling to $3,000 per month thereafter. All rents are received one month in advance.

Required

Prepare a monthly cash budget for **each** of the three months to 31 March 20X5, showing clearly any necessary workings.

Note. All workings should be in $'000.

Unless told otherwise, assume that payments are made in the month in which the costs are incurred.

(20 marks)

QUESTIONS

22 Risky Co — 18 mins

Risky Co is a retailer of sports equipment. It is run by its three directors/shareholders who started the business three years ago. Its busiest months of the year are December, January, February and March, with sales for the rest of the year being relatively insignificant.

In December the company prepares a cash budget for January, February and March. The following figures for December 20X7 through to March 20X8 are currently available. However, they may need to be revised and should be read together with the notes below.

	Dec $'000	Jan $'000	Feb $'000	Mar $'000
Sales revenue (1)	450	650	750	350
Purchases	See Notes (2) and (3)			
Staff costs (4)	45	60	70	30
Packaging costs (5)	7	10	12	6
Distribution costs (6)	35	50	58	28
Other costs (7)	50	75	85	55

Notes

1. The company does not provide any credit to customers. However, customers who join the company's members' club are given a 5% discount on all of their purchases. Half of customers are club members. The sales revenue forecasts above have been calculated before any discounts have been taken into account.

2. Purchases represent 40% of gross sales revenue. Sales revenue in November was $95,000.

3. Suppliers allow two months' credit.

4. All staff are paid at the beginning of the month for the previous month's work.

5. Packaging costs are paid one month after they are incurred.

6. Distribution costs are paid in the month in which they are incurred.

7. Other costs include depreciation of $12,000 per month. They also include rental costs of $30,000 per month, which are paid quarterly in December, March, June and September. The remainder of 'other costs' are paid in the month in which they are incurred.

8. The bank charges interest of 0.5% per month for the overdraft, calculated on the closing bank balance each month, and payable in the following month.

9. The overdraft on Cool Ski Co's bank account at 31 December 20X7 is expected to be $500,000.

10. All workings should be in $'000, to the nearest $'000.

Required

Prepare a monthly cash budget for each of the three months to 31 March 20X8, showing the cash balance at the end of each month. **(15 marks)**

23 Sporty Co — 6 mins

Sporty Co, a retailer specialising in skiwear which it currently sells through its online shop. It is considering expanding its business by branching out into the manufacture of its own brand of skiwear. It then intends to expand its customer base to include wholesale customers, such as high street retailers. The three directors/shareholders have produced a business plan and are now considering approaching a venture capital organisation for finance.

Required

Identify three factors that a venture capital organisation would take into account when deciding whether or not to invest in Cool Ski Co. **(5 marks)**

24 Print Co — 24 mins

Print Co is a printing company providing a range of printing services to commercial businesses and the public (non-commercial customers.) It has three main suppliers, which it uses for the majority of its supplies, but also uses a number of smaller suppliers for its sundry purchases. Whilst commercial customers are sometimes provided with a credit facility, non-commercial customers must pay on the day with cash, cheque, debit or credit card. Print Co prepares cleared funds forecasts on a weekly basis.

You are an accounting technician for the company and have been asked to prepare a cleared funds forecast for the period Monday 19 January to Friday 23 January 20X9 inclusive. You have been provided with the following information:

1 **Receipts**

Commercial customers

Customer name	Credit terms	Payment method	Month to: 19 Jan 20X9 sales	19 Dec 20X8 sales	19 Nov 20X8 sales
Anchor Co	2 calendar months	Cheque	$18,000	$24,000	$16,000
Beauty Co	1 calendar month	Cheque	$13,000	$18,000	$17,000
Kent Co	1 calendar month	BACS	$20,000	$18,000	$15,000
Hut Co	None	Cash	$2,200	$5,400	–
Light Co	None	Cheque	$4,500	–	$2,200

Non-commercial customers

Payment method	Mon 12 Jan.	Tue 13 Jan.	Wed 14 Jan.	Thu 15 Jan.	Fri 16 Jan.	Mon 19 Jan.	Tue 20 Jan.	Wed 21 Jan.	Thu 22 Jan.	Fri 23 Jan.
Cash	$300	$230	–	$120	–	–	$220	$350	–	$430
Cheque	$220	–	–	–	–	–	–	–	–	–
Debit card	$255	$426	–	–	–	$170	$210	–	–	–
Credit card	–	–	–	–	–	–	–	–	–	$3,500

Notes

1. Receipt of money by BACS is instantaneous.

2. All commercial customers are reliable, as cheques are always received on 19th day of each month. They are banked on the same day and clear on the fourth working day following the date of receipt.

3. Debit card payments are credited to Print Co's account on the next working day following the date of sale. They represent cleared funds as soon as they are credited.

4. Credit card receipts clear in Print Co's bank account on the fifth working day following the day of sale.

5. A 'working day' is a Monday, Tuesday, Wednesday, Thursday or Friday.

2 **Payments to suppliers**

Main suppliers

Supplier name	Credit terms	Payment method	Jan. 20X9 purchases	Dec. 20X8 purchases	Nov. 20X8 Purchases
Ink Co	1 month	Direct debit	$6,500	$5,500	$4,200
Toner Co	2 months	Direct debit	$8,500	$8,000	$10,600
Paper Co	1 month	Direct debit	$7,200	$10,500	$5,400

Notes

1. Print Co's monthly direct debit payments will leave its account on 23 January.

2. Print Co pays its sundry suppliers by cheque each month. These total $8,200 for January and will also be sent out on 23 January.

3   **Wages and salaries**

    All staff are paid a monthly salary by BACS on the 22nd day of each month. The total salaries cost for January is $9,600. BACS transactions are initiated and paid on the same day.

4   **Other payments**

    Every Monday morning, the cashier withdraws $150 from the company bank account to use as petty cash. The money leaves Print Co's bank account straight away.

5   **Other information**

    The balance on Print Co's bank account will be $35,000 on 19 January 20X9. This represents both the book balance and cleared funds.

Required

Prepare a cleared funds forecast for the period Monday 19 January to Friday 23 January 20X9 inclusive using the information provided. Show clearly the uncleared funds float and the total book balance carried forward each day. **(20 marks)**

25 Rich Co — 18 mins

Rich Co is a cash-rich company wanting to maximise the return on its cash balances over the next six months. It currently has $5,000,000 cash which it is ready to invest. Cash movements over the next six months are expected to be as follows:

	$
Cash inflow in Quarter 1	2,000,000
Cash outflow in Quarter 1	4,000,000
Cash inflow in Quarter 2	2,500,000
Cash outflow in Quarter 2	5,500,000

Based on market information available, interest rates for the year ahead have been estimated for deposits of cash with varying maturity periods. These are as follows:

Deposit period	Quarter 1 Annual rates %	Quarter 2 Annual rates %
Three month	9.4	9.6
Six month	9.7	9.8

Notes

1   A 'quarter' is a three-month period.
2   All of Rich Co's cash inflows and outflows take place on the last day of the quarter. This means that any surplus cash is available for investment from the first day of the next quarter.
3   When cash is placed on deposit for the set period of three months or six months, it is available for withdrawal on the last day of that quarter. It can be used to pay cash outflows immediately.
4   The Quarter 1 annual rates are the interest rates available as of today, for cash placed on deposit for periods of three months and six months.
5   The Quarter 2 annual rates are estimates of the annual interest rates for cash placed on deposit for periods of three months and six months.

You should assume that the annual rates given are simple rates of interest, rather than compound rates. In addition, you should assume that any interest earned during the first quarter is not available for re-investment in the second quarter.

Required

(a) Prepare a cash forecast for each of the two quarters showing clearly the opening and closing balances at the end of each quarter. **(6 marks)**

(b) Calculate which deposits should be made in order to maximise income, clearly showing the income receivable from the different options. **(9 marks)**

(Total = 15 marks)

26 Porkys Co — 18 mins

Porkys Co is an ice cream manufacturing company preparing its accounts to 31 May each year. The company's peak season occurs in the months of July, August and September and it always prepares a profit forecast for this period.

The following cash budget has been prepared for the six months ending 30 November 20X7.

	Jun $'000	Jul $'000	Aug $'000	Sept $'000	Oct $'000	Nov $'000
Receipts from sales	1,100	1,250	1,400	1,800	2,200	1,700
Sale of machinery	–	45	–	–	–	–
Total receipts	1,100	1,295	1,400	1,800	2,200	1,700
Payments						
Ingredients	250	280	360	440	340	340
Labour	350	450	550	425	275	250
Sundry expenses	75	85	95	80	70	65
Purchase of machinery	–	–	120	–	60	–
Loan repayments	50	–	50	–	50	–
Total payments	725	815	1,175	945	795	655
Receipts less payments	375	480	225	855	1,405	1,045
Opening cash balance b/f	1,400	1,775	2,255	2,480	3,385	4,790
Interest received	–	–	–	50	–	–
Closing cash balance c/f	1,775	2,255	2,480	3,385	4,790	5,835

Notes/assumptions made when preparing the cash flow forecast

1. Customers always take two months' credit.
2. The machinery to be sold for $45,000 will give rise to a profit on disposal of $3,000.
3. Depreciation of $13,000 will accrue during the three months ending 30 September 20X7.
4. One month's credit is always taken from suppliers of ingredients.
5. There are no stocks of raw materials or finished goods maintained.
6. Labour is paid by BACS on the last day of each month, for that month's work.
7. Sundry expenses are all paid in the month in which they are incurred.
8. The loan repayment relates to an interest free loan obtained from Porkys Co's parent company.
9. Interest is received by Porkys Co from the bank twice a year. The interest receivable for the peak season of July, August and September is expected to be $30,000.
10. All workings should be in $'000s to the nearest $'000.

Required

Prepare a profit forecast for the three months ending 30 September 20X7. Show all workings clearly. Where any items have been excluded from the profit forecast, include a note to justify your treatment of the item. **(15 marks)**

27 Cleared funds — 24 mins

(a) A business has $1,200 in cleared funds in its bank account at the beginning of the week (Monday). It makes all payments by cheque, and it is assumed that payments are cleared on the fourth day from the day of payment, so that if a cheque payment by cheque is sent on Monday, for example, the payment will clear through the bank account on Thursday. Receipts of payments by cheque are cleared by the bank on the third day from the day of receipt of payment. Cash payments and receipts have same-day clearing.

The business made a tax payment of $15,900 on the previous Friday, and will make payments to suppliers of $12,300 on Monday. In addition, $500 will be withdrawn for petty cash on Tuesday. In the previous week, there were receipts of payments by cheque of $8,400 on Thursday, but no cheque receipts on Friday. In the current week, it is estimated that receipts will be $2,000 per day in cash, plus the following receipts by cheque:

	$
Monday	6,000
Tuesday	6,000
Wednesday	6,000
Thursday	9,000
Friday	1,000

Required

(i) Prepare a cleared funds cash flow forecast for the week Monday to Friday.
(ii) Calculate the amount of float at the end of each day of the week. **(12 marks)**

(b) Explain briefly the purpose of cleared funds cash flow forecasts, and the reason why cleared funds forecasts are short-term forecasts only. **(8 marks)**

(Total = 20 marks)

28 Larcher Co (December 2019 exam) — 24 mins

This scenario relates to five requirements.

Tom Larcher is planning to open a small shop selling fruit and vegetables. He is concerned that he will not have enough cash to finance the venture.

Tom's estimates for the shop are as follows:

Revenues

- Sales will be $2,000 per day for the five trading days per week (Monday to Friday).
- 30% of customers, by value, will pay in cash, the remainder will pay by credit card.

Costs

- Suppliers will deliver fresh fruit and vegetables at the start of each day. Tom will pay them in full by cheque on receipt of the delivery. The gross margin on sales is 60%.
- Tom will rent a shop costing $1,800 per week, payable in advance by standing order on the Monday of each week.
- Wages will be $1,500 per week payable in arrears on Fridays, via the bankers automated clearing system (BACS).
- Utility expenses will be $500 per week payable monthly in arrears by direct debit.

Other information

- No investment in inventory or non-current assets will be required.
- Cash receipts will be banked at the end of trading on Wednesdays and Fridays.
- Receipts from credit cards will take three days to clear.
- Cheques written to suppliers will take four days to clear.
- There is $1,000 of cleared funds available to finance the venture and, in addition to this, the bank has agreed to a $900 overdraft.

(a) Prepare a daily cash budget for Tom Larcher's shop for the first five days of trading commencing on a Monday. **(6 marks)**

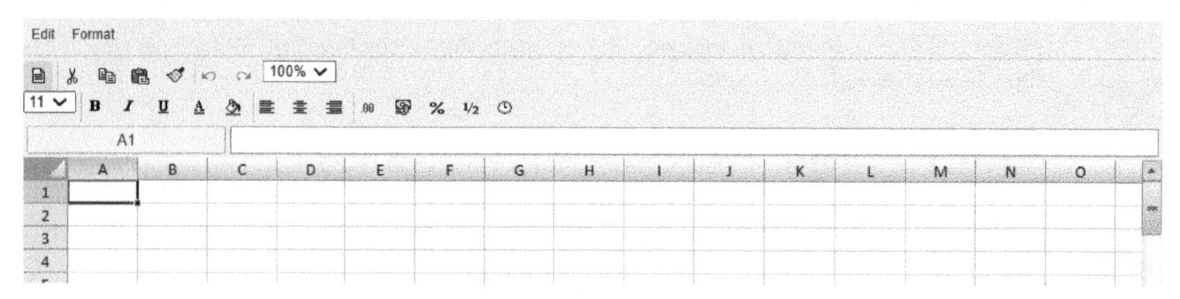

(b) Prepare a cleared funds forecast for Tom Larcher's shop for each of the first five days of trading (ignore uncleared funds). **(6 marks)**

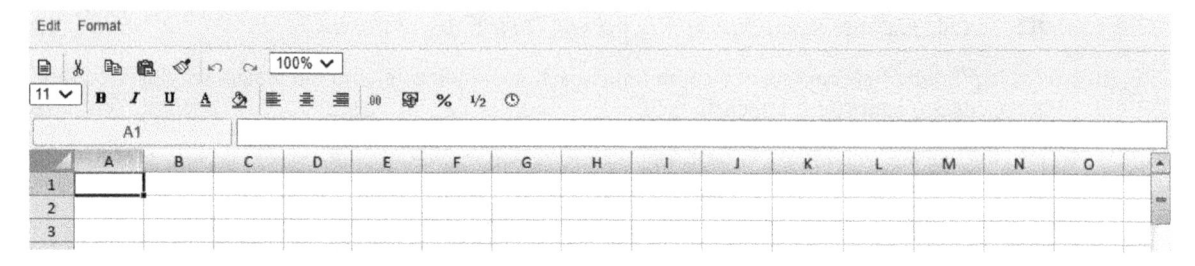

(c) Explain how the cleared funds balance would change under each of the following situations:

(i) Cash receipts were banked each day
(ii) Payments to suppliers took three days to clear

Note. marks for (i) and (ii) will be split equally **(4 marks)**

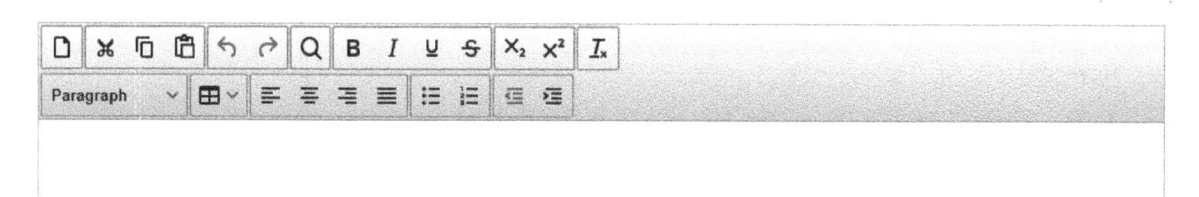

(d) Discuss the usefulness of sensitivity analysis in forecasting cash balances. **(4 marks)**

(Total = 20 marks)

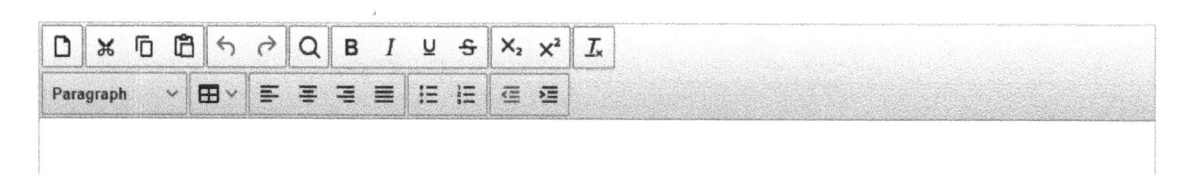

29 GES Co (June 2020 exam) — 24 mins

This scenario relates to three requirements.

GES Co manufactures a single product that has a list price of $8 per unit. Sales forecasts for the next four months are as follows:

	July	August	September	October
Sales (units)	700,000	650,000	680,000	690,000

40% of each month sales are produced in the month prior to sale and 60% are produced in the month of sale.

QUESTIONS

Cash flow forecast information

- Cash sales are expected to amount to 30% of total sales.
- Credit sales are payable in the month following sale.
- The material cost for each unit produced is $3.64.
- 50% of direct materials required for production is purchased in the month prior to being used in production and the remainder in the month of production. Purchases in September for October production will amount to $1,226,680.
- Suppliers of direct materials are paid in the month of purchase.
- Fixed overhead amounts to $1,000,000 per month of which $200,000 is depreciation.
- Conversion cost (labour and variable overhead) for each unit produced is $1.96.
- Conversion costs and fixed overhead are paid in the month incurred.
- $2 million will be paid in August for a new machine.
- Opening balances are as follows:
    - Receivables $3.5m
    - Cash $1m

Required

(a) (i) Calculate the sales budget in value and the production budget in units for EACH of the three months July, August and September. **(3 marks)**

(ii) Using the budgets calculated in part (i) prepare a cash flow forecast for EACH of the three months July, August and September. **(11 marks)**

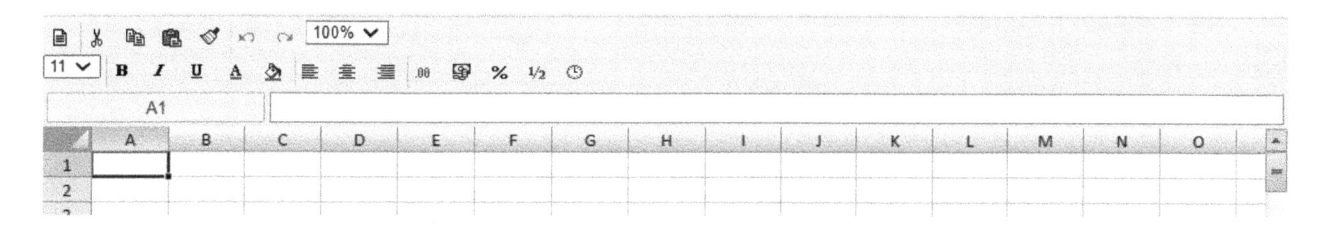

(b) explain three benefits to a company of cash budgeting. **(6 marks)**

(Total = 20 marks)

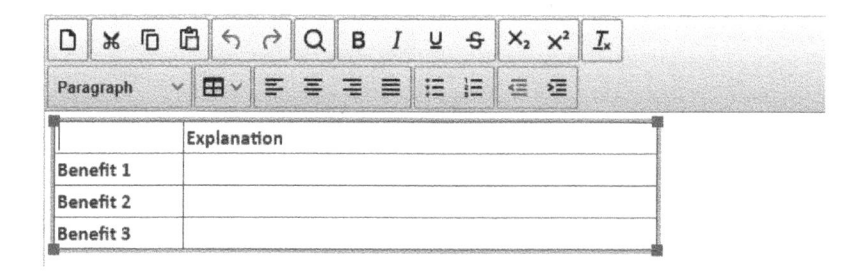

	Explanation
Benefit 1	
Benefit 2	
Benefit 3	

Do you know? – Managing cash balances

Check that you know the following basic points before you attempt any questions. If in doubt, you should go back to your BPP Interactive Text and revise first.

- .... exist to smooth the flow of funds from surplus sectors of the economy to deficit sectors. They may be either banks or other institutions.

- .... banks are banks that operate the payments mechanism and are usually called commercial banks or clearing banks. .... banks deal mostly with wholesale business in the secondary money markets, not in the High Street.

- The role of the .... bank is particularly important for the government's monetary policy. The main instrument of monetary policy is the use of .... to influence the demand for bank loans and other forms of credit, and also to influence exchange rates.

- Other functions of central banks include:
  - ....
  - ....
  - ....
  - ....
  - ....

- The 'wholesale' markets through which financial institutions borrow and lend are called the ....

- Financial instruments traded on these markets include:
  - ....
  - ....
  - ....
  - ....

- Float represents the difference between .... and .... Float is caused by .... delay, ... delay and .... delay.

- The functions of a treasurer include ...., ..., ... and ....

- Possible uses of surplus cash held by a business are:
  - ....   – ....
  - ....   – ....

- Alternatively, a business may wish to invest its surplus cash.

- The two main types of security are .... and .... securities.

- A commonly used name for government securities is ....

- A .... is an unconditional order in writing from one person/company to another, requiring the person/company to whom it is addressed to pay a specific sum of money on demand or a future date.

- Marketable securities can be ranked in order of risk and return, with the lowest risk being ...., and the highest risk being ....

- Spreading available funds across a range of separate investments can reduce risk and is called .... is risk that cannot be diversified away.

TRY QUESTIONS 30–49

Did you know? – Managing cash balances

Could you fill in the blanks? The answers are in bold. Use this page for revision purposes as you approach the exam.

- **Financial intermediaries** exist to smooth the flow of funds from surplus sectors of the economy to deficit sectors. They may be either banks or other institutions.

- **Primary** banks are banks that operate the payments mechanism and are usually called commercial banks or clearing banks. **Secondary** banks deal mostly with wholesale business in the secondary money markets, not in the High Street.

- The role of the **central** bank is particularly important for the government's monetary policy. The main instrument of monetary policy is the use of **interest rates** to influence the demand for bank loans and other forms of credit, and also to influence exchange rates.

- Other functions of central banks include:

    - **Acting as banker to government**
    - **Acting as banker to commercial banks**
    - **Issuing bank notes**
    - **Supervising banks**
    - **Acting as lender of last resort**

- The 'wholesale' markets through which financial institutions borrow and lend are called the **money markets**.

- Financial instruments traded on these markets include:

    - **Deposits**
    - **Bills**
    - **Certificates of Deposit**
    - **Commercial paper**

- Float represents the difference between **the time a payment is initiated** and **the time when the funds become available for use**. Float is caused by **transmission** delay, **lodgement** delay and **clearance** delay.

- The functions of a treasurer include **advising on capital structure, managing cash flows to minimise associated costs, maintaining good banking relationships** and **managing foreign currency transactions to avoid risk**.

- Possible uses of surplus cash held by a business are:

    - **Purchases of non-current assets**   –   **Acquisitions**
    - **Payment of dividends**   –   **Share buy-backs**

- Alternatively, a business may wish to invest its surplus cash.

- The two main types of security are **equity (share)** and **debt** securities.

- A commonly used name for government securities is **gilts**.

- A **bill of exchange** is an unconditional order in writing from one person/company to another, requiring the person/company to whom it is addressed to pay a specific sum of money on demand or a future date.

- Marketable securities can be ranked in order of risk and return, with the lowest risk being **government securities** and the highest risk being **equities**.

- Spreading available funds across a range of separate investments can reduce risk and is called **diversification**. **Systematic or market risk** is risk that cannot be diversified away.

TRY QUESTIONS 30–49

30 MCQ Question Bank 4 — 24 mins

30.1 A bond pays $4.25 for every $100 of its nominal value. If an investor values the bond at $106.50, what is the investor's required return?

- ○ 6.1%
- ○ 4.25%
- ○ 4%
- ○ 6.5%

(2 marks)

30.2 Float is caused by three types of delay. Which type refers to the delay in banking payments received?

- ○ Transmission delay
- ○ Initiation delay
- ○ Clearance delay
- ○ Lodgement delay

(2 marks)

30.3 Baumol's model is used to calculate the optimum amount of finance that a business should raise at a time. The model uses fixed and variable costs in the calculation. Which of the following is an example of a variable cost?

- ○ The opportunity cost of keeping money in the form of cash
- ○ Cost of negotiating an overdraft
- ○ Bank charges in respect of administering the finance
- ○ Transmission costs of issuing the finance

(2 marks)

30.4 In the statement of financial position of a retail bank, which of the following constitutes the largest liability?

- ○ Customers' deposits
- ○ Capital equipment
- ○ Loans to other banks
- ○ Customer overdrafts and bank loans

(2 marks)

30.5 Which of the following is an advantage of having a decentralised treasury department over a centralised one?

- ○ Larger volumes of cash are likely to be available to invest which may attract better returns.
- ○ The pool of funds held for precautionary purposes is likely to be lower.
- ○ The department is more likely to employ experts.
- ○ The department is likely to be more responsive to meet the needs of individual operating units.

(2 marks)

30.6 Which of the following are the key principles that a business should base its cash management policy on?

- (i) Safety
- (ii) Exposure
- (iii) Profitability
- (iv) Liquidity

- ○ All of them
- ○ (i), (ii) and (iv) only
- ○ (i), (iii) and (iv) only
- ○ (ii), (iii) and (iv) only

(2 marks)

30.7 Which type of investment risk is specific to market sectors?

- ○ Unsystematic risk
- ○ Systematic risk
- ○ Inflation risk
- ○ Liquidity risk

(2 marks)

30.8 What happens to the market value of a fixed interest stock with a nominal value of $100 on its maturity date?

- ○ Nothing
- ○ Falls to zero
- ○ Increases or falls to $1,000
- ○ Increases or falls to $100

(2 marks)

30.9 The motive for a business to hold cash in order to meet its regular commitments such as paying employees is known as:

- ○ The precautionary motive
- ○ The strategic motive
- ○ The transactions motive
- ○ The speculative motive

(2 marks)

30.10 In relation to shares bought for investment, what does Cum Div mean?

- ○ The purchaser is entitled to the next dividend payment.
- ○ The purchaser is not entitled to the next dividend payment.
- ○ Dividends accumulate on a cumulative basis, if they are not paid in one year they carry over and may be paid in a following year.
- ○ The share entitles the holder to the payment of a dividend each and every year.

(2 marks)

(Total = 20 marks)

31 MCQ Question Bank 5   24 mins

31.1 A bond that matures in one year's time has a par value of $100. It pays 5% interest and an investor originally paid $90 for the bond.

Assuming that the investor holds the bond to maturity, what is the gross redemption yield?

- ○ 5%
- ○ 5.6%
- ○ 10%
- ○ 16.67%

(2 marks)

31.2 One of the key principles that a business should base its cash management policy on is liquidity. Which of the following is an example of this principle?

- ○ Ensuring the business has investments which are easily convertible into cash.
- ○ Managing investments carefully to minimise costs.
- ○ Ensuring short-term investments are protected from heavy losses.
- ○ Ensuring cash and other liquid assets are secure from theft.

(2 marks)

31.3 Which of the following assets is the least liquid?

- ○ Shares
- ○ Inventory
- ○ Cash
- ○ Office buildings

(2 marks)

31.4 What impact do scrip dividends have on the issued share capital of a company?

- ○ Increase share capital
- ○ Decrease share capital
- ○ No impact on share capital
- ○ No impact on issued share capital but increase the authorised capital

(2 marks)

31.5 Float is caused by three types of delay. Which type refers to the delay incurred between posting a payment and it reaching the payee?

- ○ Clearance delay
- ○ Lodgement delay
- ○ Transmission delay
- ○ Posting delay

(2 marks)

31.6 Baumol's model of cash management is shown below. What figure is represented by i?

$$Q = \sqrt{\frac{2FS}{i}}$$

- ○ Interest cost
- ○ Inventory cost
- ○ Initiation cost
- ○ Inversion cost

(2 marks)

31.7 The following information is available for the businesses of Adele, Bianca and Caitlin. Whose business is most profitable?

	Adele $	Bianca $	Caitlin $
Non-current assets	10,000	8,000	6,000
Cash	8,000	7,000	2,000
Other current assets	1,000	1,500	2,000
Current liabilities	(500)	(1,000)	(3,000)
Net assets	18,500	15,500	7,000
Profit	2,000	2,000	2,000

- ○ All are equally profitable
- ○ Adele
- ○ Bianca
- ○ Caitlin

(2 marks)

31.8 The treasurer of Black Co can invest funds in one of three bank accounts. Which account offers the best return over one year?

Gold Saver pays 6.65% interest per annum.
Super Saver pays 6.60% interest paid monthly.
Easy Saver pays 6.55% interest paid daily.

- ○ They each offer the same return over one year
- ○ Gold Saver
- ○ Super Saver
- ○ Easy Saver

(2 marks)

31.9 On 8 September 20X8 the market price of 5% Treasury Stock 20X9 is $145. Calculate the interest yield.

- ○ 3.45%
- ○ 5.75%
- ○ 6.35%
- ○ 7.25%

(2 marks)

31.10 Which type of gilt has a life of over 15 years?

- ○ Shorts
- ○ Mediums
- ○ Longs
- ○ Undated

(2 marks)

(Total = 20 marks)

32 MCQ Question Bank 6 — 24 mins

32.1 What is a Eurocurrency deposit?

- ○ A deposit of Euros into a bank account
- ○ A deposit of Euros made in any country whose currency is also the Euro
- ○ A deposit of any currency made outside that currency's country of origin
- ○ A deposit made in one currency which is then converted into Euros by the receiving bank

(2 marks)

32.2 Which of the following are roles of a central bank?

(i) Banker to central government
(ii) Lender of last resort in the banking system
(iii) Responsible for issuing bank notes
(iv) To intervene in foreign exchange markets

- ○ All of them
- ○ (i), (ii) and (iii) only
- ○ (i), (iii) and (iv) only
- ○ (ii), (iii) and (iv) only

(2 marks)

32.3 Which type of banking is carried out by high street banks?

- ○ Retail banking
- ○ Investment banking
- ○ Casino banking
- ○ Central banking

(2 marks)

32.4 What financial deals are made on the inter-company market?

- ○ Unsecured loans between banks
- ○ Loans between companies with surplus cash and those who need to borrow
- ○ Buying and selling company shares
- ○ Buying and selling financial futures

(2 marks)

32.5 Which of the following are examples of assets of a bank?

(i) Customer current accounts
(ii) Customer overdrafts
(iii) Notes and coins
(iv) Loans to other banks

- ○ All of them
- ○ (i), (ii) and (iii) only
- ○ (i), (iii) and (iv) only
- ○ (ii), (iii) and (iv) only

(2 marks)

32.6 What is disintermediation?

- ○ The avoidance of using financial intermediaries when arranging lending or borrowing
- ○ The use of financial intermediaries to arrange lending or borrowing
- ○ The avoidance of using financial intermediaries when purchasing a company's share capital on the stock exchange
- ○ The use of financial intermediaries when purchasing a company's share capital on the stock exchange

(2 marks)

32.7 Which of the following are benefits of financial intermediaries?

(i) Pooling of risk
(ii) Aggregation of individual savings
(iii) The balancing of short and long-term lending/borrowing needs
(iv) Savers are not directly affected if a borrower defaults on their loan

○ All of them
○ (i), (ii) and (iii) only
○ (i), (iii) and (iv) only
○ (ii), (iii) and (iv) only (2 marks)

32.8 What are UK government bonds otherwise known as?

○ Certificates of deposit
○ Gilts
○ Treasury Bills
○ Stocks (2 marks)

32.9 According to Keynes, what is the only motive for holding cash that will alter the demand for money as a result of changes to interest rates?

○ Transactions motive
○ Precautionary motive
○ Speculative motive
○ Inflationary motive (2 marks)

32.10 Which type of bank deals in the wholesale money markets?

○ A central bank
○ A primary bank
○ A high street bank
○ A secondary bank (2 marks)

(Total = 20 marks)

33 Treasury function — 6 mins

Describe **TWO** advantages of having a centralised treasury department. (5 marks)

34 Cleanly Co — 24 mins

Cleanly Co is a manufacturing company producing and selling a range of cleaning products to wholesale customers. It has three suppliers and two customers. Cleanly Co relies on its cleared funds forecast to manage its cash.

You are an accounting technician for the company and have been asked to prepare a cleared funds forecast for the period Monday 2 January to Friday 6 January 20X6 inclusive. You have been provided with the following information:

(1) **Receipts from customers**

Customer name	Credit terms	Payment method	2 Jan 20X6 sales	2 Dec 20X5 sales
W Co	1 calendar month	BACS	$150,000	$130,000
X Co	None	Cheque	$180,000	$160,000

(a) Receipt of money by BACS is instantaneous.

(b) X Co's cheque will be paid into Cleanly Co's bank account on the same day as the sale is made and will clear on the third day following this (excluding day of payment).

(2) **Payments to suppliers**

Supplier name	Credit Terms	Payment method	2 Jan 20X6 purchases	2 Dec 20X5 purchases	2 Nov 20X5 Purchases
A Co	1 calendar month	Standing order	$65,000	$55,000	$45,000
B Co	2 calendar months	Cheque	$85,000	$80,000	$75,000
C Co	None	Cheque	$95,000	$90,000	$85,000

(a) Cleanly Co has set up a standing order for $45,000 a month to pay for supplies from A Co. This will leave Cleanly's bank account on 2 January. Every few months, an adjustment is made to reflect the actual cost of supplies purchased (you do **not** need to make this adjustment).

(b) Cleanly Co will send out, by post, cheques to B Co and C Co on 2 January. The amounts will leave its bank account on the second day following this (excluding the day of posting).

(3) **Wages and salaries**

	December 20X5	January 20X6
Weekly wages	$12,000	$13,000
Monthly salaries	$56,000	$59,000

(a) Factory workers are paid cash wages (weekly). They will be paid one week's wages, on 6 January, for the last week's work done in December (ie they work a week in hand).

(b) All the office workers are paid salaries (monthly) by BACS. Salaries for December will be paid on 2 January.

(4) **Other miscellaneous payments**

(a) Every Monday morning, the petty cashier withdraws $200 from the company bank account for the petty cash tin. The money leaves Cleanly's bank account straight away.

(b) The window cleaner is paid $30 from petty cash every Wednesday morning.

(c) Office stationery will be ordered by telephone on Tuesday 3 January to the value of $300. This is paid for by company debit card. Such payments are generally seen to leave the company account on the next working day.

(d) Five new computers will be ordered over the internet on 5 January at a total cost of $6,500. A cheque will be sent out on the same day. The amount will leave Cleanly Co's bank account on the second day following this (excluding the day of posting).

(5) **Other information**

The balance on Cleanly's bank account will be $200,000 on 2 January 20X6. This represents both the book balance and the cleared funds.

Required

Prepare a cleared funds forecast for the period Monday 2 January to Friday 6 January 20X6 inclusive using the information provided. Show clearly the uncleared funds float each day. **(20 marks)**

35 Waslet Co — 6 mins

Waslet Co's parent company is considering centralising the treasury function for the whole group.

List **FIVE** roles of a treasury department. **(5 marks)**

QUESTIONS

36 KM Co — 18 mins

The finance director of KM Co has recently reorganised the finance department following a number of years of growth within the business, which now includes a number of overseas operations. The company now has separate treasury and financial control departments.

Required

Describe the main responsibilities of a treasury department, and explain the advantages to KM Co of having separate treasury and financial control departments. **(15 marks)**

37 Interest rates (1) — 18 mins

The following table of London money rates shows the relationship between maturity and interest rates for four types of short-term investment, as published in the financial press.

	One month	Three months	Six months	One Year
Sterling certificates of deposit	$9^7/_8$	$10^1/_{16}$	$10^3/_{16}$	$10^5/_{16}$
Local authority bonds	$9^7/_8$	10	$10^1/_4$	$10^1/_2$
Finance house deposits	10	$10^1/_8$	$10^3/_8$	$10^9/_{16}$
Treasury bills (buy)	$9^{11}/_{16}$	$9^3/_4$	–	–

Required

Explain:

(a) The nature of the instruments listed; and **(8 marks)**
(b) The main reasons for the differences in interest rate between the instruments and over time. **(7 marks)**

(Total = 15 marks)

38 Interest rates (2) — 6 mins

In recent years there have been various pressures on interest rates to fall.

Required

Describe **THREE** likely implications to a typical company of lower interest rates. **(5 marks)**

39 Financial intermediaries (1) — 6 mins

In order to facilitate the efficient operation of financial markets, the major financial intermediaries have important roles to play.

Required

Explain what is meant by financial intermediation, giving specific examples of types of organisations that take on this role. **(5 marks)**

40 Money market instruments — 6 mins

Briefly describe **THREE** main money market instruments. **(5 marks)**

BPP LEARNING MEDIA

41 Banks and money markets — 6 mins

Banks and the money markets play an important role in a country's economy.

Required

Describe **THREE** functions of a central bank. (5 marks)

42 Banks and their customers (1) — 6 mins

The relationship between a bank and its customers arises from a legal contract between the two parties. Both parties have certain rights and duties as part of this legal contract.

Required

Describe **THREE** types of contractual relationship which may exist between bank and customer. (5 marks)

43 Banks and their customers (2) — 6 mins

Explain **THREE** duties that a bank has to its customers. (5 marks)

44 Treasury management — 6 mins

Describe **TWO** advantages of having a centralised treasury department. (5 marks)

45 Curtain Co — 6 mins

Curtain Co is a small family-run business, which makes made-to-measure curtains for its customers, who are local furnishing stores. Curtain Co does not deal directly with the general public. Its turnover for the next year is forecast to be $600,000. Curtain Co is always overdrawn and pays interest on its overdraft at 8% per annum.

Once a pair of curtains has been made, an invoice is raised and sent with the curtains to the customer. Invoices are settled by cheque for each pair of curtains, often resulting in several cheques from the same customer each month. It is now considering introducing a new system, whereby it invoices customers at the end of each month for their total despatches that month, requesting payment by standing order or direct debit within 30 days. It is expected that all Curtain Co's customers would take advantage of the full credit period, but not exceed it.

Curtain Co's owners have concerns about the cost of offering increased credit as, at present, customers pay their invoices 14 days, on average, after the month of sale. The business currently pays $1.80 for each cheque banked; it would expect to bank 2,000 cheques over the coming year if it does not make changes in the payment method. Its bank does not charge it for receipts into its account by standing order or direct debit.

Required

Calculate the new total finance costs (cheques and interest) if the new system is introduced. (5 marks)

46 Trade credit — 6 mins

For many businesses, particularly small businesses, trade credit can be a very important source of short-term finance.

Required

Explain briefly the merits and limitations of using trade finance as a source of finance for a small business. (5 marks)

QUESTIONS

47 Bills and securities (December 2019 exam) — 6 mins

Briefly explain the main features of government securities and bills of exchange. **(5 marks)**

	Explanation
Government securities	
Bills of exchange	

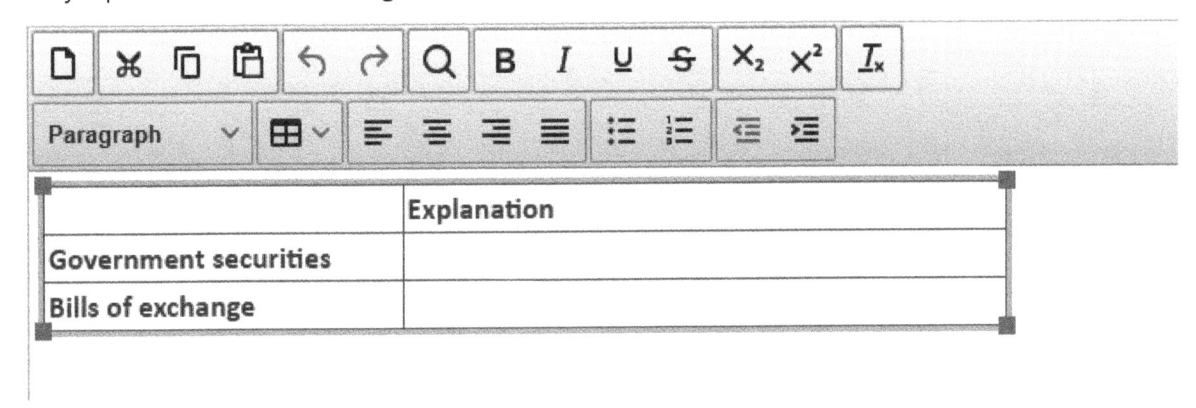

48 Surplus funds — 6 mins

A company with surplus funds may invest this money in a combination of money market accounts and equity shares in stock market companies ('listed company shares'), but when making these investments it is prudent to consider the risk-return trade-off and the management of investment risk.

Required

In the context of investing surplus funds, explain the meaning of the following terms:

(a) Risk-return trade-off
(b) Default risk **(5 marks)**

Explain why it is important to consider risk-return trade-off when investing cash. **(3 marks)**

49 Appropriate liquidity — 6 mins

Discuss briefly the appropriate levels of liquidity for a company that operates a large chain of supermarkets and suggest how the liquidity of this type of organisation may be measured and monitored: **(5 marks)**

Do you know? – Financing decisions

Check that your knowledge covers the following basic points before you attempt any questions. If in doubt, you should go back to your BPP Interactive Text and revise first.

- The government's management of the economy is directed towards certain objectives such as .... and ....

- The UK government prefers to let the money supply be regulated indirectly, through ...., rather than quantitative or qualitative controls on amounts that can be lent.

- The desire to hold money, rather than other forms of wealth, is termed '............... preference'.

- The term structure of interest rates reflects the fact that different financial instruments have different ....

- Inflation refers to a sustained increase in the general level of prices over time. Consequences of inflation include:
  - ....
  - ....
  - ....
  - ....
  - ....

- Nominal and real rates of interest, and the rate of inflation, are linked by the following formula.

  .... = (...........................) × (...........................)

- A bank's decision to lend will be based on the following factors.

  C ....   A ....
  A ....   R ....
  M ....   I ....
  P ....

- A key form of short-term finance is bank overdrafts, for which key factors to consider are:
  - ....   - ....
  - ....   - ....
  - ....   - ....

- Bank loans are more appropriate over the medium or long term, and there are three possible types of repayment: ...., ... and ....

- Leases are another source of finance. A lease can be defined as a contract between lessor and lessee for hire of a specific asset. An arrangement similar to leasing, but where ownership of the goods passes on payment of the final credit instalment, is called ....

- A stock exchange can operate as a .... market, enabling businesses to raise new finance, or as a .... market, enabling investors to sell their investments.

TRY QUESTIONS 50–72

- *Possible pitfalls*

  Write down the mistakes you know you should avoid.

Did you know? – Financial decisions

Could you fill in the blanks? The answers are in bold. Use this page for revision purposes as you approach the exam.

- The government's management of the economy is directed towards certain objectives such as **price stability** and **economic growth**.
- The UK government prefers to let the money supply be regulated indirectly, through **interest rates**, rather than quantitative or qualitative controls on amounts that can be lent.
- The desire to hold money, rather than other forms of wealth, is termed '**liquidity** preference'.
- The term structure of interest rates reflects the fact that different financial instruments have different **periods to maturity**.
- Inflation refers to a sustained increase in the general level of prices over time. Consequences of inflation include:
    - **Redistribution of wealth and income**
    - **Adverse movements in the balance of trade**
    - **Less efficient resource allocation**
    - **Resource cost of frequently changing prices**
    - **Impacts of government attempts to control inflation (for example interest rate increases affecting investment)**
- Nominal and real rates of interest, and the rate of inflation, are linked by the following formula.

    1 + nominal rate = (1 + real interest rate) × (1 + inflation rate)

- A bank's decision to lend will be based on the following factors.

    C **haracter of the customer**   A **mount of the borrowing**
    A **bility to borrow and repay**   R **epayment terms**
    M **argin of profit**   I **nsurance against non-payment**
    P **urpose of the borrowing**

- A key form of short-term finance is bank overdrafts, for which key factors to consider are:
    - **Amount**   – **Margin**
    - **Purpose**   – **Repayment**
    - **Security**   – **Benefits**
- Bank loans are more appropriate over the medium or long term, and there are three possible types of repayment: **bullet**, **balloon** and **amortising**.
- Leases are another source of finance. A lease can be defined as a contract between lessor and lessee for hire of a specific asset. An arrangement similar to leasing, but where ownership of the goods passes on payment of the final credit instalment, is called **hire purchase**.
- A stock exchange can operate as a **primary** market, enabling businesses to raise new finance, or as a **secondary** market, enabling investors to sell their investments.

TRY QUESTIONS 50–72

- *Possible pitfalls*
    - **Confusing terminology.**
    - **Not keeping your knowledge of the financial markets and the economy up to date.**

50 MCQ Question Bank 7 — 24 mins

50.1 According to Keynes, what is liquidity preference?

- ○ The desire not to run out of cash
- ○ The desire to invest cash
- ○ The desire to hold onto wealth as cash rather than to invest it
- ○ The desire to hold onto wealth in the form of notes and coins rather than to keep it in a bank account

(2 marks)

50.2 If the real rate of interest is 6% and the inflation rate is 4%, calculate the nominal rate of interest.

Your answer should be rounded up to the nearest whole percentage.

- ○ 2%
- ○ 8%
- ○ 10%
- ○ 24%

(2 marks)

50.3 Which of the following is a fiscal policy?

- ○ Interest rate setting
- ○ Reserve requirement setting
- ○ Open market operations
- ○ Changing taxation

(2 marks)

50.4 In an economy where the government borrows directly from banks, which of the following would lead to a reduction in the money supply?

(i) An increase in PSBR
(ii) A reduction in PSBR
(iii) An increase in PSDR
(iv) A reduction in PSDR

- ○ (i) and (iii) only
- ○ (i) and (iv) only
- ○ (ii) and (iii) only
- ○ (ii) and (iv) only

(2 marks)

50.5 An economy with a higher inflation rate than its trading partners will find:

(i) Its exports become relatively cheaper
(ii) Its exports become relatively expensive
(iii) Its imports become relatively cheaper
(iv) Its imports become relatively expensive

- ○ (i) and (iii) only
- ○ (i) and (iv) only
- ○ (ii) and (iii) only
- ○ (ii) and (iv) only

(2 marks)

50.6 **The following question is taken from the June 2015 exam.**

An organisation prices its goods based on actual cost plus a fixed percentage mark up.

How will the risk of inflation be split between the customer and the organisation selling the goods?

- ○ Only the customer will suffer inflation risk
- ○ Only the organisation selling the goods will suffer inflation risk
- ○ Both parties will suffer inflation risk but not equally
- ○ Both parties will share the inflation risk equally

(2 marks)

50.7 What is the real rate of interest if the nominal interest rate is 7% and the inflation rate is 3%?

Your answer should be rounded up to the nearest whole percentage.

- ○ 3%
- ○ 4%
- ○ 7%
- ○ 10%

(2 marks)

50.8 Which of the following factors have an effect on the general level of interest rates?

(i) The inflation rate
(ii) The need for the central bank to make a real return
(iii) Government monetary policy
(iv) Demand for borrowing

- ○ All of them
- ○ (i), (ii) and (iii) only
- ○ (i), (iii) and (iv) only
- ○ (ii), (iii) and (iv) only

(2 marks)

50.9 Which of the following factors can affect the volume of bank lending?

(i) Interest rate policy
(ii) Reserve requirements
(iii) Government issuing gilts
(iv) Regulation by the financial authorities

- ○ (i) only
- ○ (ii) and (iii) only
- ○ (i) and (iv) only
- ○ All of the above

(2 marks)

50.10 Loan stock is an example of short-term finance.

The above statement is:

- ○ True
- ○ False

(1 mark)

(Total = 20 marks)

51 MCQ Question Bank 8 — 24 mins

51.1 Which of the following uses for an overdraft is a bank most likely to approve of?

- ○ To purchase new machinery
- ○ To cover a temporary cash shortfall
- ○ To purchase another company's share capital
- ○ To permanently increase the level of inventories

(2 marks)

51.2 Under which type of loan repayment scheme does the borrower repay the full amount of the loan at the end of the loan period?

- ○ Balloon repayment
- ○ Amortising repayment
- ○ Straight repayment
- ○ Bullet repayment

(2 marks)

51.3 Which of the following charges may a borrower have to pay in connection with a loan?

(i) An arrangement fee
(ii) Legal fees
(iii) Interest charges
(iv) A commitment fee

○ All of them
○ (i), (ii) and (iii) only
○ (i), (iii) and (iv) only
○ (ii), (iii) and (iv) only (2 marks)

51.4 What is a rights issue?

○ An offer to existing loan stock holders to purchase a company's shares at a reduced rate
○ An offer to existing shareholders to purchase a company's shares at a reduced rate
○ The issue of company shares onto a recognised stock market
○ A dividend payment which is in the form of new shares rather than cash (2 marks)

51.5 Which of the following are common characteristics of preference shares rather than ordinary shares?

(i) They attract a fixed percentage dividend
(ii) They are payable even if the company does not have any distributable profit
(iii) The right to dividends is cumulative
(iv) Dividends are payable in priority over ordinary share dividends

○ All of them
○ (i), (ii) and (iii) only
○ (i), (iii) and (iv) only
○ (ii), (iii) and (iv) only (2 marks)

51.6 The following is a description of a method of obtaining a listing on a stock exchange.

'A sponsoring market maker arranges for most of the share issue to be purchased by a small number of investors.'

Which method of obtaining a listing does the above best describe?

○ Initial public offering
○ Prospectus issue
○ Placing
○ Introduction (2 marks)

51.7 Which UK government scheme provides security for finance provided by banks to qualifying small and medium-sized enterprises?

○ The Enterprise Finance Guarantee Scheme
○ The Enterprise Initiative
○ Development Agency schemes
○ The Enterprise Investment Scheme (2 marks)

51.8 The main drawback of business angel finance is:

○ Business angels are unlikely to want to invest in small and medium-sized enterprises
○ Business angels are likely to want to take over the day-to-day running of the business
○ Business angels are likely to impose demanding repayment schedules
○ There is no ready market to find business angel finance (2 marks)

51.9 Rite Co has just been set up by two brothers. Which of the following are appropriate sources of finance for the business?

   (i)   Trade credit
   (ii)   Bank overdraft
   (iii)   Bank loan
   (iv)   Issuing shares on a recognised stock exchange

   O   All of them
   O   (i), (ii) and (iii) only
   O   (i), (iii) and (iv) only
   O   (ii), (iii) and (iv) only   (2 marks)

51.10 Which of the following are reasons why small and medium-sized enterprises find it difficult to obtain finance?

   (i)   They have a lack of history and 'track record'
   (ii)   There is a lack of public scrutiny over their accounts as compared to larger enterprises
   (iii)   They have a lack of assets on which to secure loans
   (iv)   They are seen as 'high risk' as many similar enterprises will fail

   O   All of them
   O   (i), (ii) and (iii) only
   O   (i), (iii) and (iv) only
   O   (ii), (iii) and (iv) only   (2 marks)

(Total = 20 marks)

52 MCQ Question Bank 9   24 mins

52.1 In connection with a loan, which of the following is an example of a negative covenant?

   O   The borrower promises not to take out any further loans
   O   The borrower promises to send the bank copies of its financial statements each year
   O   The borrower promises to ensure shareholders' funds does not exceed the amount of the loan
   O   The borrower promises to meet the bank each quarter to discuss the health of the company
                                                                                                      (2 marks)

52.2 Which of the following is a benefit, to the borrower, of a loan as opposed to an overdraft?

   O   Flexible repayment schedule
   O   Only charged for the amount drawn down
   O   Easy to arrange
   O   Lower interest rates   (2 marks)

52.3 Which of the following are correct statements concerning hire purchase arrangements?

   (i)   Capital allowances are available on the full capital element of the cost.

   (ii)   The finance provider normally requires the purchaser to pay a deposit towards the purchase price at the start of the arrangement.

   (iii)   Interest payments are an allowable expense to be offset against tax.

   (iv)   Legal ownership of the asset passes to the purchaser at the start of the arrangement.

   O   All of them
   O   (i), (ii) and (iii) only
   O   (i), (iii) and (iv) only
   O   (ii), (iii) and (iv) only   (2 marks)

52.4 Which of the following is not a source of long-term finance?

- ○ Overdrafts
- ○ Retained earnings
- ○ Government grants
- ○ The capital markets (2 marks)

52.5 What are Eurobonds?

- ○ Bonds sold on an international basis
- ○ Bonds that are denominated in the Euro currency
- ○ Bonds that are sold purely in the European Union
- ○ Bonds that are issued by the European Union (2 marks)

52.6 Which of the following statements are true?

(i) Public companies can offer their shares to the general public
(ii) Private companies can offer their shares to the general public
(iii) Loan stock interest payments are tax deductible
(iv) Dividend payments are tax deductible

- ○ (i) and (iii) only
- ○ (i) and (iv) only
- ○ (ii) and (iii) only
- ○ (ii) and (iv) only (2 marks)

52.7 What is a scrip dividend?

- ○ A dividend which is paid during the financial year
- ○ A dividend which is paid in cash
- ○ A dividend which is paid by the issue of new shares
- ○ A dividend which has not been approved by the shareholders (2 marks)

52.8 Which of the following is issued at a discount to its redemption value and pays its holder no interest during its life?

- ○ A deep discount bond
- ○ A gilt-edged security
- ○ An unsecured loan note
- ○ A zero coupon bond (2 marks)

52.9 Which of the UK government schemes below gives a qualifying investor tax relief on their investment?

- ○ The Loan Guarantee Scheme
- ○ The Enterprise Initiative
- ○ Development Agency schemes
- ○ The Enterprise Investment Scheme (2 marks)

52.10 Gerry is thinking about starting up a small business. What should his initial source of finance be?

- ○ A bank loan
- ○ A bank overdraft
- ○ A venture capitalist
- ○ His own personal resources (2 marks)

(Total = 20 marks)

53 Question with help: Money supply — 6 mins

Explain what is meant by the term 'the money supply'. **(5 marks)**

Approaching the answer

Use this answer plan to construct your answer if you are stuck.

Define the money supply.

Outline the concepts of narrow and broad money.

Outline the role of the commercial banks in the creation of money.

54 Question with help: Commercial banks — 6 mins

Give **three** reasons why a commercial bank might operate with various different interest rates. **(5 marks)**

Approaching the answer

Use this answer plan to construct your answer if you are stuck.

Factors influencing interest rates:

- Risk
- Duration
- Size
- Margin
- Overseas

55 Trob Co (June 2020 exam) — 6 mins

This scenario relates to one requirement.

The following is an extract from Trob Co's financial statements:

	$
Revenue	500,000
Gross profit	275,000
Operating profit	200,000
Non-current assets	800,000
Inventory	50,000
Receivables	100,000

Assuming there are 365 days in a year, calculate the following ratios for Trob Co:

- Operating margin
- Return on capital employed
- Net asset turnover
- Quick (acid test) ratio
- Payable days

(5 marks)

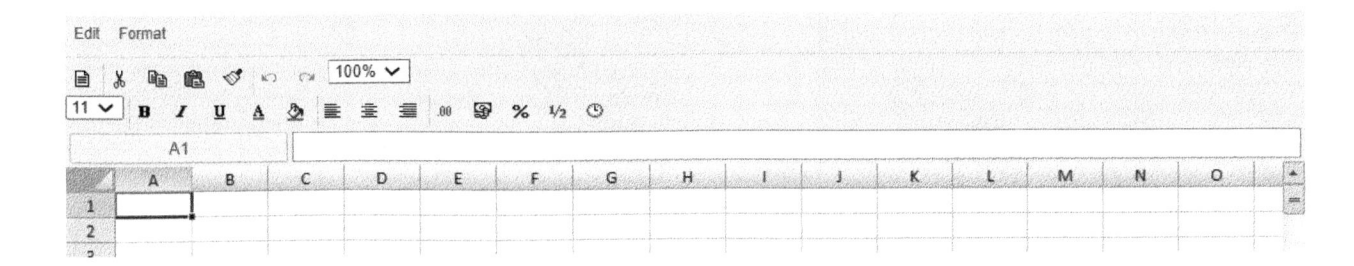

56 Retailer Co — 24 mins

Retailer Co operates a chain of retail and wholesale stores throughout the country. The Board of Directors undertook a strategic review of operations two years ago, which also involved a detailed profitability analysis of each of the company's outlets. Resulting from this appraisal, a strategic withdrawal from certain markets was agreed and this strategy is now almost complete. The Board of Directors wishes to have the recent financial performance of the company reassessed, relative to the industry average, following the implementation of the withdrawal strategy.

Extracts from the financial statements of Retailer Co

Statement of profit or loss

	Y/e 30 Nov 20X2 $'000	Y/e 30 Nov 20X1 $'000
Revenue	2,500	3,000
Gross profit	275	300
Finance cost	(35)	(50)
Profit before tax	240	250
Income tax expenses	(60)	(62)
Profit after tax	180	188

Statement of financial position

	as at 30 Nov 20X2 $'000	$'000	as at 30 Nov 20X1 $'000	$'000
Assets				
Non-current assets				
Property, plant and Equipment		860		862
Current assets				
Inventory	250		300	
Receivables	100		150	
Bank	40		–	
		390		450
		1,250		1,312
Equity and liabilities				
Equity				
5c ordinary shares (5m issued)		250		250
Share premium		100		100
Retained earnings		380		200
		730		550

FFM FOUNDATIONS IN FINANCIAL MANAGEMENT

	Statement of financial position as at 30 Nov 20X2		Statement of financial position as at 30 Nov 20X1	
	$'000	$'000	$'000	$'000
Non-current liabilities				
10% Convertible debentures (20X5)	300		300	
12% Secured debenture (20X5) Note 3	–		100	
		300		400
Current liabilities				
Bank overdraft	–		100	
Payables	160		200	
Income tax	60		62	
		220		362
		1,250		1,312

Other information:

	20X2	20X1
(1) Industry average statistics		
Return on capital employed	29%	30%
Return on shareholder's capital	28%	28%
Operating profit margin	10%	10%
Asset turnover ratio	2.8 times	2.8 times
Current ratio	1:1	1:1
Quick ratio (Acid test)	0.7:1	0.7:1
Receivables days	12 days	12 days
Gearing ratio (Medium and long term debt as a % of equity based on book value)	60%	50%
Interest cover (Times interest earned)	4 times	5 times

Note. All averages are based on year end values.

(2) Retailer Co's operating profit is expected to grow by 10% per annum for the next two years.

(3) The secured debenture was redeemed in December 20X1.

(4) Each convertible debenture is convertible into 1,000 shares (per $100 nominal value) at any time during 20X5. The convertible debenture is held by a venture capital organisation, which provided finance for Retailer Co to modernise its retail outlets in 20W9. The venture capitalist currently also holds 20% of the company's ordinary shares.

Required

Assess the financial performance and financial position of Retailer Co in comparison to the industry average.

(11 marks are available for calculations and 9 marks are available for appropriate commentary) **(20 marks)**

57 Clean Lens Co
6 mins

Clean Lens Co is a contact lens manufacturer and distributor producing an extensive range of contact lenses that are distributed direct to customers via the internet. It is a small company with five shareholders, all of whom are involved in the running of the company.

The company is in the preliminary stages of developing a new type of contact lens, made of a unique material that moulds to the shape of the eye, providing revolutionary comfort for the lens wearer. The company's projections show that profits of $1.3 million per annum are expected over the first five years, once sales commence.

In order to proceed with the project, further finance of $1.5 million is required. Clean Lens Co expects to fund the project through a mix of debt and equity finance, and is considering approaching venture capital organisations.

Required

Briefly explain **three** factors that Clean Lens Co should take into account when deciding on the mix of debt and equity finance. **(5 marks)**

58 Caterer Co — 24 mins

Caterer Co produces a standard meal for consumption by airline passengers, which it sells to various airlines throughout Europe. Each meal is sold to the airlines for $2.00.

At present, the company's plant is operating at full capacity and it is not possible to increase sales above the current level, unless further investment is made in premises and equipment.

The most recent set of company accounts reveals the following.

STATEMENT OF PROFIT OR LOSS FOR YEAR ENDING 31 MAY 20X1

	$m
Revenue (2m meals)	4.0
Less variable costs	(2.0)
	2.0
Less fixed costs	(1.0)
Profit before finance cost and taxation	1.0
Less finance cost	(0.2)
Profit before tax	0.8
Less income tax cost (25%)	(0.2)
Profit after tax	0.6

STATEMENT OF FINANCIAL POSITION EXTRACTS AS AT 31 MAY 20X1

	$m	$m
Share capital (equity)		
5m ordinary shares (par value 50c)	2.5	
Share premium	2.0	
Retained earnings	0.5	
		5.0
Medium term finance		
10% debentures 20Y0		2.0
		7.0

Notes

1 The production manager has indicated that the building of an extension and the installation of a new packaging process at a cost of $2 million will increase output by 20%. It is expected that this additional capacity will be fully utilised.

2 This expansion would be financed by $2 million 10% debentures, issued at par.

3 The new proposed investment will reduce variable costs of all meals by 20c per meal, but will increase fixed costs by $200,000 per annum.

4 Installation of the new facilities could be put in place immediately.

5 There is no change expected in the tax rate.

Required

(a) Assuming the company decides to install the new facilities immediately, prepare a projected statement of profit or loss for the year ended 31 May 20X2. **(12 marks)**

(b) Calculate and comment on the following ratios at 31 May 20X1 and those projected at 31 May 20X2:

  Gearing ratio (Total debt/total equity)
  Interest cover (Times interest earned) **(4 marks)**

(c) Identify and discuss **two** practical factors that are likely to have an influence on the level of gearing which can be achieved. (Where possible, relate your answer to a company such as Caterer Co.) **(4 marks)**

(Total = 20 marks)

59 Zimmer Co — 18 mins

Zimmer Co is a listed company specialising in the manufacture and distribution of mobility aids, ranging from walking sticks to wheelchairs. The company directors are considering branching out into the manufacture and distribution of stair lifts. Such expansion would require considerable capital investment and the company is therefore considering how it could finance the project.

Required

Explain:

(a) The advantages and disadvantages, to a company, of debt finance over equity finance; **(10 marks)**

(b) The reasons why a company may choose to issue preference shares rather than ordinary shares or debt. **(5 marks)**

(Total = 15 marks)

60 Gym Jam Co — 18 mins

Gym Jam Co is a well-established company that hires out a range of top quality treadmills to gyms across the country, under operating leases.

Over recent months, Gym Jam Co's client base has expanded so rapidly that the company has struggled to finance the level of treadmill purchases required to supply its new clients. The company used a loan from its local bank to assist with its last bulk order of treadmill purchases two years ago. Interest on this loan was variable, being linked to the bank's base rate, and Gym Jam Co saw its interest charges steadily increasing over the two-year period. It is now considering using a lease (fixed interest) to acquire the next bulk order of treadmills.

In the last year, the company's receivables days have increased from an average of 30 days to 45 days, partly because accounts receivable ledger staff could not cope with the increased workload. Currently, all customers are invoiced every three months (quarterly) for the hire of the treadmills, and most of them pay by cheque. Invoices are raised manually and state on them that payment terms are 30 days from invoice date.

You are an accounting technician for the company, and have been asked to assist in resolving these problems.

Required

(a) Briefly describe **two** advantages of a lease for Gym Jam Co. **(4 marks)**

(b) Identify **four** weaknesses in Gym Jam Co's invoicing and credit control system and indicate how they can be rectified. **(8 marks)**

(c) Explain why the interest charges on Gym Jam Co's loan kept increasing. **(3 marks)**

(Total = 15 marks)

61 Sources of finance — 18 mins

Financial analysts will use ratios to compare performance of companies in the same industry.

Lenders will frequently use ratio analysis to help them decide whether to lend to an individual in the first place and whether to continue their financial support. Business owners and managers also use ratios to assess the financial performance of their business. Such ratios may include earnings per share, interest cover, gearing and net profit margin.

Required

(a) Outline **four** sources of finance (short and/or long-term) available to small and medium-sized businesses. Ignore government grants, leasing and factoring. **(12 marks)**

(b) Discuss **two** limitations of ratio analysis. **(3 marks)**

(Total = 15 marks)

62 Slim Jim Co — 6 mins

Slim Jim Co is a five-year old private company specialising in the manufacture of a range of health drinks, foods and supplements aimed at the fitness market. At present, their biggest customers are health food shops and fitness centres. However, now that their brand has become established, the wealthy owners, who also manage the business, are convinced that sales could be increased dramatically through the opening of an internet shop. They are currently considering how best to fund the expansion of the business.

Funds would be needed to set up the website, expand manufacturing at the factory, and employ more staff to deal with administration, despatch and delivery of the web orders.

It is estimated that $2 million would be needed for the expansion. At present, the market value of the company's equity is $4 million and the company has loans of $0.5 million, repayable in six months' time. The company also has cash built up from retained earnings of $1.3 million.

Required

Outline **three** appropriate sources of medium/long-term finance that may be available to Slim Jim Co to finance its expansion. (Presume that government grants and leasing are **not** appropriate.) **(5 marks)**

63 Convertible loan notes (June 2020 exam) — 6 mins

Explain the main features of convertible loan notes and explain TWO reasons why a company might issue them. **(5 marks)**

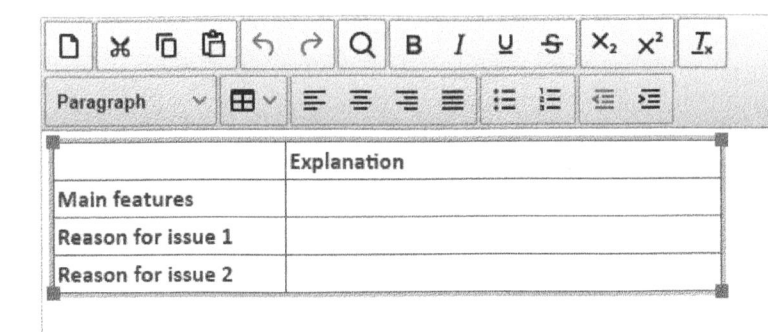

	Explanation
Main features	
Reason for issue 1	
Reason for issue 2	

64 Educate Co — 18 mins

Educate Co is a fast-growing company specialising in the provision of adult education. It currently has ten language schools and three information technology schools. It is estimated that the education sector will grow by 15% over the next five years. The company is keen to take advantage of the opportunities which are available and is seeking to raise funds to finance its growth.

Since the company is 'highly geared' its advisors have suggested that it should seek to raise funds through some sort of share capital issue, rather than a loan.

Required

(a) Explain **four** reasons why a company might seek a stock exchange listing. **(10 marks)**

FFM FOUNDATIONS IN FINANCIAL MANAGEMENT

(b) Explain the meaning of the term 'highly geared' and why it is important to a company trying to raise extra finance. **(5 marks)**

(Total = 15 marks)

65 Venture capital (December 2019 exam) — 6 mins

Describe THREE main conditions a venture capitalist may require when investing in a business. **(5 marks)**

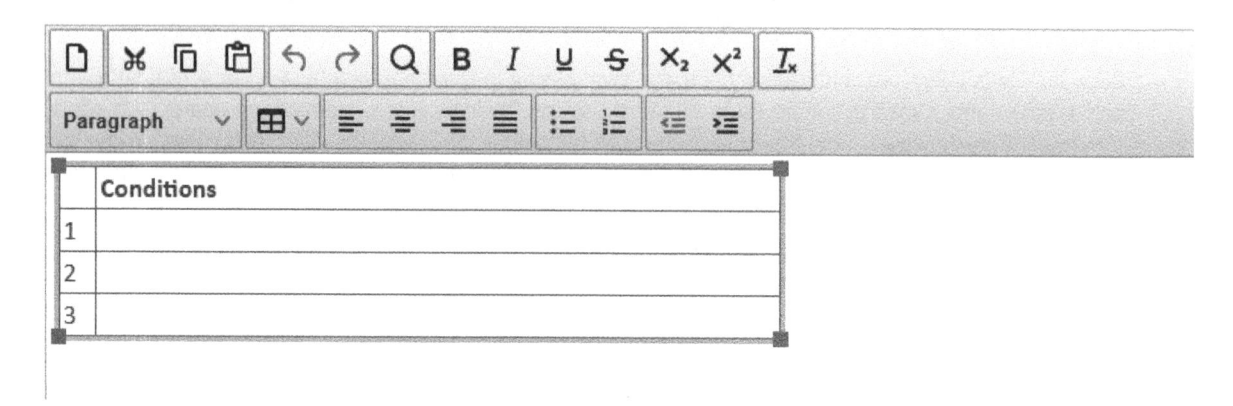

	Conditions
1	
2	
3	

66 Skint Co — 6 mins

Skint Co is a small family owned company that makes fuses for electrical plugs. It was set up 25 years ago by its main shareholder, Mr Holmes, who is also managing director of the company.

The company is facing short-term cash flow difficulties. It is already a highly geared company and Mr Holmes is concerned that the bank will not lend it any more money. He is considering applying for a personal loan or giving a personal guarantee in order to solve the company's short-term cash flow difficulties.

Required

List and explain **two** general factors that will be taken into account by a bank when deciding whether or not to lend money to a client. **(5 marks)**

67 Lease and hire purchase (June 2020 exam) — 6 mins

Explain the main similarities and differences between a lease and a hire purchase agreement. **(5 marks)**

68 Leasing and hire purchase — 6 mins

A business may decide to finance the acquisition of machines or equipment by means of a leasing or hire purchase arrangement.

Explain the benefits of these methods of financing. **(5 marks)**

QUESTIONS

69 Gearing and EPS 18 mins

Two companies Company A and Company B are identical in every respect, with the exception of their capital structure. Both companies have assets of $2,000,000, and both have annual profits before interest and tax of $200,000. However, Company A is an all equity company, with 2,000,000 shares of $1, and Company B is a 50%-geared company, with 1,000,000 shares of $1 and $1,000,000 of 6% debt. The rate of taxation is 25%.

Required

(a) Calculate the earnings per share for each company. (5 marks)

(b) Calculate the earnings per share if the annual profit before interest and tax increases by 50% to $300,000. (5 marks)

(c) Explain what the relevance of the financial gearing of the company to the change in earnings per share given the change in pre-tax profit. (5 marks)

(Total = 15 marks)

70 Blimp Company 18 mins

The statement of financial position of Blimp Company (Blimp) as at 31 December 20X5 is as follows:

	$m
Non-current assets	33.0
Current assets	66.9
Total assets	99.9
Equity and liabilities	
$0.50 ordinary shares	12.0
Accumulated profits	31.2
Total equity	43.2
10% Debentures	20.0
Current liabilities	36.7
Total equity and liabilities	99.9

A statement of profit or loss for the year to 31 December 20X5 is as follows:

	$m
Sales	153.8
Profit before interest and taxation	22.8
Interest payable	2.0
Profit before taxation	20.8
Tax (25%)	5.2
Profit after taxation	15.6

The company wishes to expand its production facilities to meet an increase in sales demand for its products. It will need $10 million of new capital to invest in equipment. It is expected that annual profit before interest and taxation will increase by $4 million.

Blimp is considering the following possible methods of financing the expansion programme:

(a) Issuing 5 million $0.50 equity shares at a premium of $1.50 per share

(b) Issuing 2 million $0.50 equity shares at a premium of $1.50 per share and $6 million 10% Debentures at par

Assume that the rate of tax on profits is 25%.

Required

For each of the financing schemes under consideration:

(a) Calculate the earnings per share for the year to 31 December 20X5. (2 marks)
(b) Calculate the expected earnings per share for the year ended 31 December 20X6. (9 marks)

(c) Compare the effect on EPS of the two proposed methods of financing the new investment. **(4 marks)**

(Total = 15 marks)

71 Internally-generated funds — 6 mins

Briefly explain the importance of internally-generated funds for a company. **(5 marks)**

72 New company — 18 mins

A company was established about one year ago by an individual who has developed a patented product. They own 100% of the company. Trials of the product have been successful and early sales have been encouraging. The owner now needs additional finance to expand the business to increase production capacity and sales. They are aware, however, that small companies can have great difficulty in obtaining finance for growth.

Required

(a) In the context of the financing problem for many small companies, explain briefly the nature of:

    (i) Funding gap
    (ii) Maturity gap
    (iii) Inadequate security. **(7 marks)**

(b) Indicate the sources of finance that the company may be able to obtain to finance a major expansion of the business. **(4 marks)**

(c) Indicate, with brief reasons, sources of finance that are sometimes available to small and medium-sized companies but which are unlikely to be available to this company. **(4 marks)**

(Total = 15 marks)

Do you know? – Investment decisions

Check that you know the following basic points before you attempt any questions. If in doubt, you should go back to your BPP Interactive Text and revise first.

- A .... cost is a future cash flow arising as a direct result of a decision.

- .... cost is the benefit which could have been earned, but has been given up, by choosing one option instead of another.

- .... expenditure is expenditure on non-current assets, examples of which are:

  - ....
  - ....
  - ....
  - ....

- Expenditure for the purpose of the trade, or to maintain non-current assets, is called .... expenditure.

- There are various methods of evaluating capital projects.

- The .... method, also called the return on investment method, calculates the estimated average profits as a percentage of the estimated average investment.

- The .... is the time taken for the initial investment to be recovered in the cash inflows from the project. This is particularly relevant if there are liquidity problems, or if distant forecasts are very uncertain.

- .... techniques take account of the time value of money. As with payback, these techniques use cash figures before depreciation in the calculations.

- The .... method calculates the present value of all cash flows, and sums them to give the NPV. If this is positive, then the project is acceptable. The .... is the period by which the .... is expected to become positive.

- The .... technique uses a trial and error method to discover the discount rate which produces a .... of zero. This discount rate will be the return forecast for the project.

- Discounted cash flow (DCF) methods of appraisal have a number of advantages over other appraisal methods.

  - ....
  - ....
  - ....
  - ....

  TRY QUESTIONS 73–92

- *Possible pitfalls*

  Write down the mistakes you know you should avoid.

Did you know? – Investment decisions

Could you fill in the blanks? The answers are in bold. Use this page for revision purposes as you approach the exam.

- A **relevant** cost is a future cash flow arising as a direct result of a decision.
- **Opportunity** cost is the benefit which could have been earned, but has been given up, by choosing one option instead of another.
- **Capital** expenditure is expenditure on non-current assets, examples of which are:

    – Land and buildings   – Plant and machinery
    – Motor vehicles   – Fixtures and fittings

- Expenditure for the purpose of the trade, or to maintain non-current assets, is called **revenue** expenditure.
- There are various methods of evaluating capital projects.
- The **accounting rate of return** method, also called the return on investment method, calculates the estimated average profits as a percentage of the estimated average investment.
- The **payback period** is the time taken for the initial investment to be recovered in the cash inflows from the project. This is particularly relevant if there are liquidity problems, or if distant forecasts are very uncertain.
- **Discounted cash flow** techniques take account of the time value of money. As with payback, these techniques use cash figures before depreciation in the calculations.
- The **net present value** method calculates the present value of all cash flows, and sums them to give the NPV. If this is positive, then the project is acceptable. The **discounted payback period** is the period by which the **net present value** is expected to become positive.
- The **internal rate of return** technique uses a trial and error method to discover the discount rate which produces a **net present value** of zero. This discount rate will be the return forecast for the project.
- Discounted cash flow (DCF) methods of appraisal have a number of advantages over other appraisal methods.

    – **The time value of money is taken into account.**
    – **All of a project's cash flows are taken into account.**
    – **The timing of cash flows is allowed for.**
    – **There are universally accepted methods of calculating the NPV and IRR.**

    TRY QUESTIONS 73–92

- *Possible pitfalls*

    – **Including non-relevant costs and sunk costs when appraising investments.**
    – **Treating depreciation as a cash flow.**
    – **Not stating your assumptions.**

73 MCQ Question Bank 10 — 12 mins

73.1 Why is the present value of a future cash flow always less than the amount of the future cash flow?

The present value of a cash flow is lower than the future cash flow because:

- ○ The amount of the future cash flow is uncertain, and the present value is lower because of this uncertainty.
- ○ The effect of inflation means that a future cash flow is not worth as much as its present day equivalent.
- ○ It is an alternative amount of money to a future cash flow, and so must be quoted at a discount.
- ○ A present value is the amount that could be invested now to obtain the future cash flow, given a return on investment equal to the discount rate. **(2 marks)**

73.2 An investor with £10,000 to invest puts the money into a three-year savings bond. Although the bond is marketed as a 4% bond, interest is credited to the account at 2% compound every six months. What will be the value of this investment after three years?

- ○ $11,040.81
- ○ $11,200.00
- ○ $11,248.64
- ○ $11,261.62 **(2 marks)**

73.3 At a higher discount rate, the present value of a future cash flow will be:

- ○ Lower
- ○ Higher
- ○ The same
- ○ Impossible to say **(2 marks)**

73.4 **The following question is taken from the December 2015 exam.**

A company is considering two mutually exclusive projects. The cash flows for each project are as follows:

Year	0	1	2	3
Project X	$(15,000)	$8,000	$8,000	$8,000
Project Y	$(15,000)			$26,000

Which project(s) should the company undertake?

- ○ Both projects
- ○ Project X only
- ○ Project Y only
- ○ Neither project **(2 marks)**

73.5 Which of the following cash flows has the highest present value at a discount rate of 9%? Use present value tables for your answer.

- ○ $25,000 at the end of Year 4
- ○ $30,000 at the end of Year 6
- ○ $20,000 at the end of Year 2
- ○ $50,000 at the end of Year 12 **(2 marks)**

(Total = 10 marks)

74 MCQ Question Bank 11 — 24 mins

74.1 Which of the following are examples of revenue expenditure?

(i) Purchasing inventory
(ii) Maintenance of production equipment
(iii) Purchasing a factory building
(iv) Paying employee salaries

○ (i), (ii) and (iii) only
○ (i), (ii) and (iv) only
○ (i), (iii) and (iv) only
○ (ii), (iii) and (iv) only

(2 marks)

74.2 **The following question is taken from the June 2016 exam.**

T Co has been asked to quote for a one-off project which will require 60 hours of skilled labour. Skilled labour is currently fully utilised elsewhere in the company where it earns a contribution of $5 per hour. Skilled labourers are paid $6.40 per hour. T Co can only hire an additional 30 hours of labour. The additional labour will be paid 25% more than T Co pays its own skilled labour.

Using relevant costing principles, what is the cost of skilled labour that should be included in the quotation?

○ $384
○ $582
○ $432
○ $684

(2 marks)

74.3 Raven Co is considering a new investment and is following the steps of the decision making and control cycle. Which step of the cycle follows immediately after detailed evaluation?

○ Implementation
○ Consideration
○ Authorisation
○ Decision

(2 marks)

74.4 The following information is available for Project Go.

	$
Profit	
Year 1	1,000
Year 2	2,000
Year 3	3,000
Year 4	2,000
Total	8,000
Initial investment	7,500
Residual value	2,500

Calculate the accounting rate of return for Project Go.

○ 27%
○ 40%
○ 80%
○ 106%

(2 marks)

74.5 Guild Co is considering purchasing a new machine. The relevant cash flows are:

	$
Cost	125,000
Cash inflows	
Year 1	35,500
Year 2	45,500
Year 3	52,000
Year 4	27,000
Total	160,000

Calculate the simple payback period of the new machine.

- ○ Two years and six months
- ○ Two years and eight months
- ○ Two years and ten months
- ○ Three years exactly

(2 marks)

74.6 Motor Co is considering purchasing new equipment. The relevant cash flows are:

	$	Present value factor
Cost	85,000	1
Cash inflows:		
Year 1	15,000	0.909
Year 2	20,000	0.826
Year 3	45,000	0.751
Year 4	37,000	0.683
Total	117,000	

Calculate the discounted payback period of the new machine.

- ○ Three years and two months
- ○ Three years and five months
- ○ Three years and seven months
- ○ Three years and ten months

(3 marks)

74.7 Tilly will receive an annuity starting after three years. It will pay her $1,500 per year for three years and her cost of capital is 10%.

Using the annuity rates below, calculate the present value of the annuity.

Year	Annuity rate 10%
1	0.909
2	1.736
3	2.487
4	3.170
5	3.791
6	4.355

- ○ $1,778
- ○ $2,802
- ○ $4,755
- ○ $10,263

(2 marks)

74.8 The results of a net present value analysis for Project Green are as follows:

	$
NPV using 10% cost of capital	5,000
NPV using 15% cost of capital	(2,000)

Calculate the internal rate of return (IRR) for Project Green.

- ○ 11.6%
- ○ 12.6%
- ○ 13.6%
- ○ 14.6%

(2 marks)

74.9 **The following question is taken from the December 2014 exam.**

An organisation is considering a project with the following cash flows:

Time	Description	Cash flow $
0	Initial investment	(60,000)
0–7	Yearly costs	(12,000)
4–10	Yearly revenues	35,000

Using a cost of capital of 10%, which annuity factors should be used to discount the yearly costs and yearly revenues?

	Yearly costs	Yearly revenues
○	5.868	4.355
○	4.868	4.355
○	4.868	3.658
○	5.868	3.658

(2 marks)

74.10 How do public sector capital budgeting decisions differ from private sector ones?

- ○ They do not seek to make a profit
- ○ The payback period is the key appraisal tool used rather than net present value analysis
- ○ The cost of capital used is the Bank of England base rate
- ○ They take into account social costs and social benefits

(2 marks)

(Total = 20 marks)

75 Financing concepts — 6 mins

(a) Explain briefly:

(i) The difference between simple and compound interest
(ii) The connection between the present value and the future value of a cash flow. **(3 marks)**

(b) An investor invests $20,000 for three years at 4% annual compound interest, after which the annual interest rate changes to 2% compound. What will be the value of the investment after seven years?

(2 marks)

(Total = 5 marks)

QUESTIONS

76 Question with help: Two capital projects — 24 mins

The following information relates to two possible capital projects of which you have to select one to invest in. Both projects have an initial capital cost of $200,000 and only one can be undertaken. Profit is calculated after deducting straight line depreciation.

Project	X	Y
Expected profits	$	$
Year 1	80,000	30,000
2	80,000	50,000
3	40,000	90,000
4	20,000	120,000
Estimated resale value at end of Year 4	40,000	40,000

The cost of capital is 16%, relevant discount factors being as follows.

End of year	
1	0.862
2	0.743
3	0.641
4	0.552
5	0.476

Required

(a) Calculate:

　(i) The payback period to one decimal place
　(ii) The accounting rate of return using average investment
　(iii) The net present value **(11 marks)**

(b) Advise the board which project in your opinion should be undertaken, giving reasons for your decision. **(3 marks)**

(c) State **three** ways in which risk can be taken into account when making a capital investment decision. **(6 marks)**

(Total = 20 marks)

Approaching the answer

Use this answer plan to construct your answer if you are stuck.

(a) Will give you some basic practice of three commonly used appraisal techniques. Remember the following rules.

- Cash flows are used in payback and net present value calculations. If you are given accounting profits (as in this question) you must add back the depreciation charge in order to convert the figures from profits to cash flows.

- Accounting profits are used in calculating the accounting rate of return. Accounting profits are taken after depreciation.

(b) Involves explaining which is the best of the three methods, and why, and also what the implications might be if either of the other methods suggest a different recommendation. Risks can be accounted for in a number of different ways in (c). Risk criteria can be set, an adjustment made to the calculation or a range of outcomes considered.

77 Taxi Co — 24 mins

Taxi Co is a long established company providing high quality transport for customers. It currently owns and runs 350 cars and has a turnover of $10 million per annum.

The current system for allocating jobs to drivers is very inefficient. Taxi Co is considering the implementation of a new computerised tracking system called 'Kwictrac'. This will make the allocation of jobs far more efficient.

You are an accounting technician for an accounting firm advising Taxi Co. You have been asked to perform some calculations to help Taxi Co decide whether Kwictrac should be implemented. The project is being appraised over five years.

The costs and benefits of the new system are set out below.

(i) The central tracking system costs $2,100,000 to implement. This amount will be payable in three equal instalments: one immediately, the second in one year's time, and the third in two years' time.

(ii) Depreciation on the new system will be provided at $420,000 per annum.

(iii) Staff will need to be trained how to use the new system. This will cost Taxi Co $425,000 in the first year.

(iv) If Kwictrac is implemented, revenues will rise to an estimated $11 million this year, thereafter increasing by 5% per annum (ie compounded). Even if Kwictrac is not implemented, revenues will increase by an estimated $200,000 per annum, from their current level of $10 million per annum.

(v) Despite increased revenues, Kwictrac will still make overall savings in terms of vehicle running costs. These cost savings are estimated at 1% of the post Kwictrac revenues each year (ie the $11 million revenue, rising by 5% thereafter, as referred to in note (iv)).

(vi) Six new staff operatives will be recruited to manage the Kwictrac system. Their wages will cost the company $120,000 per annum in the first year, $200,000 in the second year, thereafter increasing by 5% per annum (ie compounded).

(vii) Taxi Co will have to take out a maintenance contract for the Kwictrac system. This will cost $75,000 per annum.

(viii) Interest on money borrowed to finance the project will cost $150,000 per annum.

(ix) Taxi Co's cost of capital is 10% per annum.

Required

(a) Calculate the net present value of the new Kwictrac project to the nearest $'000. Use the discount factors provided at the end of the question. **(12 marks)**

(b) Calculate the discounted payback period for the project and interpret the result. **(3 marks)**

(c) Taxi Co wants to ensure that it has enough cash available to pay the second and third instalments for the Kwictrac system, when they fall due. The company has therefore decided to invest the cash on time deposits with its local bank. The rates of interest paid by the bank are as follows:

Six months deposits	7% per annum
One year deposits	8% per annum
Two year deposits	9% per annum
Three year deposits	10% per annum

Interest is paid once a year, at the end of the year.

Required

Calculate the total amount of cash that Taxi Co needs to put on deposit immediately in order to meet the final two instalments for Kwictrac. **(5 marks)**

Note. You should assume that all cash flows occur at the end of the year, unless otherwise stated.

(Total = 20 marks)

QUESTIONS

78 Quick Freeze Foods Co — 24 mins

Quick Freeze Foods Co produces a range of convenience processed foods for a number of supermarket chain stores. Its success has been based on the expertise and customer-driven emphasis of its research and development team.

The R&D team has identified two mutually exclusive projects which could be undertaken. The finance director has recruited you as assistant accountant to carry out a financial evaluation of each project.

Details of the three projects' cash flows are shown below.

Cash flow timing

	Indian range $	Chinese range $
Initial outlay	(80,000)	(20,000)
1	26,500	5,000
2	26,500	6,000
3	26,500	8,000
4	26,500	10,000

Assume that cash flows occur at the ends of each of the years shown.

Required

(a) Using each of the following appraisal methods rank the projects in order of their investment potential.

    (i) Net present value (NPV) at 10% **(8 marks)**
    (ii) Approximate internal rate of return (IRR) **(8 marks)**

(b) Critically compare each of the above investment appraisal methods. **(4 marks)**

(Total = 20 marks)

79 Weavers Co — 24 mins

Weavers Co is engaged in the manufacture of carpets and is considering an expansion of production facilities to meet an anticipated increase in demand over the next five years. The board of directors is currently considering two mutually exclusive options.

The first option is to acquire an additional loom.

(i) The loom will have an initial cost of $800,000 and will have a life of five years. At the end of year five it will have a zero scrap value.

(ii) The loom will produce an additional 1,000 carpets per annum for the next five years.

(iii) The sales price of each carpet is $1,000 which has been fixed for the next five years by Government price control.

(iv) Each carpet produced by this loom requires:

    (1) Material costing $400.
    This will remain constant for the next five years.

    (2) Direct labour of ten hours at $10 per hour in year one.
    For each of the subsequent four years, pay will increase by 2% of the preceding year's level.

    (3) Machine time of 20 hours at $10 per hour.
    This will remain constant for the next five years.

(v) Depreciation is on a straight line basis.

The second option is to subcontract production of an additional 1,000 carpets per annum under a fixed contract for the next five years.

(i) There is an annual subcontract fee payable at the end of each of the next five years commencing at the end of year one at $150,000. For each of the subsequent four years this fee will increase by 5% of the preceding year's level.

(ii) Over the next five years the subcontractor has agreed to produce and deliver up to a maximum 1,000 carpets each year to the company for an agreed cost per carpet of $700 (in addition to the annual fee in (i)).

(iii) The sales price of each carpet is $1,000 which has been fixed for the next five years by Government price control.

(iv) Under the contract Weavers Co must agree to accept a minimum of 750 carpets per annum.

(v) Weavers Co has already spent $100,000 conducting research into the viability of this subcontract arrangement.

The cost of capital is 10%.

Ignore taxation.

Required

(a) Calculate the net present value of each of the options to the nearest $'000. State clearly any assumptions made. **(18 marks)**

(b) On the basis of the calculation made in (a) above, which of the two options would you choose and why? **(2 marks)**

(Total = 20 marks)

80 Rainbow Co — 24 mins

Rainbow Co, a medium-sized company specialising in the manufacture and distribution of equipment for babies and small children, is evaluating a new capital expenditure project. Together with another company outside the group, it has invented a remote controlled pushchair, one of the first of its kind on the market. It has been unable to obtain a patent for the invention, but is sure that it will monopolise the market for the first three years. After this, it expects to be faced with stiff competition.

The details are set out below.

(1) The project has an immediate cost of $2,100,000.

(2) Sales are expected to be $1,550,000 per annum for years 1 to 3, falling to $650,000 per annum for the two years after that. No further sales of the product are expected after the end of this five-year period.

(3) Cost of sales is 40% of sales.

(4) Distribution costs represent 10% of sales.

(5) 20% of net profits are payable to their co-inventor the year after the profits are earned.

(6) The company's cost of capital is 5%.

Required

(a) Calculate the net present value of the project at the company's required rate of return. Assume that all cash flows arise annually in arrears unless otherwise stated. Conclude whether the project is financially viable. **(15 marks)**

(b) Calculate the project's internal rate of return (IRR) to the nearest percent, using discount factors of 5% and 10%. **(5 marks)**

Note. Calculations should be in $'000, to the nearest $'000

(Total = 20 marks)

81 Pills Co — 24 mins

Pills Co is a medium-sized medical research company, engaged in the development of new medical treatments. To date, the company has invested $250,000 in the development of a new product called 'Gravia'. It is estimated that it will take a further two years of development and testing before Gravia is approved by medical industry regulators.

The company believes it can sell the patent for Gravia to a multinational pharmaceutical company for $1,000,000, when it has been fully developed.

The directors of Pills Co are currently reviewing the Gravia project, as there is some concern about the size of the required finance to complete the development work.

The project manager has provided the following information.

(1) To complete the development, Pills Co will need to acquire additional type A material expected to cost $150,000 per annum over the next two years.

(2) Type B material will also be required. Currently, there is a sufficient stock of type B material to last for the two years of the project. This material originally cost $50,000. Its replacement cost is $75,000. Instead of using it on this project, it could immediately be sold as scrap for $20,000. It has no other alternative use.

(3) If it is decided to continue with the Gravia project, specialist equipment will need to be purchased immediately for $100,000. This equipment could eventually be sold at the end of the project for $25,000.

(4) Two chemists currently employed for an annual salary of $20,000 each will be made redundant whenever the Gravia project ends. Redundancy payments are expected to be one full year's salary each.

(5) Laboratory technicians currently employed by Pills Co are working on the Gravia project at a total annual cost of $85,000. The company has a variety of other projects to which the technicians could be transferred whenever the Gravia project ends.

(6) Annual fixed overheads allocated to this project of $100,000 include $60,000 general Head Office overheads and $40,000 overheads which are specifically incurred as a direct consequence of the project.

(7) If the development project does not proceed, a foreign dictator has offered immediately to buy the existing Gravia formula from Pills Co for military use at a cost of $250,000.

(8) Interest on money borrowed to finance the project will cost $20,000 per annum.

(9) All cash flows occur at the end of the year unless otherwise stated.

(10) Pills' estimated cost of capital is 10%.

Required

(a) Briefly explain **TWO** main principles used to identify relevant costs for decision-making using examples from the question. **(6 marks)**

(b) (i) Calculate the project's net present value to the nearest $'000. **(12 marks)**

    (ii) Based on financial analysis, determine whether the company should proceed with the project. **(2 marks)**

(Total = 20 marks)

82 Soke Co — 18 mins

Soke Co, an international soft drinks company, has recently acquired Fizz Co, which produces high quality soft drinks for its local domestic market. Following the acquisition, the finance department of Soke Co examined the capital investment appraisal procedures in Fizz Co.

The report summary was critical of processes in use and concluded that:

(1) There is no apparent structure or formalised process for evaluation of capital investment projects.
(2) Post completion controls do not exist in any meaningful way.

Required

(a) As the Financial Assistant, prepare a draft report to the Finance Director, identifying and briefly explaining the major stages in evaluating and controlling expenditure projects. **(10 marks)**

(b) Identify and briefly explain **TWO** advantages of a post completion audit. **(5 marks)**

(Total = 15 marks)

83 Silly Filly Co — 24 mins

Silly Filly Co is a recently established company specialising in the manufacture of talking toy horses for children. The Silly Filly range currently comprises three key products – all of which are toy horses – plus approximately thirty accessories to complement the range, from stables to grooming kits.

The Silly Filly range has been such a success in the last year that the management is considering producing an animated film to accompany the range. This is in accordance with the company's long-term expansion plans, culminating in a stock exchange flotation in three years' time.

The film will take one year to make. In the year following that, sales of the film will commence.

You, an accounting technician for the company, have been asked to assist in appraising the project to decide whether it should go ahead. The following information is relevant to your calculations.

(i) Market research has already been carried out at a cost of $1.2 million.

(ii) The services of a company specialising in animation will be required at a total cost of $520,000. 50% of these costs will be paid immediately with the remainder being paid in one year's time.

(iii) Two producers will be employed throughout the first year of the project. They will each be paid salaries of $120,000.

(iv) Other production costs during the year are expected to be $650,000.

(v) A film director will be employed immediately on a one-year contract at a cost of $160,000.

(vi) The animated film is expected to generate revenues of $1.2 million in the first year of sales, $2.2 million in the second year, and $1.6 million in the third year.

(vii) The two producers and the director will each be paid royalties from the film. These will be paid at the rate of 1.5% of gross revenues for **each** of the producers and 2% for the director. They will always be payable one year in arrears.

(viii) Specialist equipment will need to be purchased immediately for the film production. This will cost $2.3 million but can be sold at the end of the year for $1.7 million.

(ix) A loan for $1 million will be taken out to assist in financing the project. The loan will be repayable in two years' time, with interest of 8% per annum being payable for its duration.

(x) The company's cost of capital is 10% per annum.

(xi) Assume that all cash flows occur at the end of each year, unless otherwise stated.

Required

(a) Calculate the project's net present value (NPV) at the company's cost of capital. Conclude as to whether the company should proceed with the project, giving a reason for your conclusion. **(16 marks)**

(b) List **FOUR** costs associated with a new equity issue. **(4 marks)**

(Total = 20 marks)

84 Mr Food — 24 mins

Mr Food owns a café and currently sells hot drinks and food such as sandwiches, crisps and cakes. Annual net income is currently $200,000.

He wants to offer cooked meals and plans to extend his buildings and build a kitchen and a restaurant. In the new buildings, Mr Food will be able to incorporate a kitchen which will meet the necessary hygiene standards and have a restaurant which will be able to seat up to 60 people. Architect's fees of $8,000 have already been incurred in drawing up the plans and the building work is expected to take one year.

Building work

The total cost of building is estimated to be $200,000. This will be paid 25% at the beginning of the project and 75% on completion of the building work, one year later. Depreciation will be charged over 25 years on a straight-line basis.

The building work will cause disruption, which will cause some of the existing clients to leave. Mr Food estimates that the effect of this will be to reduce the current annual net income from the café by 10% for the duration of the building work. Mr Food believes that the current annual net income from the café will return to 95% of its original level once the building work is completed, and will remain at this level.

Running costs (these will arise only when new operations commence in year two)

Cleaners will be employed costing $8,000 for each year the restaurant is open to diners.

Chefs will need to be employed, each earning $10,000 per year. The number of chefs employed will depend on the estimated number of weekly diners and will be calculated using the following table.

Number of weekly diners	Number of chefs to be employed
0–150	1
151–250	2
251–350	3
351–450	4

The minimum number of chefs will be employed.

Waiting staff will be employed, costing $5,000 per year per member of waiting staff. The number of waiting staff required is estimated to be two in the first year the restaurant is open to diners, and then three in each subsequent year.

Cash overheads are currently $30,000 per year. Mr Food estimates that the expansion will cause overheads to increase by 8% in the first year the restaurant is open to diners and that they will then continue at this level.

Net income from the new operations (ie revenue less food costs)

People who frequent the restaurant Friday–Sunday are estimated to generate a net income of $10 per diner per day, whereas those frequenting the restaurant Monday–Thursday are estimated to generate a net income of $7 per diner per day.

The estimated number of diners per week:

Year	Friday–Sunday per day	Monday–Thursday per day
2	40	20
3	50	30
4	60	35
5	60	35

Required

Using the discount tables provided, calculate the net present value of the restaurant project over a five-year period. On the basis of your calculation conclude whether the expansion should take place (assume 52 weeks in a year). Ignore tax in your calculation. **(20 marks)**

85 Nippers — 24 mins

Nippers is a children's nursery. It is a profitable business and demand for child places always exceeds supply because of the great shortage of local nurseries. It is owned and managed by a lady called Mrs Dibble. All the staff at the nursery are either relatives or good friends of Mrs Dibble's and even the shortest-serving member of staff has worked at the nursery for ten years. Mrs Dibble is planning on retiring on her sixtieth birthday in six years' time, at which point she hopes to sell the business to one or some of the existing staff. She wants to work full-time until then since she enjoys working so much.

She is currently considering whether to extend the building in order to create more space so that she can meet the demand for nursery places. Mrs Dibble's brother has offered to do the extension, by himself, at a very competitive price. He is currently unemployed and he faces bankruptcy if he does not find work soon.
Mrs Dibble estimates that, with the extension, she would be able to sell the business as a going concern for $600,000 in six years' time. Without the extension, she would expect to sell it for $500,000 in six years' time.

A local builder has recently approached Mrs Dibble with an unexpected offer to buy the nursery now for $850,000. He hopes to build apartments on the land.

Mrs Dibble needs to decide whether to carry on in business without the extension (Option 1), have the extension built (Option 2), or sell to the developer (Option 3). The following information is available.

(1) Mrs Dibble has already obtained preliminary planning permission for the extension at a cost of $1,200.

(2) Mrs Dibble's building costs are estimated to be $85,000. Of this amount, $45,000 relates to materials and must be paid immediately. The balance of the building costs relates to labour and will be paid on completion of the work. The work would take one year to complete. The nursery would still be open as usual during the year so revenue would be unaffected by the building work.

(3) The nursery currently generates net cash inflows of $98,000 per annum. With the extension, these would rise to $135,000 once the work is complete. Mrs Dibble pays herself a salary, but this amount has already been deducted before arriving at the $98,000.

(4) The nursery's cost of capital is 10% per annum.

(5) Assume that all cash flows occur at the end of each year, unless otherwise stated.

Required

(a) Calculate the net present value (NPV) of each option at the business's cost of capital. Based on these calculations, conclude as to which option Mrs Dibble should choose. **(16 marks)**

(b) List **two** non-financial factors that Mrs Dibble should consider. **(4 marks)**

(Total = 20 marks)

86 Robo Clean Co — 24 mins

Robo Clean Co is a recently established innovation company. It currently has one product on the market, the 'Robovac', a robotic floor cleaner. This has been extremely successful. The company is currently developing a new robotic cleaner called 'Robomum' that vacuums, dusts and presses.

To date $120,000 has been spent on developing the product. The company has also incurred $250,000 of market research costs, although the invoice for these costs has only just been received and will be paid in January.

Since the set-up costs are substantial, a final decision now needs to be made as to whether it is viable to manufacture and sell 'Robomum'. The following revenues and costs have been estimated:

1. A new factory, to be used solely for the production of 'Robomum', will need to be built. This will take nearly a year to build and is expected to cost $11.75 million in total, payable in two installments. The first installment of $6m will be paid at the start of the building work and the second installment for the remaining balance will be paid when the building work has been completed at the end of the year.

2. Robo Clean Co will immediately enter into a one-year contract with a project management company, who will oversee the building of the factory. The total cost of this during the year will be $250,000.

    Two production lines will need to be installed in the factory at a further cost of $1,500,000 payable at the end of the build in one year's time.

3. The machinery for the production of 'Robomum' also needs to be built-to-order and is expected to cost $2.5 million, payable in one year's time. Its terminal value is nil. Depreciation will be charged as soon as production commences (as soon as the build finishes in one year's time) at 10% per annum on a straight-line basis. Maintenance costs for the machinery are estimated at $250,000 per annum.

4. Production and Sales will commence in the year following the build. Sales quantities and prices for 'Robomum' are expected to be as follows:

Years	1	2	3 and 4	5 to 9 (inclusive)
Sales volume ('000 units)	5	10	30	50
Sales price ($)	1,000	800	700	500

    It is anticipated that by the beginning of year 10, a new robotic helper will have replaced 'Robomum', hence there will be no further sales.

5. Material costs for 'Robomum' are estimated at $125 per unit.

6. Labour costs are estimated at $100 per unit.

7. Fixed production overheads on the new factory are estimated at $240,000 per annum. Variable production overheads are expected to be $50 per unit.

8. Head office costs of $4.5 million per annum will be allocated to 'Robomum' when production commences. Of these costs, only $3.7 million is incremental.

9. The introduction of 'Robomum' is expected to adversely affect sales of 'Robovac'. It is thought that, for every two units of 'Robomum' sold, one unit of 'Robovac' will be lost. 'Robovac' is currently sold for $150 per unit and generates a net cash flow of $50 per unit.

10. The company's cost of capital is 5%.

11. Assume that all cash flows occur at the end of the year, unless stated otherwise.

12. All workings should be in $'000, to the nearest $'000.

Required

Calculate the net present value (NPV) of the project at the company's cost of capital. Conclude as to whether Robo Clean Co should proceed with the project.

(20 marks)

87 Go Green Co 24 mins

Go Green Co is a small company specialising in the manufacture of a small range of environmentally friendly toiletries and cleaning products. It is considering extending its production lines to include environmentally friendly soap and washing-up liquid.

The company's research and development department has already spent $450,000 developing the products and a further $325,000 on test marketing them. If the company decides to proceed with the project, new machinery will be purchased immediately and production will commence straight away.

Notes

1   Forecast sales in '000 units, are as follows:

	Years				
	1	2	3	4	5
Soap	250	200	150	90	30
Washing up liquid	240	280	320	170	50

2   Forecasts for the revenues and costs per unit for each of the new products have been made, as detailed below. However, these may need to be revised as per notes (a) to (c) below.

	Soap $	Washing-up liquid $
Selling price	1.75	1.60
Direct materials	(0.15)	(0.35)
Direct labour (Note a)	(0.25)	(0.12)
Variable overheads (Note b)	(0.50)	(0.24)
Allocated fixed overheads (Note c)	(0.65)	(0.65)
	0.20	0.24

(a)   The product cost cards for both products above have been prepared on the basis that each factory worker is paid a standard hourly rate of $6. Further details of labour requirements are as follows:

Year one

Production of each unit of soap requires 2.5 minutes of one factory worker's time. However, all workers are currently working to full capacity. Therefore, for the first year's production of soap, they will have to work overtime, for which they are paid $7.20 per hour.

Production of each unit of washing-up liquid requires 1.2 minutes of one factory worker's time. During the first year, temporary workers provided by an agency will be used to produce the washing-up liquid at a cost to the company of $7 per hour.

Years two to five

New permanent staff will be recruited to produce both soap and washing-up liquid. They will be paid at the company's standard hourly rate of $6 per hour.

(b)   Variable overheads represent factory power costs, which vary according to labour hours worked.

(c)   Allocated fixed overheads comprise factory rental costs of $0.10 per unit and depreciation of $0.55 per unit.

3   The company will need to purchase a new piece of machinery immediately costing $500,000 if the project is to proceed. Some modifications will need to be made to the machinery on site. They will take place as soon as the machinery is purchased and will take two days to complete. The cost of these will be $150,000 payable on completion. The machinery will have no scrap value at the end of the project.

4   There are currently two production lines that are not in use on the top floor of the factory. If the project goes ahead, these two lines will be used for production. If the project does not go ahead the top floor will be rented out immediately to a third party, producing income of $125,000 per annum, receivable annually in arrears.

5   Go Green Co's cost of capital is 10% per annum.

6   Assume that all cash flows occur at the end of the year unless otherwise stated.

7   All workings should be in $'000 to the nearest $'000.

Required

Calculate the net present value of the proposed project over five years and conclude whether the project should be accepted. **(20 marks)**

88 Wicker Co   24 mins

Wicker Co manufactures chairs. It has recently been approached by one of its customers, Chill Co, a garden furniture retailer, who has asked it to enter into a three-year contract to supply a particular range of chairs. The chairs will form part of Chill Co's new luxury collection that they plan to start selling in three months' time. Production would therefore have to commence as soon as possible.

There are three types of chairs in the collection – The Recliner (R), The Soother (S) and The Handy (H). Wicker Co has collated the following information:

1   Chill Co estimates that it would purchase the following quantities of R, S and H over the three year period:

	Year 1	Year 2	Year 3
R	20,000	22,000	24,200
S	25,000	27,500	30,250
H	30,000	33,000	36,300

Wicker Co's intention is not to hold any finished goods inventory at the end of each year.

2   Chill Co will pay $200 for each R purchased, $100 for each S and $70 for each H.

3   Wicker Co will need to use a high-tech machine to make the chairs. This could be purchased immediately at a cost of $200,000 and would have no scrap value at the end of the three years. Alternatively, Wicker Co has another machine on site, for which it no longer has any use, which could be modified at an immediate cost of $75,000. This machine would then be equivalent to the high-tech machine in terms of its capacity to make chairs. This machine was bought two years ago at a cost of $300,000. If it is not used for the Chill Co contract, it will be sold immediately for $100,000. If modified, it would have no scrap value at the end of the three years.

4   Wicker Co would also use some additional existing machinery to carry out the work on the chairs. Depreciation of $45,000 per annum would be allocated to this contract.

5   Materials usage for each of the three chairs are as follows:

	R	S	H
Wood X (m^2)	1	2	3
Fabric (m)	3	2	1

6   Materials costs are as follows:

Wood X $14 per m^2
Fabric $22 per m

Wicker Co already has 160,000m^2 of Wood X in inventory, which it ordered in error last month. Wood X cost $20 per m^2. If Wicker does not use Wood X for this contract, it will either be used immediately as a substitute for Wood Y, which currently costs $13 per m^2, or sold for $11 per m^2.

Also, Wicker Co already has 294,000m of fabric in inventory. The fabric cost the company $20 per metre. If it does not use this fabric for the Chill Co contract, the fabric would be sold immediately for $10 per metre since it has no other use for it.

7   Labour costs incurred will be as follows:

	Year 1	Year 2	Year 3
Labour	1,590	1,980	2,179

8   Variable overheads will be $900,000 in Year 1, and increase by 10% per year after Year 1.

9   Fixed overheads are expected to be $400,000 per annum. Of these, $220,000 relates to apportionment of factory rent. The factory space that would be used for the contract is currently unused and Wicker Co does not foresee it being used at all in the future unless this contract is entered into. The remainder of the fixed overhead cost relates to a new warehouse that would be rented to cope with the increased storage space required for the Chill Co contract.

10 The company's cost of capital is 11%.

Required

Calculate the net present value of the contract and recommend whether Wicker Co should enter into the contract. Workings should be in $'000, to the nearest $'000. **(20 marks)**

89 Painless Co — 24 mins

Painless Co is a pharmaceutical company making both ibuprofen-based and paracetamol-based pain relief tablets. It is considering outsourcing its whole packaging operation. The following information is available:

1   A total of 170 staff would be made redundant immediately. All staff are currently graded from A to D, with grade A staff being the lowest paid. Details of the staff to be made redundant are shown below:

Grade	No. of redundancies	Salary per annum per employee $'000
A	130	16
B	20	19
C	15	32
D	5	64

All redundant Grade A and B employees would immediately receive 70% of their annual salary; Grade C and D employees would immediately receive 85% of their annual salary.

2   The packaging warehouse, which will no longer be required if the outsourcing goes ahead, is rented from a local company under a lease that still has five years to run. There is no clause for the Painless Co to terminate the lease early. The company paid a $100,000 lump sum at the start of the lease five years ago. Painless Co spreads the cost of this lump sum over the life of the lease, charging $10,000 each year as an expense in its statement of profit or loss. In addition to this, the annual rental costs are $25,000 per annum, also an expense in the statement of profit or loss. The company pays the rent annually in advance, the last payment having been made yesterday. Painless Co hopes to sub-let this warehouse for $30,000 per annum, but expects it to take one year before a suitable tenant is found. Rent will then be charged annually in advance.

3   The company owns the packaging factory. If this proposal goes ahead, the factory will either be sold or leased immediately. The company has already met a potential buyer for the factory who would pay $300,000 for it immediately. However, the interested party would alternatively be prepared to lease the factory for a five-year period at a rental of $55,000 per annum, payable annually in advance. The value of the factory, in present value terms, at the end of the rental period would be $65,000.

4   Annual sales of the company's paracetamol and ibuprofen tablets are expected to be 64,000 and 67,200 respectively. These are expected to remain the same for the next five years.

5   The total costs (excluding labour, which is dealt with in note 1) of making one thousand boxes of paracetamol tablets and one thousand boxes of ibuprofen tablets are $7.80 and $7.50 respectively. Alternatively, the respective costs, per thousand, of buying the boxes in are $13 for paracetamol and $14.20 for ibuprofen.

6   The company's cost of capital is 10%.

7   Assume that all cash flows occur at the end of each year, unless told otherwise.

8   Answers should be given in $'000s.

QUESTIONS

Required

Calculate the net present value of the proposal to outsource the manufacture of the packaging, using the discount table extracts provided, and conclude whether the proposal should go ahead.

(20 marks)

90 Discounted payback period (December 2019 exam) — 6 mins

The company is evaluating an investment in a pressing machine. The machine will cost $500,000 and have a useful life of 10 years. At the end of this time its residual value would be $50,000. Annual profits are expected to be $100,000. The company has a cost of capital of 8% and uses straight line depreciation.

Calculate the discounted payback period of the proposed investment in the pressing machine. **(5 marks)**

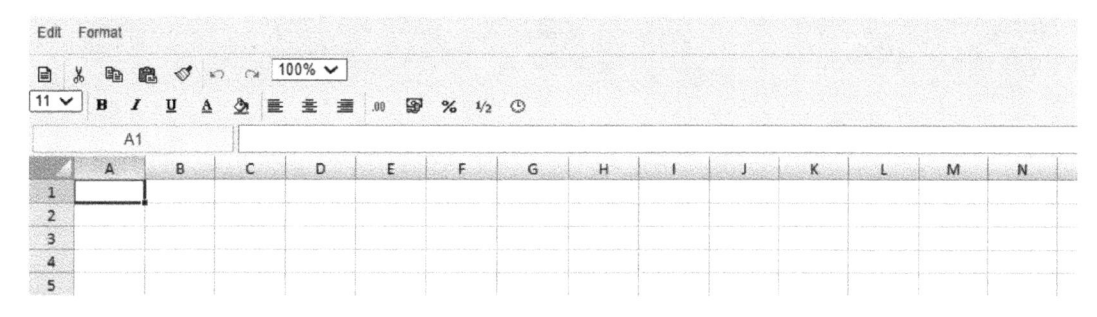

91 Edgely Co (December 2019 exam) — 18 mins

This scenario relates to two requirements.

Edgely Co wishes to evaluate a proposal to launch a new product. The following information is available:

Non-current asset

- A machine required to make a new product will cost $34,000 and it will have a useful economic life of four years.

- Based on an estimate of its residual value at the end of four years, the machine will be depreciated at $7,000 per year on a straight-line basis.

Costs and revenues

- Sales will be $20,000 in its first year and are expected to grow by 5% in each subsequent year.

- Direct material costs will be 30% of sales value each year.

- Labour costs will be $4,000 in the first year and are expected to increase by 2% in each subsequent year.

Note. there will be no inventories of raw materials or finished goods

(a) Calculate the accounting rate of return of the new product based upon average investment. **(9 marks)**

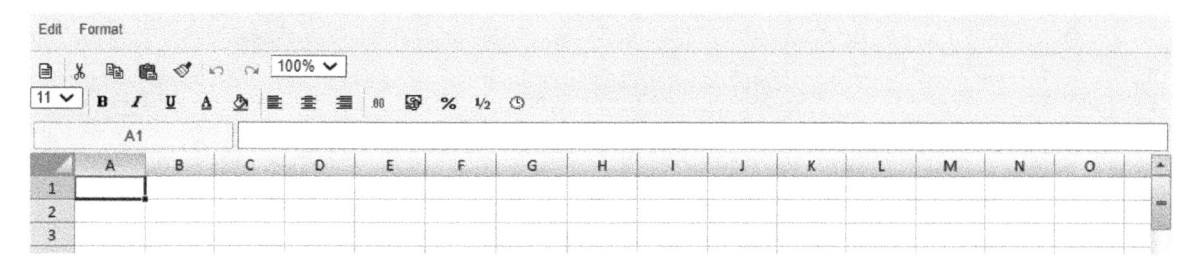

(b) Discuss three benefits of using net present value (NPV) instead of accounting rate of return to appraise new investments.

(6 marks)

(Total = 15 marks)

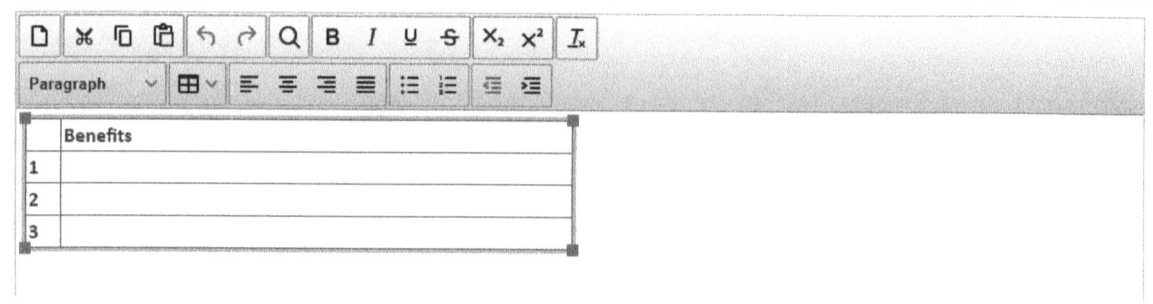

	Benefits
1	
2	
3	

92 Mem Co (June 2020 question) — 18 mins

This scenario relates to two requirements.

Mem Co manufacturers a specialist component and is considering buying a replacement machine costing $2.5 million. This machine would operate for five years after which time it would be sold for $100,000.

The replacement machine would have a production capacity of 300,000 components per year which is 50,000 more components per year than the existing machine produces. Mem Co is able to sell all components produced.

Other information

- If Mem Co purchased the replacement machine it would require a concrete foundation which would cost $15,000. The site has already been assessed as suitable for the foundation by a surveyor who charged a $3000 fee. This fee has not yet been paid.

- If the existing machine was scrapped it could be sold for $48,000 cash now. Otherwise it would last for a further five years at which time its scrap value would be zero.

- The selling price of $14.00 per components would not change if the replacement machine were purchased.

- Variable costs are currently $6.60 per component and the replacement machine's variable costs would be $5.00 per component.

- Cash fixed costs would increase by $43,000 per year if the existing machine were replaced.

- Mem Co uses a 9% cost of capital to evaluate projects of this type.

(a) Calculate the net present value (NPV) of the replacement machine and conclude whether Mem Co should buy the replacement machine. Show all calculations.

(10 marks)

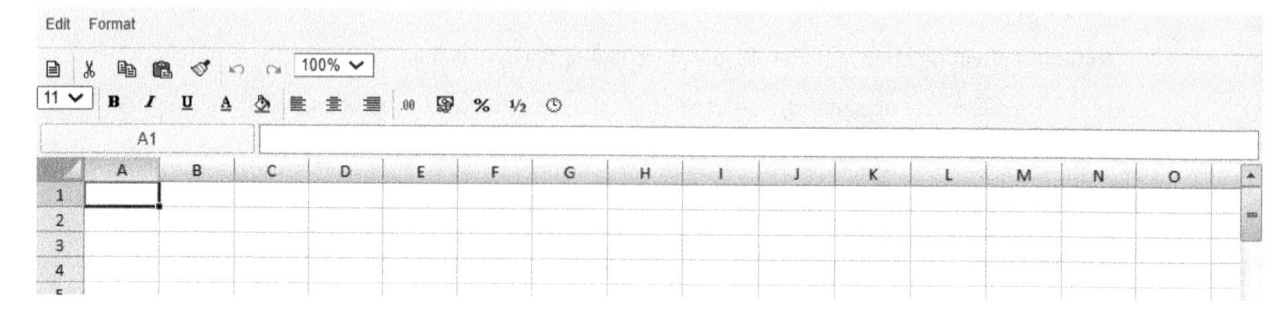

(b) Discuss the benefits of NPV compared to the Accounting rate of return. **(5 marks)**

(Total = 15 marks)

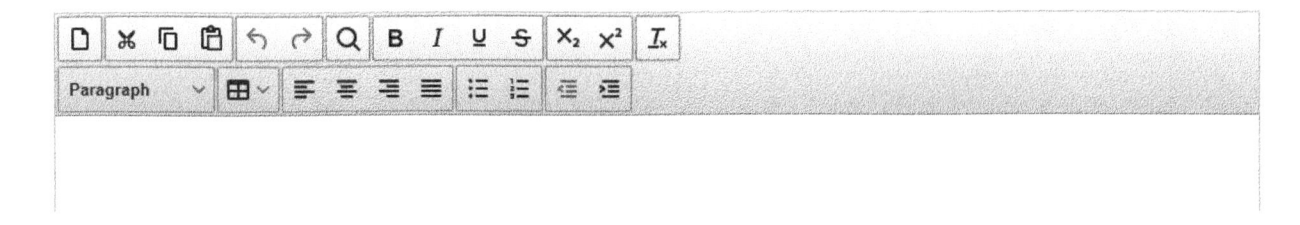

Do you know? – Credit management

Check that you know the following basic points before you attempt any questions. If in doubt, you should go back to your BPP Interactive Text and revise first.

- When a company has receivables, it is effectively lending money interest-free. Receivables can therefore be a major cost. Strict control must be maintained to ensure that credit limits are not exceeded and that customers pay by the due date.
    - Discounts may be allowed for prompt payment. .... must be compared with ....
    - If credit terms are relaxed to increase sales, ... must be compared with ....

- Credit control deals with a firm's management of its working capital. .... credit is offered to business customers. .... credit is offered to household customers.

- A firm must consider suitable payment terms. .... can be offered, if cost-effective and if they improve liquidity.

- Credit risk is the possibility that .... High risk customers can be profitable, but need to be managed carefully.

- Data about potential customers can be obtained from a number of sources.
    - .... owe a duty of care to their customers and to the enquirer: their assessments of a customer's credit statement are likely to be precisely worded.
    - .... references are useful, but should not be used uncritically.
    - .... agencies supply legal and business information and give suggested ratings.

- .... analyses can be prepared by customer or in any useful aggregation. Aggregated information may highlight disputed items or overdues as a percentage of receivables.

- Factoring can be *with* or *without* .... Where the factor is exposed to the risk of bad debts the fees are likely to be higher.

- Credit insurance can be obtained against .... However, the insurers will rarely insure the entire debt portfolio.

- Some customers are reluctant to pay. A staged process of reminders and demands, culminating in ...., is necessary.

TRY QUESTIONS 93–108

- *Possible pitfalls*

Did you know? -- Credit management

Could you fill in the blanks? The answers are in bold. Use this page for revision purposes as you approach the exam.

- When a company has receivables, it is effectively lending money interest-free. Receivables can therefore be a major cost. Strict control must be maintained to ensure that credit limits are not exceeded and that customers pay by the due date.
    - Discounts may be allowed for prompt payment. **The interest saving from obtaining prompt payment** must be compared with **the cost of the discount**.
    - If credit terms are relaxed to increase sales, **the benefit from increased sales** must be compared with **the interest cost and any increased bad debt cost**.
- Credit control deals with a firm's management of its working capital. **Trade** credit is offered to business customers. **Consumer** credit is offered to household customers.
- A firm must consider suitable payment terms. **Settlement discounts** can be offered, if cost-effective and if they improve liquidity.
- Credit risk is the possibility that **a debt will go bad**. High risk customers can be profitable, but need to be managed carefully.
- Data about potential customers can be obtained from a number of sources.
    - **Banks** owe a duty of care to their customers and to the enquirer: their assessments of a customer's credit statement are likely to be precisely worded.
    - **Trade** references are useful, but should not be used uncritically.
    - **Credit reference** agencies supply a variety of legal and business information, and give suggested ratings.
- **Receivables ageing** analyses can be prepared by customer or in any useful aggregation. Aggregated information may highlight disputed items or overdues as a percentage of receivables.
- Factoring can be *with* or *without* **recourse**. Where the factor is exposed to the risk of bad debts the fees are likely to be higher.
- Credit insurance can be obtained against **bad debts**. However, the insurers will rarely insure the entire debt portfolio.
- Some customers are reluctant to pay. A staged process of reminders and demands, culminating in **debt collection or legal action**, is necessary.

    TRY QUESTIONS 93–108

- *Possible pitfalls*
    - **Not calculating costs and benefits of new policies carefully, from the point of view of the business.**

93 MCQ Question Bank 12   24 mins

93.1 Which of the following is **NOT** an essential element of a contract?

- ○ Intention to create legal relations
- ○ Offer
- ○ Consideration
- ○ *Quantum meruit* (2 marks)

93.2 What is the main contract law remedy available to a business which has a customer who refuses to pay an invoice?

- ○ Damages
- ○ Specific performance
- ○ Termination
- ○ Action for the price (2 marks)

93.3 In 20X8 the share capital of Milly Co was as follows:

	$
Ordinary shares of $1 each	1,750,000
8% Preference shares of $1 each	250,000
	2,000,000

In the same year the company made a profit of $1,500,000.

Calculate Milly Co's earnings per share (EPS) ratio for 20X8.

- ○ 75c
- ○ 85c
- ○ 88c
- ○ $6 (2 marks)

93.4 Which of the following statements describes debt factoring?

- ○ The sale of a selection of invoices to a third party at a discount to their actual value.
- ○ An arrangement whereby a third party takes over the collection of trade debt and advances a proportion of the money it is due to collect.
- ○ A form of insurance that protects a business from bad debt.
- ○ A government scheme that provides guarantees to banks in respect of loans they provide to qualifying small businesses. (2 marks)

93.5 In terms of sale of goods contracts, what is lien?

- ○ The seller's right to sue for damages if the purchaser refuses to pay.
- ○ The seller's right to retain title for goods until they are paid for.
- ○ The seller's right to hold onto goods that have been sold, if the purchaser does not pay for them and they are still in their possession.
- ○ The seller's right to deliver goods only once they have been paid for. (2 marks)

93.6 Which types of contracts must be in writing?

- (i) Sale of land contracts
- (ii) Consumer credit agreements
- (iii) An agreement to purchase items from a shop
- (iv) Commercial agreements to supply raw materials

- ○ All of them
- ○ (i) and (ii) only
- ○ (i) and (iv) only
- ○ (ii) and (iii) only (2 marks)

93.7 In terms of contract law, what is consideration?

- ○ The process the Judge goes through when coming to a decision as to whether the terms of the contract have been breached.
- ○ What each party brings to the contract. Usually it is a promise from one party in return for payment by the other.
- ○ The measure of value placed on work done by one party when the contract has been breached by the other.
- ○ A statement made in the course of contractual negotiations.

(2 marks)

93.8 M Co recently declared a dividend of $0.15 per share. The market value of its shares currently stands at $2.85 cum div and its earnings per share (EPS) is $0.50.

Calculate M Co's price earnings (P/E) ratio.

- ○ 5.4
- ○ 5.7
- ○ 6.0
- ○ 0.19

(2 marks)

93.9 In relation to insolvency and bankruptcy, which of the following describes administration?

- ○ A moratorium over a company's debts while an insolvency practitioner seeks a good resolution for all creditors.
- ○ Where secured creditors appoint a receiver to manage or realise the secured assets until they can be paid.
- ○ A procedure where the assets of a company are sold, debts are paid out of the proceeds and the company is eventually dissolved.
- ○ An arrangement between a company and its creditors whereby a compromise is reached as to how much of its debts will be repaid.

(2 marks)

93.10 Which of the following methods of chasing debts is the most expensive?

- ○ Letters
- ○ Telephone
- ○ Email
- ○ Personal visit

(2 marks)

(Total = 20 marks)

94 Collecting debts — 18 mins

(a) In its dealings with regular commercial customers, a company may agree a written contract containing terms and conditions of their commercial dealings. In practice, some terms and conditions that may seem beneficial to the supplier are of limited practical value.

Required

Explain the nature of the following clauses in a contract with a credit customer, and explain why they may be of limited practical value:

(i) Retention of title clause
(ii) Interest on late payments clause.

(6 marks)

(b) Describe briefly the legal procedures that are necessary for the collection of overdue unpaid debts from a customer.

(5 marks)

(c) Explain briefly the difference between bankruptcy and insolvency.

(4 marks)

(Total = 15 marks)

QUESTIONS

95 Doha Co — 6 mins

Doha Co is currently in dispute with one of its suppliers, Petcoats Co. Pooch Co is unsure of its legal obligations regarding an agreement it made with Petcoats Co. The Financial Director of Pooch Co has asked you, an accounting technician, to explain certain legal terms to them.

Required

Define the following legal terms.

(a) 'Offer' **(2 marks)**
(b) 'Acceptance' **(2 marks)**
(b) 'Consideration' **(1 mark)**

(Total = 5 marks)

96 Receivables analysis — 18 mins

Efficient collection of money owed by customers requires efficiency in the monitoring of accounts receivable.

Required

(a) Describe briefly the main contents of accounts receivable records for a credit customer. **(5 marks)**

(b) A business has the following unpaid accounts receivable:

Customer	Invoice amount $	Invoice date
AB	250	4/10
	500	16/11
CD	800	11/11
	460	27/9
EF	720	4/10
GH	640	30/10
IJ	910	21/10
	160	30/8
KL	225	15/10
MN	430	3/11
OP	370	15/9
QR	660	14/11
ST	880	22/8

Required

(i) Prepare an aged receivables report as at the end of November (30/11) in the following format:

Customer	Less than 1 month $	1–2 months $	2–3 months $	Over 3 months $	Total $

(ii) Comment on the information in the report. **(10 marks)**

(Total = 15 marks)

89

FFM FOUNDATIONS IN FINANCIAL MANAGEMENT

97 Monitoring accounts receivable — 6 mins

A company with a large number of credit customers should monitor accounts receivable using the most suitable information available.

Required

Describe briefly the main internal sources of information for monitoring accounts receivables. **(5 marks)**

98 VDO Co — 24 mins

VDO Co manufactures and sells DVD playing devices for use with conventional video recorders, avoiding the need for customers to replace their existing video player in order to move to DVD technology. In recent years, the business has been growing rapidly as the availability of films on DVD has increased.

In the last year, the company has encountered cash flow difficulties and the board of directors has become increasingly concerned about this development. Extracts from VDO Co's financial statements are as follows.

	Statement of financial position as at 31 May 20X1		Statement of financial position as at 31 May 20X0	
	$'000	$'000	$'000	$'000
Assets				
Non-current assets				
Property, plant and equipment		550		450
Current assets				
Inventory	250		100	
Receivables	250		120	
Bank	–		80	
		500		300
		1,050		750
Equity and Liabilities				
Equity				
$0.1 ordinary shares		50		50
Retained earnings		600		550
		650		600
Non-current liabilities				
Bank term loan		200		–
Current liabilities				
Payables		200		150
		1,050		750

	Statement of profit or loss y/e 31 May 20X1	Statement of profit or loss y/e 31 May 20X0
	$'000	$'000
Revenue	4,000	2,000
Profit before finance cost	120	120
Finance cost	(20)	–
Profit before tax	100	120
Corporation tax expense (20%)	(20)	(24)
Profit for the year	80	96
Dividends	(30)	(36)

Other information

	20X1	20X0
(1) Industry average statistics		
Receivables days	35 days	33 days
Current ratio	2:1	2:1
Total debt: total equity	20%	20%

		20X1	20X0
	(Book value)		
	P/E ratio	20 times	18 times
	ROCE	20%	18%
(2)	Average market value of VDO Co's shares	240c	346c

Required

(a) Assess the financial performance of VDO Co in comparison to the industry average. (8 marks are available for calculations and 8 marks are available for relevant comments.) **(16 marks)**

(b) Identify and briefly discuss **two** possible reasons, other than overtrading, for a manufacturing company such as VDO Co to experience cash shortages, despite the considerable growth in sales. **(4 marks)**

(Total = 20 marks)

99 Noise Co — 6 mins

Noise Co makes and sells sound equipment to a range of clients. Its main supplier, Speak Co, has never offered discounts for early payment so Noise Co has always taken the full 60 days' credit allowed by Speak Co.

Speak Co has recently been having problems collecting its debts on time. Following this, a decision has been made to offer customers a 2% discount for all invoices paid within two weeks (14 days) of purchase.

Noise Co can invest cash to obtain an annual return of 12%.

Required

Determine whether it is financially viable for Noise Co to take advantage of the early payment discount.

(5 marks)

100 Credit control — 6 mins

Discuss **two** features of a credit control system that would encourage customers to pay on time. **(5 marks)**

101 Trade references (December 2019 exam) — 6 mins

Explain and discuss the usefulness of trade references and visits to customers premises when checking the creditworthiness of potential new customers. **(5 marks)**

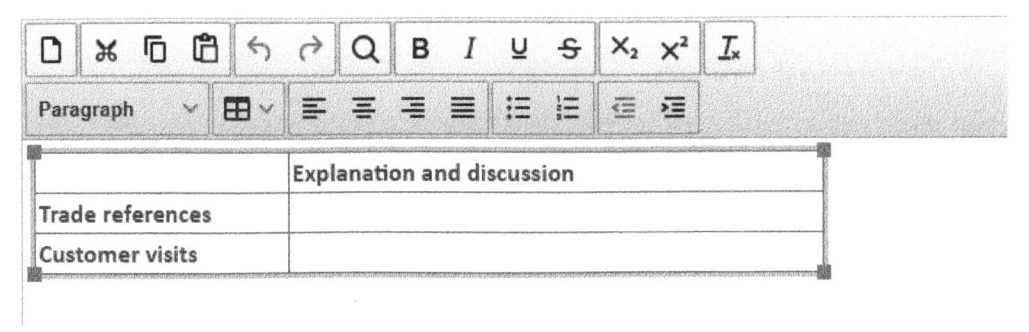

	Explanation and discussion
Trade references	
Customer visits	

102 Expander Co — 24 mins

Expander Co has recently decided to set up a new factory so it can enter as both a manufacturer and wholesaler into the rapidly expanding mobile telephone market.

Expander Co will manufacture a single type of mobile telephone and sell it to a variety of retail outlets. The retail outlets have been categorised into three distinct groupings.

(1) Mobile telephone shops

(2) Chain stores specialising in a variety of telecommunications equipment

(3) Internet service providers who include mobile telephones which can be linked to the internet as part of their product range

The new telephone will be launched on 1 January 20X0. Forecast sales data for the first year are as follows.

Customer type	Sales price $	January 20X0 sales Units	Monthly compound growth %	Credit period allowed Months
Mobile phone shops	50	2,000	5	1
Specialist chain stores	40	5,000	5	3
Internet service providers	30	5,000	10	3

All sales to retail outlets are on credit and are invoiced at month end, except for 10% of mobile telephone shop sales, which will be for cash.

The company is currently experiencing liquidity difficulties due to the rate of expansion being undertaken. The recently appointed financial controller is concerned about the financial implications of launching the new product, particularly in light of the fact that at present there is no credit control function in the company. This is a new market sector for the company and there will be a need to assess the creditworthiness of new customers.

Required

(a) Prepare two aged receivables schedules, one for each of the first two months of 20X0. These schedules should show the amount outstanding for each customer type, and the business as a whole appropriately aged. **(14 marks)**

(b) Identify and briefly discuss **two** factors which need to be considered when assessing the creditworthiness of new customers. **(6 marks)**

(Total = 20 marks)

103 Beff Co (June 2020 exam) — 18 mins

This scenario relates to three requirements.

Beff Co is a successful and profitable company with credit sales of $3 million per year. Sales are spread evenly over the year and there are no irrecoverable debts.

Beff Co is falling behind with its credit control activities as although standard credit terms are 30 days, receivable days are currently 80 days. Receivables are financed by a bank overdraft at a cost of 5% per year.

To improve credit control Beff Co is considering either employing the services of a factor company or employing a full-time credit controller.

Employ the services of a factor company - Option 1

A factor company would:

- Reduce the receivable days to 30 days.
- Advance Beff Co 75% of receivables at an interest rate of 8% per annum.
- Charge an admin fee equal to 2% of all credit sales.

Employ a full-time credit controller - Option 2

A credit controller would:

- Be paid a salary of $18,000 per year.
- Reduce the receivable days to 35 days.

(a) (i) Calculate the current cost of financing trade receivables. **(2 marks)**

(ii) Calculate the net cost or benefit of EACH of the two options and state which (if either) Beff Co should choose. **(9 marks)**

Note. assume there are 365 days in a year.

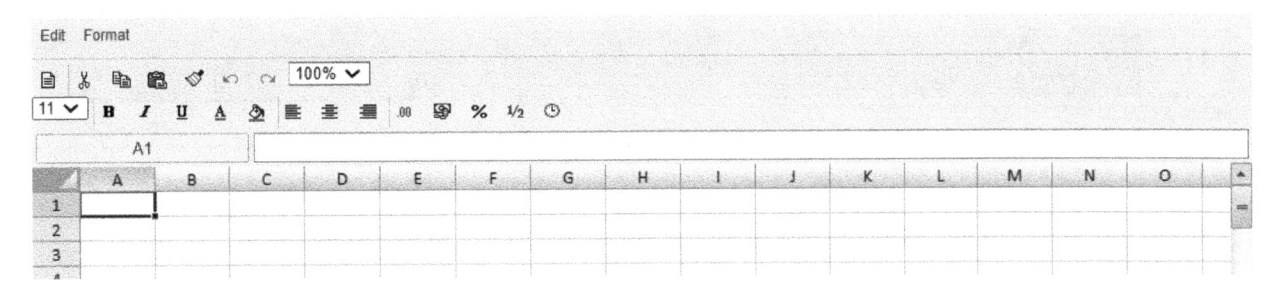

(b) Explain TWO benefits of employing a factor company. **(4 marks)**

(Total = 15 marks)

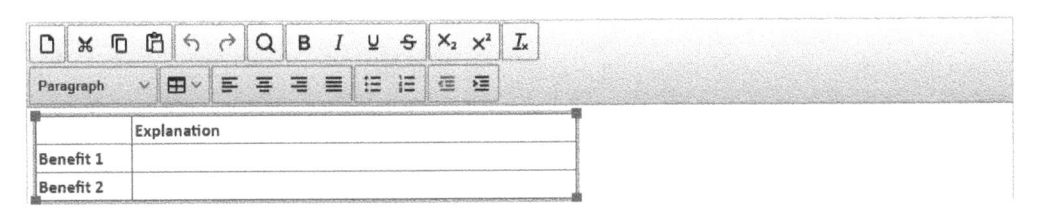

	Explanation
Benefit 1	
Benefit 2	

104 Waste Co — 24 mins

Waste Co is a waste management company, with one sole shareholder/director, Mr Trusty. It collects two types of waste from businesses – recyclable waste and confidential waste. Since companies have increasingly become aware of both the need for recycling and the need to protect confidential information, Waste Co's client base has expanded rapidly over the last two years.

As the business has expanded Mr Trusty has had less time available to focus on credit control. This has resulted in a steady deterioration in accounts receivable collection and a rapid increase in Mr Trusty's overdraft, despite high profits. Mr Trusty's bank has now refused to extend his overdraft any further and has suggested that he either employ a credit controller or factor his accounts receivable.

The following information is available:

1. Credit sales for the year ending 30 November 20X7 were $2,550,000 and average accounts receivable days were 60. Sales are expected to increase by 25% over the next year.

2. If Mr Trusty employs a good credit controller, the cost to the business will be $47,000. It is anticipated that the accounts receivable days can then be reduced to 40 days.

3. A local factoring organisation has offered to factor the company's accounts receivable on the following terms:

    (i) An advance of 80% of the value sales invoices (which Mr Trusty would fully utilise).
    (ii) An estimated reduction in accounts receivable days to 35 days.
    (iii) An annual administration fee of 1.3% of turnover.
    (iv) Interest charge on advances of 12% per annum.

4. Current overdraft rates are 10% per annum.

5. Assume there are 365 days in a year.

Required

(a) Explain the meaning of 'debt factoring' (accounts receivable factoring) to Mr Trusty, distinguishing between 'with recourse' and 'without recourse' agreements. **(5 marks)**

(b) Explain how debt factoring is different from 'invoice discounting'. **(3 marks)**

(c) Calculate whether it is financially beneficial for Waste Co to factor its accounts receivables for the next year, as compared to employing a credit controller. **(12 marks)**

(Total = 20 marks)

105 Jay Co — 18 mins

Jay Co manufactures furniture. It has come under pressure in recent years to reduce prices in order to compete with some larger competitors in the market. The company's aim has therefore been to maintain sales levels, with the effect that receivables control has been allowed to deteriorate. The company has always had a target of keeping the receivables period at an average of 45 days.

Receivables as at 31 May 20X7 are $323,654. Sales for the year ending 31 May 20X7 were $1,581,743. This figure included $14,250 of cash sales. During this time, debts of $26,784 were written off. All $26,784 relates to sales made in the year ending 31 May 20X7.

Required

(a) Calculate the current receivables collection period, in days, from the above information. **(4 marks)**

(b) How much of the year-end receivables' balance would have to be immediately recovered in order to reduce the receivables collection period to the target level? **(3 marks)**

(c) Calculate the company's bad debt ratio for the year ended 31 May 20X7. **(2 marks)**

(d) List **three** procedures that could be used to pursue the overdue debts. **(6 marks)**

(Total = 15 marks)

106 Light Co — 24 mins

Light Co is a privately owned company specialising in the manufacture of lighting equipment. It supplies lighting to customers, who take an average of 30 days to pay. It has an overdraft on its current account of $2 million. The compound annual interest rate charged on this account is 12%, with interest being charged to the account daily.

In order to reduce its overdraft, Light Co is now considering introducing discounts to customers who pay within seven days.

Required

(a) Calculate the maximum discount that Light Co should offer for payment within seven days if it wants to avoid any increase in its overall finance costs and explain the basis of your calculation. **(5 marks)**

(b) One year later, despite introducing a tempting discount to customers, Light Co has found that very few customers have paid early and taken the discount. In fact, receivables days have increased significantly, as has the company's overdraft. Light Co is therefore considering factoring its debts in the coming year.

Credit sales for the last year totalled $12 million, with average receivables of $2 million. Next year, sales are expected to increase by 10%. Receivables days are expected to increase to 70 days if the factoring arrangement is **not** entered into. A factoring company has put forward the following proposal to Light Co:

(i) Receivables days will be reduced to 28 days as a result of stricter credit control procedures.
(ii) The factor will charge interest of 13% per annum on the advances.
(iii) The factor will charge an administration fee of 1.5% of turnover for the service.
(iv) The factor will advance 80% of the value of sales invoices.

Should Light Co enter into the agreement, it will make its credit controller redundant. They earn a salary of $18,000 per annum. Current bank overdraft rates have remained the same at 12% per annum.

Required

Evaluate whether it is financially viable for Light Co to factor its debts in the coming year. **(15 marks)**

(Total = 20 marks)

107 Waste Co — 6 mins

Waste Co is a waste management company, with one sole shareholder/director, Mr Trusty. As the business has expanded rapidly over the last two years, Mr Trusty has had less time to focus on credit control. This has resulted in a steady deterioration in accounts receivable collection and a rapid increase in Mr Trusty's overdraft despite high profits. Mr Trusty's bank has now refused to extend his overdraft any further and has suggested that he either employ a credit controller or factor his accounts receivable.

Required

Explain the meaning of 'debt factoring' (accounts receivable factoring) to Mr Trusty, distinguishing between 'with recourse' and 'without recourse' agreements. **(5 marks)**

108 Mr Allan — 6 mins

Mr Allan, the owner of a small cleaning company, is considering undertaking some company contract work to supplement the income from current domestic jobs. If Mr Allan changes to commercial contracts, he expects revenue for the next year to be $75,000, with customers paying within the 30-day limit set. It would cost him $2,000 per annum to employ someone one day a week to invoice customers and collect debts for him. Alternatively, his local bank has offered to provide a factoring service for him, including the advance of 80% of his sales invoices. They would charge 2% of revenue for the administration and charge interest of 8% per annum on advances. However, the bank would not invoice Mr Allan's customers. He would need to employ somebody for half a day a week to do this, at a cost of $1,000 per annum.

Mr Allan pays interest at the rate of 10% per annum on his overdrawn bank account.

Without factoring, his costs are:

		$
Overdraft cost: $75,000 × 30/365 @ 10%	=	616
Wages	=	2,000
Total cost	=	2,616

Mr Allan thinks that customers will pay within 30 days regardless of which option is selected.

Required

Calculate the cost to Mr Allan of factoring his debts. **(5 marks)**

Mixed bank questions

109 Mixed bank 1 — 24 mins

109.1 Which of the following is a variable expenditure cost within a cash budget?

- ○ Raw material purchases
- ○ Depreciation of machinery
- ○ Administrators' salaries
- ○ Marketing expenses

(2 marks)

109.2 One unit of Product G costs $35 to make and generates $15 in profit. Calculate the margin on Product G.

- ○ 30%
- ○ 35%
- ○ 38%
- ○ 43%

(2 marks)

109.3 Which of the following is the accounts payable payment period ratio?

- ○ $\dfrac{\text{Purchases on credit terms}}{\text{Average payables}} \times 365 \text{ days}$
- ○ $\dfrac{\text{Average payables}}{\text{Purchases on credit terms}} \times 365 \text{ days}$
- ○ $\dfrac{\text{Total purchases}}{\text{Average payables}} \times 365 \text{ days}$
- ○ $\dfrac{\text{Average payables}}{\text{Total purchases}} \times 365 \text{ days}$

(2 marks)

109.4 In contract law, what is *quantum meruit*?

- ○ Damages payable for breach of contract
- ○ A measure of the value of work done under a contract
- ○ The consideration agreed for a contract
- ○ The payment due on performance of a contract.

(2 marks)

109.5 Which of the following is the lender of last resort within an economy?

- ○ A clearing bank
- ○ A merchant bank
- ○ A central bank
- ○ A retail bank

(2 marks)

109.6 According to the Fisher effect, what nominal interest rate would an investor need in order to achieve a 7% return in one year's time if the inflation rate is 10%?

- ○ 3%
- ○ 3.3%
- ○ 17%
- ○ 17.7%

(2 marks)

109.7 A bank which sets limitations on a borrower's financial position as a term of the loan agreement has issued a:

- ○ Negative covenant
- ○ Positive covenant
- ○ Qualitative covenant
- ○ Quantitative covenant

(2 marks)

109.8 Over a sufficiently long enough period, all costs will eventually become:

- ○ Variable costs
- ○ Relevant costs
- ○ Marginal costs
- ○ Fixed costs

(2 marks)

109.9 A company is considering undertaking a contract for a new client. The contract requires 100 kg of material A. It has 200 kg in inventory, which it bought last year at a cost of $10 per kg. The current resale value is $8, although to replace the material today would cost $15 per kg. There is no other use for the material, except as a substitute for material B, which costs $14 per kg.

What is the relevant price per kg of material A?

- ○ $10
- ○ $14
- ○ $8
- ○ $15

(2 marks)

109.10 The following information is available for a project:

Year		$	Present value factor at 10%
0	Investment	10,000	1.000
1	Cash inflow	2,000	0.909
2	Cash inflow	5,000	0.826
3	Cash inflow	7,000	0.751

Calculate the net present value of the project.

- ○ $1,205
- ○ $2,255
- ○ $11,205
- ○ $21,205

(2 marks)

(Total = 20 marks)

110 Mixed bank 2   24 mins

110.1 Float causes the difference in a company's cash position between:

- ○ The cash book and cash flow forecast
- ○ The cash book and cleared funds statement
- ○ The cleared funds statements and cash flow forecast
- ○ The cash book and petty cash

(2 marks)

110.2 Which of the following can cause cash flow problems for a company?

(i) Trading losses   (iii) Growth
(ii) Inflation   (iv) Seasonal business

- ○ All of them
- ○ (i), (ii) and (iii) only
- ○ (i), (ii) and (iv) only
- ○ (ii), (iii) and (iv) only

(2 marks)

110.3 What does it mean if a company is low geared?

- ○ It has a low proportion of debt to equity
- ○ It has a low proportion of cash to debt
- ○ It has a low proportion of equity to debt
- ○ It has a low proportion of debt to cash

(2 marks)

110.4 Which of the following are allowable expenses that may be set off against a company's tax charge?

(i) Interest payable on loan notes
(ii) General provisions for doubtful debt
(iii) Interest payable under a lease agreement
(iv) Interest payable under a hire purchase agreement

○ All of them
○ (i), (ii) and (iii) only
○ (i), (iii) and (iv) only
○ (ii), (iii) and (iv) only

(2 marks)

110.5 Which of the following is a source of business angel finance?

○ The stock exchange
○ The government
○ Development agencies
○ Business and personal contacts

(2 marks)

110.6 Which of the following would not be an appropriate use of a long-term loan?

○ To purchase a new office building
○ To purchase new production equipment
○ To purchase inventory
○ To purchase a fleet of company vehicles

(2 marks)

110.7 If the nominal rate of interest is 4% and the inflation rate is 2%, calculate the real rate of interest.

○ 1.92%
○ 1.96%
○ −1.92%
○ −1.96%

(2 marks)

110.8 Which of the following costs of a project are relevant costs?

(i) Depreciation
(ii) Lost profit from alternative projects that cannot proceed if the project goes ahead
(iii) Overheads directly attributable to the project
(iv) Variable costs of the project

○ All of them
○ (i), (ii) and (iii) only
○ (i), (iii) and (iv) only
○ (ii), (iii) and (iv) only

(2 marks)

110.9 The following information is available for a project:

	5% cost of capital	10% cost of capital
Net present value	$2,500	($3,000)

Calculate the IRR of the project.

○ 5.27%
○ 7.27%
○ 7.73%
○ 12.27%

(2 marks)

110.10 What would be the effect if capital expenditure items were treated as revenue expenditure in a company's accounts?

○ Profit and non-current assets both understated
○ Profit overstated, non-current assets understated
○ Profit understated, non-current assets overstated
○ Profit and non-current assets both overstated

(2 marks)

(Total = 20 marks)

QUESTIONS

111 Mixed bank 3 — 24 mins

111.1 The following statements have been made about the benefits of debt finance compared to equity finance:

Statement 1: Interest payments on debt attract tax relief.
Statement 2: Control of the company is diluted.

Which of the above statements is/are true?

- ○ Both of them
- ○ Statement 1 only
- ○ Statement 2 only
- ○ Neither of them (2 marks)

111.2 Extracts from a company's accounts show the following balances:

	$'000
Inventories	114
Receivables	216
Cash	42
Payables	180
Loans	60

Which of the following is the company's quick ratio, calculated to the nearest two decimal places?

- ○ 1.55
- ○ 1.08
- ○ 2.07
- ○ 1.43 (2 marks)

111.3 The net present value of a proposed project is $20,000 at a discount rate of 5% and $(28,000) at 10%.

What is the internal rate of return of the project, to the nearest one decimal place?

- ○ 7.1 %
- ○ 7.5 %
- ○ 2.3 %
- ○ 8.6% (2 marks)

111.4 Which of the following will increase the length of the cash operating cycle?

(i) An increase in the period of credit given by suppliers
(ii) A decrease in the period of credit given by suppliers
(iii) An increase in the period of credit given to customers
(iv) A decrease in the period of credit given to customers

- ○ (i) and (iii) only
- ○ (ii) and (iv) only
- ○ (ii) and (iii) only
- ○ (i) and (iv) only (2 marks)

111.5 The following statements have been made about the probable long-term effects of introducing a just-in-time system of inventory management:

(i) Inventory holding costs increase
(ii) Labour productivity improves
(iii) Manufacturing lead times decrease

Which of the above statements are true?

- ○ (i), (ii) and (iii)
- ○ (i) and (ii) only
- ○ (i) and (iii) only
- ○ (ii) and (iii) only (2 marks)

111.6 The following statements have been made about a bank's rights in relation to its customers:

(i) The bank has the right to be repaid overdrawn balances on demand, except where the overdraft terms require a period of notice.

(ii) The bank can use the customers' money in any legally or morally acceptable way that it chooses.

(iii) A customer's money must always be available for immediate withdrawal, irrespective of the terms of the deposit.

Which of the above statements are true?

- ○ (i) and (ii) only
- ○ (i), (ii) and (iii)
- ○ (i) and (iii) only
- ○ (ii) and (iii) only

(2 marks)

111.7 The net present value of a proposed project is a positive $56,000 at a discount rate of 10% and a negative $28,000 at 20%.

What is the internal rate of return of the project, to the nearest whole percentage?

- ○ 17%
- ○ 13%
- ○ 30%
- ○ 8%

(2 marks)

111.8 The following data relates to a manufacturing company:

Average finished goods inventory	$25,000
Average raw materials inventory	$15,000
Average WIP	$30,000
Sales for the period	$400,000
Gross profit margin	25%

WIP is 50% complete as regards materials and conversion costs.

What is the average production period (work-in-progress) to the nearest whole day?

- ○ 37 days
- ○ 73 days
- ○ 30 days
- ○ 18 days

(2 marks)

111.9 The following statements have been made about the essential elements of a contract:

(i) All contracts need to be in a strict legal form in order to be binding
(ii) Both parties must have intended the contract to be legally binding
(iii) Offer and acceptance must both have taken place

Which of the above statements are true?

- ○ (i), (ii) and (iii)
- ○ (i) and (iii) only
- ○ (ii) and (iii) only
- ○ (i) and (ii) only

(2 marks)

111.10 Which of the following is a potential remedy when one party has breached a contract?

(i) Specific performance
(ii) Termination
(iii) Quantum merit
(iv) Damages

- ○ All of the above
- ○ (iv) only
- ○ (i) and (iv) only
- ○ (i), (ii) and (iv) only

(2 marks)

(Total = 20 marks)

112 Mixed bank 4 — 24 mins

The following information relates to questions 112.1 and 112.2

Annual sales	$2,500,000
Costs as a percentage of sales:	
Raw materials	10%
Direct labour	15%
Production overheads	5%

Working capital statistics:

Average raw materials holding period	Four weeks
Average finished goods holding period	Two weeks
Average receivables collection period	Six weeks
Average payables collection period	Eight weeks

All finished goods values include raw materials, direct labour and production overheads. Assume there are 52 weeks in the year.

112.1 How much working capital is required to finance finished goods inventory, to the nearest $?

- ○ $28,846
- ○ $9,615
- ○ $57,962
- ○ $24,038

(2 marks)

112.2 How much working capital is required to finance receivables?

- ○ $384,615
- ○ $86,538
- ○ $115,385
- ○ $288,462

(2 marks)

112.3 Which of the following is **NOT** a money market instrument?

- ○ Treasury bills
- ○ Certificates of deposit
- ○ Cash
- ○ Commercial paper

(2 marks)

112.4 Assumption 1: Amounts of cash required in future periods can be predicted with certainty.

Assumption 2: The opportunity cost of holding cash is known and it does not change over a period of time.

Which of the above, if either, is an assumption on which Baumol's model of cash management is based?

- ○ **Both** Assumption 1 and Assumption 2
- ○ Assumption 1 **only**
- ○ Assumption 2 **only**
- ○ **Neither** Assumption 1 **nor** Assumption 2

(2 marks)

112.5 Are the following statements about systematic and unsystematic risk true or false?

1. Systematic risk can be diversified away
2. Unsystematic risk can be diversified away

- ○ Both statements are true
- ○ Statement 1 is true and statement 2 is false
- ○ Statement 2 is true and statement 1 is false
- ○ Both statements are false

(2 marks)

112.6 A company purchases a non-current asset with a useful economic life of ten years for $1.25 million. It is expected to generate cash flows over the ten year period of $250,000 per annum before depreciation. The company charges depreciation over the life of the asset on a straight-line basis. At the end of the period it will be sold for $250,000.

What is the accounting rate of return for the investment (based on average profits and average investment)?

- ○ 20%
- ○ 15%
- ○ 33%
- ○ 25%

(2 marks)

112.7 Bee Co is deciding whether to make components X and Y or buy them in from an outside supplier. The supplier would charge $50 per unit of X and $55 per unit of Y.

Production cost ($ per unit)	X	Y
Direct material	12	13
Direct labour	25	27
Variable overhead	8	7
Fixed overhead	7	6

Which of the components, if any, should be bought in from outside?

- ○ X only
- ○ Y only
- ○ Both X and Y
- ○ Neither X nor Y

(2 marks)

112.8 A company has material B in its inventory, which it purchased in error at a cost of $800. The company is deciding whether to: (i) use it as a substitute for material A which would cost $500 to buy in; or (ii) sell material B for $510 cash LESS selling costs of $20; or (iii) use it in another contract.

If the company decides to use the material in another contract, what is its relevant cost?

- ○ $800
- ○ $510
- ○ $500
- ○ $490

(2 marks)

112.9 Statement 1: Simple payback period takes into account the time value of money and uses cash flows rather than profits.

Statement 2: Internal rate of return takes into account the time value of money and uses cash flows rather than profits.

Which of the above statements is/are true?

- ○ Statement 1 only
- ○ Statement 2 only
- ○ Both statement 1 and statement 2
- ○ Neither statement 1 nor statement 2

(2 marks)

112.10 Statement 1: Positive covenants are promises by a borrower to do something.

Statement 2: Quantitative covenants are promises to keep within financial limits set by the lender.

Which of the above statements is/are true/false?

	Statement 1	Statement 2
○	False	True
○	False	False
○	True	False
○	True	True

(2 marks)

(Total = 20 marks)

113 Mixed bank 5 — 24 mins

113.1 A company has the following non-current assets:

	20X5	20X6
Non-current assets at closing net book value	$200,000	$250,000

Depreciation for the 20X6 statement of profit or loss is $30,000. No disposals were made in the period.

What is the correct figure for cash purchases of non-current assets during 20X6?

- ○ $50,000
- ○ $80,000
- ○ $250,000
- ○ $20,000

(2 marks)

113.2 An investment of $100,000 is made in a project. The scrap value is expected to be $15,000 at the end of the project. Four equal annual cash inflows of $35,000 will arise from the project, the first of which arises two years after the initial investment.

What is the payback period and the accounting rate of return (based on initial investment) of the project?

	Payback	Accounting rate of return
○	3.9 years	11%
○	3.9 years	28%
○	2.9 years	11%
○	2.9 years	28%

(2 marks)

113.3 Which of the following statements is/are true with respect to investment appraisal methods?

(i) The accounting rate of return takes into account the timing of the cash inflows and outflows.

(ii) Shareholders should benefit if a project is accepted which has a positive net present value.

(iii) The internal rate of return calculation will always produce a unique answer. What is the maximum amount of inventory that should be held?

- ○ (i) and (ii)
- ○ (ii) only
- ○ (i) and (iii)
- ○ (ii) and (iii)

(2 marks)

113.4 Which of the following would usually be considered to be the least liquid asset?

- ○ Accounts receivable
- ○ Short-term investments
- ○ Inventory
- ○ Cash at bank

(2 marks)

113.5 Company X has been offered a 2% discount if they pay their suppliers within 10 days of the invoice. Payments are usually made after 30 days.

What is the compound annual cost of not taking the discount to the nearest percentage point?

- ○ 24%
- ○ 28%
- ○ 45%
- ○ 27%

(2 marks)

113.6 A company sells inventory for cash.

What will be the effect on the quick ratio (acid test) and the accounts receivable payment period?

Quick ratio	Accounts receivable payment period
○ Increase	Decrease
○ Decrease	No change
○ No change	Increase
○ Increase	No change

(2 marks)

113.7 Which of the following is the first stage in a bankruptcy procedure?

- ○ A trustee in bankruptcy is appointed
- ○ A statutory demand for payment is issued
- ○ The company is wound up
- ○ The assets of the company are wound up

(2 marks)

113.8 A company sells goods on credit and is expecting the following sales:

	$
March	20,000
April	15,000
May	25,000
June	30,000

The following are the expected payments from accounts receivables:

50% in the month of sale   15% two months after sale
30% one month after sale   5% are bad debts

What is the expected cash inflow in May?

- ○ $18,250
- ○ $19,375
- ○ $20,000
- ○ $25,000

(2 marks)

113.9 What is risk that can be diversified away known as?

- ○ Systematic risk
- ○ Unsystematic risk
- ○ Currency risk
- ○ Investment risk

(2 marks)

113.10 A company is preparing a quotation for a project, based on relevant costing principles. The project will require 100 kg of material X. The following information about material X is available:

Units already in inventory	Original cost price per kg	Net realisable value per kg	Current purchase price per kg
50 kg	$6	$7	$8

The material is used frequently by the company.

What is the relevant cost of the material to be included in the quotation?

- ○ $750
- ○ $700
- ○ $600
- ○ $800

(2 marks)

(Total = 20 marks)

QUESTIONS

114 Mixed bank 6 — 24 mins

114.1 Exactly one year ago, $100 of treasury bill was issued with a coupon rate of 4%, redeemable at par nominal value two years after issue. The treasury bill currently has a market value of $102.25.

What is the interest yield on the treasury bill, calculated to the nearest two decimal places?

- ○ 3.91%
- ○ 4.00%
- ○ 1.71%
- ○ 2.20%

(2 marks)

114.2 Quilt Co grants credit terms of 30 days net to customers but offers an early settlement discount of 1% for payment within seven days.

What is the compound percentage cost of the discount to Quilt Co, to the nearest percentage?

- ○ 17%
- ○ 18%
- ○ 19%
- ○ 20%

(2 marks)

114.3 A company is negotiating a contract with a customer for ongoing supply of goods on credit.

Which of the following are optional terms and conditions that might be included in the contract from the outset?

(1) A retention of title clause
(2) The period of free credit

- ○ 1 only
- ○ 2 only
- ○ 1 and 2
- ○ Neither 1 or 2

(2 marks)

114.4 Which of the following statements is/are true/false?

Statement 1: Positive covenants are promises by a borrower to do something.
Statement 2: Quantitive covenants are promises to keep within financial limits set by the lender.

	Statement 1	Statement 2
○	False	True
○	False	False
○	True	False
○	True	True

(2 marks)

114.5 'An unconditional order in writing to pay the addressee a specified sum of money either on demand or at a future date'.

What does the above definition describe?

- ○ Bill of exchange
- ○ Loan stock
- ○ Preference shares
- ○ A bond

(2 marks)

FFM FOUNDATIONS IN FINANCIAL MANAGEMENT

114.6 A company purchases a non-current asset with a useful economic life of ten years for $1.25 million. It is expected to generate cash flows over the ten year period of $250,000 per annum before depreciation. The company charges depreciation over the life of the asset on a straight-line basis. At the end of the period it will be sold for $250,000.

What is the accounting rate of return for the investment (based on average profits and average investment)?

- ○ 20%
- ○ 15%
- ○ 33%
- ○ 25% **(2 marks)**

114.7 The following statements have been made about a bank's rights in relation to its customers:

(i) The bank has the right to be repaid overdrawn balances on demand, except where the overdraft terms require a period of notice.

(ii) The bank can use the customers' money in any legally or morally acceptable way that it chooses.

(iii) A customers' money must always be available for immediate withdrawal, irrespective of the terms of the deposit.

Which of the above statements are true?

- ○ (i) and (ii) only
- ○ (i), (ii) and (iii)
- ○ (i) and (iii) only
- ○ (ii) and (iii) only. **(2 marks)**

114.8 A company has material B in its inventory, which it purchased in error at a cost of $800. The company is deciding whether to: (i) use it as a substitute for material A which would cost $500 to buy in; or (ii) sell material B for $510 cash LESS selling costs of $20; or (iii) use it in another contract.

If the company decides to use that material in another contract, what is its relevant cost?

- ○ $800
- ○ $510
- ○ $500
- ○ $490 **(2 marks)**

114.9 The following statements have been made about the probable long-term effects of introducing a just-in-time system of inventory management:

(i) Inventory holding costs increase
(ii) Labour productivity improves
(iii) Manufacturing lead times decrease

Which of the above statements are true?

- ○ (i), (ii) and (iii)
- ○ (i) and (ii) only
- ○ (i) and (iii) only
- ○ (ii) and (iii) only **(2 marks)**

114.10 A company has the following non-current assets:

	20X7	20X8
Non-current assets at closing net book value	$220,000	$270,000

Depreciation for the 20X8 statement of profit or loss is $40,000. No disposals were made in the period.

What is the correct figure for cash purchases of non-current assets during 20X8?

- ○ $50,000
- ○ $80,000
- ○ $270,000
- ○ $90,000

(2 marks)

(Total = 20 marks)

115 Mixed bank 7 — 24 mins

115.1 If a company regularly fails to pay its suppliers by their normal due dates, it may lead to the following:

- (i) Reduction in credit rating
- (ii) Trade receivables days may increase
- (iii) Difficulty in obtaining credit from new suppliers
- (iv) Having insufficient cash to settle trade payables

Which **TWO** of the above could arise as a result of exceeding suppliers' credit terms?

- ○ (iii) and (iv)
- ○ (ii) and (iii)
- ○ (i) and (iv)
- ○ (i) and (iii)

(2 marks)

115.2 Quilt Co grants credit terms of 30 days net to customers but offers an early settlement discount of 1% for payment within seven days.

What is the compound percentage cost of the discount to Quilt Co, to the nearest per cent?

- ○ 17%
- ○ 18%
- ○ 19%
- ○ 20%

(2 marks)

115.3 The following information relates to the inventory of Swiss Co:

	Maximum	Minimum
Usage levels	1,000 kg per day	300 kg per day
Lead times	Ten days	Five days

What is the maximum amount of inventory that should be held?

- ○ 10,000
- ○ 9,500
- ○ 1,500
- ○ 8,500

(2 marks)

115.4 'An unconditional order in writing to pay the addressee a specified sum of money either on demand or at a future date.'

What does the above definition describe?

- ○ Bill of exchange
- ○ Convertible bond
- ○ Preference share
- ○ Long term loan

(2 marks)

115.5 Mint Co is considering using the services of a factor. Its annual sales are $5,000,000 with customers taking an average of 60 days to pay. The cost of financing these is currently $65,753 per annum.

The factor will advance 70% of Mint Co's sales invoices at a promotional rate of 8% of amounts advanced, the same rate that the company pays on its overdraft. In addition, the factor will reduce the average receivables period to 30 days. It will also take over the administration of the sales ledger, for which it will charge an annual fee of 1% of sales.

What is the cost or benefit of employing the services of the factor compared to continuing without the factor?

- ○ $17,124 cost
- ○ $17,124 benefit
- ○ $15,753 benefit
- ○ $15,753 cost

(2 marks)

115.6 Which of the following manages the government's debt?

- ○ The central bank
- ○ Investment banks
- ○ Debt factors
- ○ The treasury

(2 marks)

115.7 An investment project has a positive net present value of $33,274 when discounted at the cost of capital of 10% per annum. The estimated after tax net cash inflows at the end of each year of the project's five-year life are $64,000. The annuity factor at 10% per annum for five years is 3.791.

What is the investment amount in Year 0?

- ○ $275,898
- ○ $286,726
- ○ $273,350
- ○ $209,350

(2 marks)

115.8 The following statements relate to a manufacturing company:

Statement 1: Being listed on a recognised stock exchange is a disadvantage for a company that wants to facilitate its growth by acquisition.

Statement 2: Being listed on a recognised stock exchange can enhance a company's image.

Which of these statements is/are correct?

- ○ Only statement 1
- ○ Only statement 2
- ○ Both statements 1 and 2
- ○ Neither statement 1 nor statement 2

(2 marks)

115.9 Exactly one year ago, $100 of treasury stock was issued with a coupon rate of 4%, redeemable at par two years after issue. The stock currently has a market value of $102.25.

What is the stock's interest yield, calculated to the nearest two decimal places?

- ○ 3.91%
- ○ 4.00%
- ○ 1.71%
- ○ 2.20%

(2 marks)

115.10 A company has determined that the net present value of an investment project is positive $24,800 when using a 5% discount rate and negative $12,400 when using a 10% discount rate.

What is the internal rate of return of the project, to the nearest 1%?

- ○ 6%
- ○ 7%
- ○ 8%
- ○ 9%

(2 marks)

(Total = 20 marks)

116 Mixed bank 8 (December 2019 real exam) — 36 mins

116.1 Which of the following statements relating to the centralisation of the treasury function in a divisionalised company is/are true?

(1) Treasury will be more responsive to the needs of individual divisions
(2) Borrowing can be arranged in bulk giving access to lower interest rates
(3) The company's precautionary cash balance will increase

- 1 only
- 2 only
- 3 only
- 1 and 2

(2 marks)

116.2. Which of the following statements relating to short-term borrowing is/are true?

(1) The interest rate is normally lower than for long-term borrowing
(2) It should be used to finance long term investment projects

- 1 only
- 2 only
- Both 1 and 2
- Neither 1 nor 2

(2 marks)

116.3. Which of the following was NOT identified by Keynes as a motive for holding cash?

- Transactions
- Precautionary
- Speculative
- Inflationary

(2 marks)

116.4. A company has in issue $400,000 equity shares with a nominal value of $0.25 each. They are currently trading at $5.00 each.

It is considering making a one for three rights issue at a 10% discount on current market price.

How much cash will the rights issues raise if it is fully subscribed?

- $600,000
- $2,400,000
- $5,400,000
- $2,666,667

(2 marks)

116.5. Which of the following is a right of an ordinary shareholder?

- To vote at company Annual General Meetings
- To receive a guaranteed dividend payment each year
- To sell their shares back to the company at the purchase price they paid
- To rank for payment before debt holders in the event of the company's liquidation

(2 marks)

116.6. An investor requires a real return of 2% each year. In the coming year inflation is forecast to be 5%.

What nominal rate of return does the investor require to one decimal place?

- 2.9%
- 3.0%
- 7.0%
- 7.1%

(2 marks)

116.7. A company has an operating profit of $20 million and a profit after tax of $16 million. It has declared a preference dividend of $2 million. It has issued 7,000,000 ordinary shares and one million preference shares.

What is the company's earnings per share?

- ○ $1.75
- ○ $2.00
- ○ $2.50
- ○ $2.29

(2 marks)

116.8. Which of the following factors have been identified as problems faced by the SMEs (smaller and medium-sized enterprises) sector when seeking external finance?

(1) Lack of assets to provide security for loans
(2) Lack of a trading track record
(3) Lack of innovative ideas

- ○ 1 and 2 only
- ○ 1 and 3 only
- ○ 2 and 3 only
- ○ 1, 2 and 3

(2 marks)

116.9. Which of the following routes cannot be pursued by the creditors of an insolvent company to recover money owed?

- ○ Bankruptcy
- ○ Liquidation
- ○ Receivership
- ○ Administration

(2 marks)

116.10. A company has current assets of $m, and current liabilities of $1.2m.

What would be the effect on its current ratio and acid test (quick) ratio if the company buys $0.4m of inventory using its cash balance?

- ○ Current ratio decreases, Acid test decreases
- ○ Current ratio unchanged, Acid test decreases
- ○ Current ratio decreases, Acid test unchanged
- ○ Current ratio unchanged, Acid test increases

(2 marks)

116.11. A company requires its customers to pay within 60 days of the invoice date. It is considering offering a settlement discount of 2% for payment within seven days of the invoice date.

What is the annual percentage cost of the discount? Assume a 365-day year.

- ○ 13.77%
- ○ 2.04%
- ○ 14.61%
- ○ 14.93%

(2 marks)

116.12. A company has trade receivables of $6.4m which it finances using a bank overdraft costing 8% per year. A debt factoring company offers the company an 80% advance of its receivables at an interest rate of 9% per year.

What is the increase in interest payable if the company accepts the factor's offer?

- ○ $51,200
- ○ $64,000
- ○ $576,000
- ○ $460,800

(2 marks)

116.13. What is a loan covenant?

- An agreement by the lender not to increase interest rates
- A record capped by the lender of the amount borrowed and the interest rate charged
- An annual statement of the balance of the loan outstanding
- An agreement by the borrower to obligations over and above repaying the loan

(2 marks)

116.14. A company needs equity finance for a new project. It is considering the following actions.

(1) A scrip (or bonus) issue of new equity shares
(2) A reduction in dividend paid
(3) Sale of redeemable preference shares

Which would increase the amount of equity finance a company has available for the new project?

- 1 only
- 2 only
- 3 only
- 1 and 3

(2 marks)

116.15. Which of the following services are offered by debt factors?

(1) Credit control administration
(2) Finance provision
(3) Bad debt insurance

- 1 and 2 only
- 1 and 3 only
- 2 and 3 only
- 1, 2 and 3

(2 marks)

(Total = 30 marks)

117 Mixed bank 9 (June 2020 real exam) — 36 mins

117.1. Which of the following calculates working capital

- Current assets less inventory
- Current assets plus current liabilities
- Current assets less current liabilities
- Capital employed less current liabilities

(2 marks)

117.2. A company uses 1,200 units of component X per month. Component X costs $2 per unit.

The holding costs for one unit for one year is 10% of purchase cost. The company has a fixed ordering cost of $4,800 per year plus a variable element of $100 per order. The company carries no safety inventory.

If the company uses the economic order quantity (EOQ) model to manage inventory, what is the total cost of ordering and holding component X per year (to the nearest $)?

- $5,559
- $5,019
- $5,258
- $759

(2 marks)

117.3. Two of Mel Co's suppliers have recently changed their credit terms. Details are as follow:

Supplier A

Old terms: net 45 days or 2% discount for payments made within seven days
New Terms: net 45 days or 3% discount for payments made within seven days

Supplier B

Old terms: net 30 days or 2% discount for payments made within seven days
New Terms: net 30 days or 2% discount for payments made within ten days

Which supplier(s) new terms are more attractive financially than their old terms to Mel Co?

- ○ Supplier A only
- ○ Supplier B only
- ○ Both Supplier A and Supplier B
- ○ Neither Supplier A nor Supplier B

(2 marks)

117.4. Which of the following is a correct ranking of short-term investment opportunities in terms of risk (highest risk first)?

- ○ Ordinary shares, certificates of deposit, government stock
- ○ Ordinary shares, government stock, certificates of deposit
- ○ Government stock, ordinary shares, certificates of deposit
- ○ Certificates of deposit, ordinary shares, government stock

(2 marks)

117.5. What is the purpose of the primary market of a stock exchange?

- ○ To enable companies to raise new finance
- ○ To provide a market for existing investors in a company to sell their shares
- ○ To regulate takeover activity
- ○ To enforce rules of conduct for listed companies

(2 marks)

117.6. Which of the following is LEAST likely to be the responsibility of a company's treasury department?

- ○ Liquidity management
- ○ Foreign exchange risk management
- ○ Banking relationships
- ○ Preparation of the company's annual report

(2 marks)

117.7. Which of the following form part of a government's monetary policy?

(1) Interest rate policy
(2) Taxation policy
(3) Open market operations in gilts

- ○ 1 only
- ○ 1 and 2
- ○ 1 and 3
- ○ 2 and 3

(2 marks)

117.8. Which of the following do NOT act as financial intermediaries in the capital markets?

- ○ Insurance companies
- ○ Venture capital organisations
- ○ Accountancy firms
- ○ Unit trusts

(2 marks)

117.9. A company has the following issued share capital.

	$m
Ordinary shares (nominal value $0.50)	10
8% Preferred shares (nominal value $0.10)	5

Profit before tax is $12m. Tax on these profits is $4m.

What is the company's earnings per share (EPS) (to the nearest $0.01)?

- ○ $0.40
- ○ $0.80
- ○ $0.38
- ○ $0.76

(2 marks)

117.10. A project requires an immediate investment of $10,000 and will generate a $5,000 net cash inflow at the end of each of the next five years.

The project's NPV at an interest rate of 12% has been correctly calculated as $8,025.

By how much can the annual cash inflow reduce before the project is no longer financially viable?

- ○ $2,226
- ○ $1,605
- ○ $1,387
- ○ $2,774

(2 marks)

117.11. Which of the following reorder levels would ensure that a company did not run out of inventory?

- ○ Maximum usage (units per day) × maximum lead time (days)
- ○ Minimum usage (units per day) × minimum lead time (days)
- ○ Maximum usage (units per day) × minimum lead time (days)
- ○ Minimum usage (units per day) × maximum lead time (days)

(2 marks)

117.12. Which of the following will it experience a decrease in wealth because of an increase in the rate of inflation?

(1) Households receiving pensions that are fixed in money terms
(2) Companies buying goods under long term fixed price contracts
(3) Banks who have lent money on fixed interest rate terms

- ○ 1 and 2 only
- ○ 2 and 3 only
- ○ 1 and 3 only
- ○ 1, 2 and 3

(2 marks)

117.13. A company has received an order from a customer to make a bespoke product. The company is currently operating at full capacity and to make the bespoke product it will need to take skilled labour off existing work where it is earning a contribution of $5 per skilled labour hour. Skilled labour is paid $20 per hour.

What is the relevant cost of skilled labour per hour for the bespoke product?

- ○ $5
- ○ $15
- ○ $20
- ○ $25

(2 marks)

117.14. Which of the following can be used to obtain a quotation on a Stock Exchange?

(1) An offer for sale
(2) A prospectus issue
(3) A rights issue

○   1 and 2 only
○   2 and 3 only
○   1 only
○   1, 2 and 3

(2 marks)

117.15. Which of the following is/are true?

(1) Low capital gearing means that the value of the company's equity is low compared to the value of its prior charge capital.

(2) By investing in a project with a pre-tax return on capital of 9% and financing the project entirely by debt capital costing 6% a company will increase its earnings per share.

○   1 only
○   2 only
○   1 and 2
○   Neither 1 nor 2

(2 marks)

(Total = 30 marks)

Answers

ANSWERS

1 MCQ Answer Bank 1

1.1 The answer is Current assets less inventories/Current liabilities.

The other options are the current ratio, the profit margin and gearing.

1.2 The answer is over-capitalised.

An excess of current assets when compared to current liabilities indicates a business is over-capitalised.

1.3 The answer is 1,800 kg

Maximum inventory level = reorder level + reorder quantity − (minimum usage × minimum lead time).

Reorder level = maximum usage × maximum lead time.

Reorder level = 250 kg × 7 days = 1,750 kg

Maximum inventory level = 1,750 kg + 125 kg − (25 kg × 3 days)
= 1,875 kg − 75 kg = 1,800 kg

1.4 The answer is Total quality management.

Getting things done right first time is the key principle of total quality management.

1.5 The answer is zero.

Working capital consists of current assets less current liabilities. In Peter Co's case it is inventory plus receivables less payables less overdraft (12,000 + 8,000 − 2,500 − 17,500) = zero.

1.6 The answer is 32 days

The cash cycle is the length of time raw materials and finished goods are held in inventory, plus the length of time the company takes to collect payment from customers, less the credit period it receives from its suppliers. In Pop Co's case it is (3 + 23 + 34 − 28) = 32 days.

1.7 The answer is 157 days

Working capital cycle = 170 − 35 + 22 days = 157 days.

1.8 The answer is 23 days

The average production period is

$$\frac{\text{Average WIP inventory}}{\text{Cost of sales} \times \text{degree of completion}} \times 365$$

$$\frac{85,000}{2,250,000 \times 0.6} \times 365 = 23 \text{ days}$$

1.9 The answer is 114 units

$Q = \sqrt{\frac{2cd}{h}}$ where:

c = cost of placing one order

d = demand in units for one year

h = holding cost per unit

$Q = \sqrt{\frac{2 \times 1,000 \times 65}{10}} = 114$ units

1.10 The answer is Inventory turnover period + receivables collection period − payables payment period

2 Question with help: Seats Co

The annual costs and revenues for Comfyseat will be as follows.

Expected annual sales volume (units)		25,000
Selling price per unit		$100
		$'000
Sales		2,500
Materials (40% × 100/125 × 2,500)		800
Labour (30% × 100/125 × 2,500)		600
Overheads (30% × 100/125 × 2,500)		600
Total cost		2,000

The average value of current assets will be as follows.

		$'000	$'000
Raw materials	4/52 × 800		62
Work in progress			
Materials (100% complete)	4/52 × 800	62	
Labour (40% complete)	40% × 4/52 × 600	18	
Overheads (40% complete)	40% × 4/52 × 600	18	
			98
Finished goods			
Materials (100% complete)	3/52 × 800	46	
Labour (100% complete)	3/52 × 600	35	
Overheads (100% complete)	3/52 × 600	35	
			116
Receivables	6/52 × 2,500		288
Total current assets			564
Current liabilities			
Materials	5/52 × 800	(77)	
Labour	1/52 × 600	(12)	
Overheads	6/52 × 600	(69)	
			(158)
Total working capital requirement			406

The annual costs and revenues for Bigseat will be as follows.

Expected annual sales volume (units)		25,000
Selling price per unit		$245
		$'000
Sales revenue		6,125
Materials	50% × 100/140 × 6,125	2,188
Labour	25% × 100/140 × 6,125	1,094
Overheads	25% × 100/140 × 6,125	1,094
Total cost		4,376

The average value of current assets will be as follows.

		$'000	$'000
Raw materials	6/52 × 2,188		252
Work in progress			
Materials (100% complete)	4/52 × 2,188	168	
Labour (40% complete)	40% × 4/52 × 1,094	34	
Overheads (40% complete)	40% × 4/52 × 1,094	34	
Finished goods			236
Materials (100% complete)	3/52 × 2,188	126	
Labour (100% complete)	3/52 × 1,094	63	
Overheads (100% complete)	3/52 × 1,094	63	

	$'000	$'000
Receivables	8/52 × 6,125	252
		942
Total current assets		1,682
Materials	5/52 × 2,188	(210)
Labour	1/52 × 1,094	(21)
Overheads	3/52 × 1,094	(63)
		(294)
Total working capital requirement		1,388

The total working capital requirement is therefore $406,000 + $1,388,000 = $1,794,000

3 Pooch Co

Working capital requirement

Annual costs:	$	$
Raw materials		
15% of 2.2m	330,000	
Labour		
20% of 2.2m	440,000	
Variable overheads		
11% of 2.2m	242,000	
Fixed overheads		
10% of 2.2m	220,000	
Other costs		
12% of 2.2m	264,000	

Current assets

	$	$
Raw materials		
= 4/52 × 330,000		25,385
WIP		
Materials 75% complete		
= 75% × 2/52 × 330,000	9,519	
Labour 50% complete		
= 50% × 2/52 × 440,000	8,462	
Variable overhead 50% complete		
= 50% × 2/52 × 242,000	4,654	
Fixed overhead 50% complete		
= 50% × 2/52 × 220,000	4,231	
		26,866
Finished goods		
Materials		
= 4/52 × 330,000	25,385	
Labour		
= 4/52 × 440,000	33,846	
Variable overhead		
= 4/52 × 242,000	18,615	
Fixed overhead		
= 4/52 × 220,000	16,923	
		94,769
Receivables		
= 6/52 × 2,200,000		253,846
		400,866

	$	$
Current liabilities		
Materials		
= 4/52 × 330,000	25,385	
Labour		
= 1/52 × 440,000	8,462	
Variable overhead		
= 8/52 × 242,000	37,231	
Fixed overhead		
= 5/52 × 220,000	21,154	
Other costs		
= 12/52 × 264,000	60,923	
		153,155
Working capital required is		
400,866 – 153,155		247,711

4 Shoes for You Co

Helping hand. Remember the cash operating cycle is the number of days a business takes to convert its raw materials into cash. It is calculated by the formula:

Cash operating cycle equals:

The average time raw materials remain in stock

Less the credit period given by suppliers

Plus the time taken to produce the goods

Plus the time finished goods remain in stock until sold

Plus the credit period given to customers

Each can be calculated using the working capital ratios

Raw materials inventory holding period   Days

$$\frac{\text{Raw materials inventory}}{\text{Materials Purchases}} \times 365 = \frac{133,000}{630,000} \times 365 = \qquad 77$$

Credit given by suppliers

$$\frac{\text{Average trade payables}}{\text{Total overheads on credit terms}} \times 365 = \frac{73,000}{(350,000+320,000)} \times 365 = (40)$$

Note. Staff wages are paid daily in cash so are not on credit terms.

Average work in progress period

$$\frac{\text{Average work in progress}}{(\text{Cost of sales} \times \text{degree of completion})} \times 365$$

Cost of sales

	£
Production wages	450,000
Materials purchases	630,000
Other production overheads	350,000
	1,430,000

Work in progress is 65% complete.

$$\frac{195,000}{(1,430,000 \times 0.65)} \times 365 = \frac{195,000}{929,500} \times 365 = \qquad 77$$

ANSWERS

Inventory turnover period

$$\frac{\text{Inventory value}}{\text{Cost of sales}} \times 365 = \frac{325{,}000}{1{,}430{,}000} \times 365 = \qquad 83$$

Note. Cost of sales was calculated above.

Credit period given to customers

$$\frac{\text{Average trade receivables}}{\text{Total sales on credit terms}} \times 365 = \frac{410{,}000}{2{,}500{,}000} \times 365 = \qquad 60$$

Note. The question stated all sales are on credit terms.

Total cash operating cycle $\quad \underline{257}$

The total cash operating cycle of Shoes for You Co is 257 days.

5 Victory Co

Helping hand. Make sure that you know the Economic Order Quantity formula and that you can apply it to a problem such as this. Always note how long it will take to deliver orders as this is an important detail, even though it isn't brought into the economic order quantity calculation.

In (a) (iii) and (b) you need to bring purchasing costs into the calculations as they will be affected by the discount.

(a) (i) Using the economic order quantity (EOQ) model:

$$Q = \sqrt{\frac{2C_oD}{C_h}}$$

where: C_o = cost of making one order = $75
    D = annual demand = 200 × 52 = 10,400
    C_h = holding cost per unit per annum = $2
    Q = $\sqrt{(2 \times \$75 \times 10{,}400)/\$2}$
    Q = $\sqrt{780{,}000}$
    Q = 883.2 units

The economic order quantity is therefore 883 units (to the nearest unit).

(ii) Demand is fixed at 200 bottles per week, and delivery from the supplier takes two weeks. Victory must therefore reorder when stocks fall to 400 units (two weeks demand).

(iii) The total cost of stocking Buzz for one year will be:

		$
Purchase cost		
10,400 units $20 each		208,000
Ordering cost		
Annual demand (units)	10,400	
Order size (units)	883	
Number of orders per year	11.78	
Cost of placing one order	$75	
Annual ordering cost		883
Holding cost		
Average inventory (883/2)	441.5	
Holding cost per unit pa	$2	
Annual holding cost		883
Total annual cost		209,766

(b) The factors for the new supplier are as follows:

Co = $250
D = 10,400
Ch = $1.80

$$Q = \sqrt{\frac{2 \times \$250 \times 10,400}{\$1.80}} = 1,699.7$$

The economic order quantity is therefore 1,700 units (to the nearest unit).

To determine whether it is financially viable to change supplier we must calculate the total annual cost of ordering from this supplier and to compare this with the existing annual cost.

		$
Purchase cost		
10,400 units $19 each		197,600
Ordering cost		
Annual demand (units)	10,400	
Order size (units)	1,700	
Number of orders per year	6.12	
Cost of placing one order	$250	
Annual ordering cost		1,530
Holding cost		$
Average inventory (1,700/2)	850	
Holding cost per unit pa	$1.80	
Annual holding cost		1,530
Total annual cost		200,660

This is $9,106 less than the existing annual purchasing cost, and therefore it would be financially beneficial to switch suppliers.

6 Rant Co

> **Helping hand.** You will not necessarily be given the definition of the terms in the EOQ formula therefore it is a good idea to learn what the terms actually mean.

(a) Symptoms of overtrading include:

(i) **Increased revenue**, well above normal or usually sustainable levels
(ii) **Increased inventory**, **receivables** and **cash** (and hence increased debt ratios)
(iii) **Increased non-current assets**
(iv) **Increased payables** and **loan finance**, without any corresponding increase in equity
(v) **Reduced liquidity ratios** as a result

As far as Rant is concerned, sales have increased by 250% over the last year to satisfy increasing demand for its products, and non-current assets have risen by 75%. Current assets too are on the increase. There has been a rapid increase in creditor finance (trade payables and exceeding bank overdraft limits), without any potential for an injection of new capital from the shareholders (existing or new). These are sure signs that Rant is overtrading.

(b) The **economic order quantity (EOQ)** model can assist in reducing inventory costs by determining the optimum order size for inventories, which minimizes ordering and holding costs. The calculation is based upon the following assumptions:

(i) It assumes that **annual demand** is constant. In reality there may be peaks and troughs, increasing the risk of running out of stock at certain times of the year.

(ii) The calculation does not take into account the **credit terms** and **discount policies** that may be offered by different suppliers. It assumes that purchase costs are constant.

(iii) It is assumed that the **lead time is constant** and therefore that suppliers are completely dependable.

(c) **EOQ calculation**

$$\sqrt{\frac{2C_oD}{C_h}} = \sqrt{\frac{2 \times \$150 \times 150{,}000}{\$15}} = \sqrt{3{,}000{,}000} = 1{,}732$$

7 Fleet Co

> **Helping hand.** Holding, ordering and purchase cost formulas are good to learn as they are often needed in questions such as this. You will not necessarily be given the definition of the terms in the EOQ formula therefore it is a good idea to learn what they are.

Marking scheme

		Marks
(a)	EOQ – 0.5 mark for demand, 0.5 for holding cost, 0.5 for order cost if in the correct place and 0.5 for correct answer	2
(b)	Holding costs (1 mark for cost at each of 80,000 and 100,000 pairs)	2
	Order costs (1 mark for cost at each of 80,000 and 100,000 pairs)	2
	Total costs (1 mark for purchase cost at each of 80,000 and 100,000 pairs)	2
	Conclusion – based on OFR total cost for 80,000 and 100,000	1
		7
(c)	WCC explained – 1 mark for each point made	2
	Increase order size – 1 mark for each point made	2
	Liquidity effect – 1 mark for each point made	2
		6
Total marks		**15**

(a) **EOQ**

$$EOQ = \sqrt{\frac{2C_oD}{C_h}}$$

Where

C_o = the cost of placing one order
D = the annual demand in units
C_h = the cost of holding one unit per annum.

$$EOQ = \sqrt{\frac{2 \times 500 \times 800{,}000}{0.125}} = 80{,}000 \text{ pairs of shoes}$$

(b) The answer would be presented in a spreadsheet such as this:

I11   fx   =C11+E11+G11

	A	B	C	D	E	F	G	H	I
1									
2	Working		Price pre discount		5				
3									
4	Demand		800000						
5									
6	Order size		Holding cost		Ordering cost		Purchasing cost		Total cost
7			(order size/2 x holding cost)		(demand / order size x order cost)				
8									
9	80000		5000		5000		4000000		**4010000**
10									
11	100000		6250		4000		3900000		**3910250**
12									
13	Fleet Co should increase its order size to 100,000 pairs of shoes as total cost per year will reduce by $99,750.

Tutorial note. The solution spreadsheet is constructed using the following formulae; these would be visible to the marker and are shown below as an example:

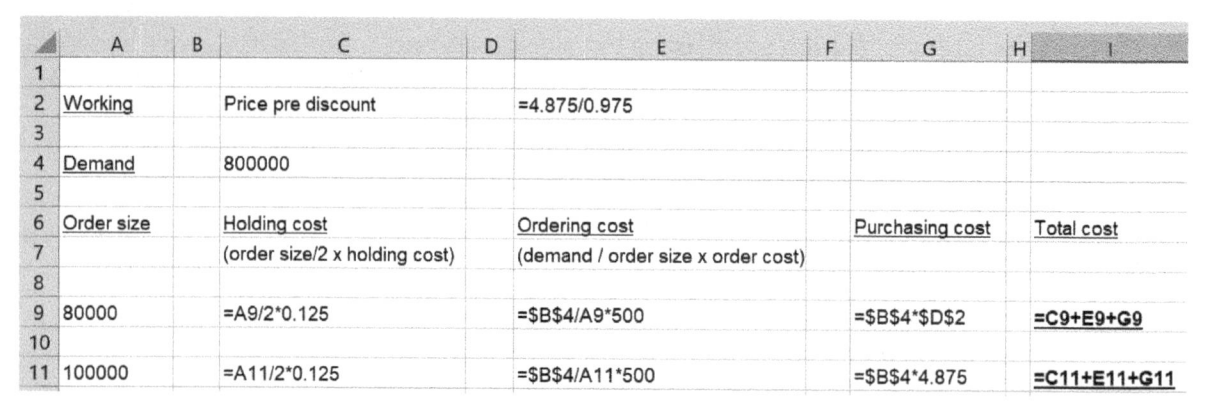

	A	B	C	D	E	F	G	H	I
1									
2	Working		Price pre discount		=4.875/0.975				
3									
4	Demand		800000						
5									
6	Order size		Holding cost		Ordering cost		Purchasing cost		Total cost
7			(order size/2 x holding cost)		(demand / order size x order cost)				
8									
9	80000		=A9/2*0.125		=$B$4/A9*500		=$B$4*$D$2		=C9+E9+G9
10									
11	100000		=A11/2*0.125		=$B$4/A11*500		=$B$4*4.875		=C11+E11+G11

(c)

Explanation of the working capital cycle

The working capital cycle (also known as the cash operating cycle) is the period between suppliers being paid and cash being received from customers. In the case of a wholesaler like Fleet Co, the length of the cycle will be the sum of the period of credit given to suppliers (receivables days) and its inventory holding period (inventory days), less the time taken to pay its suppliers (payables days). Given the 90 days Fleet Co takes to pay its suppliers, its working capital cycle is likely to be negative, meaning that it receives cash from its customers before it has to pay its suppliers.

Impact of increasing order size

Increasing the order size will mean that Fleet Co's stock levels will increase, and this will lengthen its inventory days. This will increase its working capital cycle. Everything else being equal, this will increase the amount of money tied up in inventory and reduce the amount of cash held, thus reducing the company's liquidity.

8 Overtrading

Marking scheme

	Marks
Allow up to 3 marks for both definition and symptoms	5
Total marks	5

ANSWERS

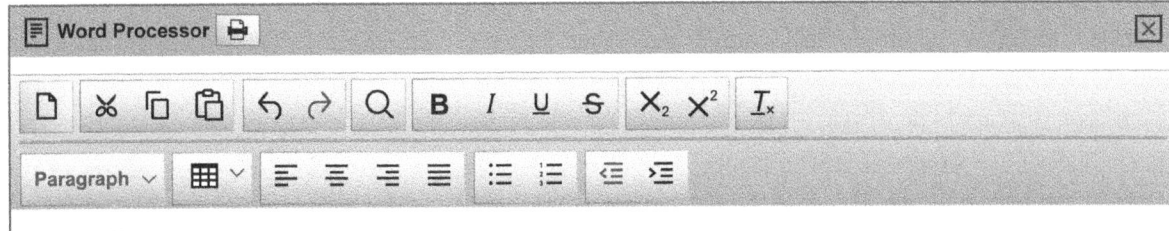

Overtrading

When a business transacts a higher level of sales than its working capital can normally sustain, without sufficient long-term capital available, it is overtrading. Many companies which overtrade are profitable and commercially successful, but an increase in sales demand leads to higher receivables and inventory which reduces liquidity and the ability to pay debts as they fall due. Without new capital (or better control of growth and working capital) companies which overtrade risk liquidity problems and insolvency.

Symptoms

- A rapid increase in revenue. An increase in demand for a company's products will often be accompanied by an increase in receivables. In effect, a cash out-flow.
- An increase in inventories. Inventories are necessary to ensure that sales demand can be achieved but financing the inventory and its safe storage causes cash deficits.
- An increase in current liabilities. In order to finance the receivables and inventory, payments to suppliers are delayed.

The above can occur because the company is not financing growth using long-term capital but is trying to grow using short-term credit. The insufficient provision of long-term finance will result in a reduction in a company's liquidity ratios.

9 The Kitchen Co

Helping hand. There is much to cover in this question, so beware of getting bogged down on a particular part. It is important to allocate your time carefully and not to overrun.

(a) **Overtrading**

A company is said to be overtrading when its sales are expanding too quickly for it to finance them. Further explained, this means that the volume of sales is too large given the level of long-term capital at the company's disposal.

(b) The Kitchen Co's **turnover** has increased by 100% over the last year. However, since this is a **new company** and the 'FishEye' is an innovative product for which this company is the sole retailer, one would expect to see a large increase in turnover.

Similarly, since sales have increased so much, **trade receivables** would have been expected to increase proportionately, which they did. Since a 100% increase in turnover is effectively a doubling in turnover, the doubling of trade receivables was to be expected.

Again, **inventory levels** have doubled. This is also linked to the doubling of turnover. Inventory levels would have been increased in order to meet the increase in demand.

The company is relying heavily on its **overdraft** but it is not exceeding it; nor is it uncommon for a new business to rely on this form of short-term finance to fund its working capital.

Whilst the **current ratio** has deteriorated it is still 2.5:1, which is higher than the industry norm.

In conclusion then, whilst the company's financial position needs to be monitored carefully to ensure that sales do not spiral out of control, the company **does not** currently appear to be overtrading.

(c) (i) **Re-order level** = max. lead time × usage × 125%

$$= 1,000 \times 20 \times 1.25$$
$$= 25,000 \text{ units}$$

(ii) **Economic order quantity**

$$Q = \sqrt{\frac{2C_O D}{C_H}} = \sqrt{\frac{2 \times 650 \times 48 \times 5 \times 1,000}{2}} = 12,490 \text{ units}$$

(iii) **Maximum inventory level** = reorder level + reorder quantity – (minimum usage × minimum lead time)
= 25,000 + 12,490 – (1000 × 10) = 27,490

10 Brush Co

> **Helping hand.** You are not given cost of sales so you will have to calculate it from the information provided. Don't forget that any credit period given to Bush Co by suppliers will reduce the working capital cycle period.

(a) **Working capital cycle**

		$	Days
Inventories:			
Raw materials:	$\dfrac{\text{Raw materials}}{\text{Purchases}} \times 365$ =	$\dfrac{82,000}{378,000} \times 365$	79
Work in progress:	$\dfrac{\text{Work in progress}}{\text{Cost of sales (w.1)} \times \text{degree of completion}} \times 365$ =	$\dfrac{58,000}{1,018,000 \times 70\%} \times 365$	30
Finished goods:	$\dfrac{\text{Finished goods}}{\text{Cost of sales}} \times 365$ =	$\dfrac{210,000}{1,018,000} \times 365$	75
Credit allowed to customers:	$\dfrac{\text{Receivables}}{\text{Sales}} \times 365$ =	$\dfrac{356,000}{1,500,000} \times 365$	87
Credit taken from suppliers: Materials:	$\dfrac{\text{Payables}}{\text{Raw materials costs}} \times 365$ =	$\dfrac{45,000}{378,000} \times 365$	(43)
Overheads:	$\dfrac{\text{Payables}}{\text{Variable/fixed overheads}} \times 365$ =	$\dfrac{75,000}{400,000} \times 365$	(68)
Labour:	$\dfrac{\text{Payables}}{\text{Direct labour costs}} \times 365$ =	$\dfrac{9,000}{240,000} \times 365$	(14)
			146

ANSWERS

	$
Working 1: Cost of sales	
Raw material costs	378,000
Direct labour	240,000
Variable production overheads	215,000
Apportioned fixed production overheads	185,000
	1,018,000

(b) **Concerns about Brush Co's working capital cycle (choose any two)**

- The receivables payment period is 87 days. This is too long, given that Brush Co only allows 60 days credit to customers. Also, it is twice as long as the payment period for raw material supplies.

- The payment period for raw material supplies is 43 days and for overheads it is much higher, at 68 days. These periods are both longer than the agreed credit period of 30 days. This could lead to interest being charged by suppliers and a deterioration in the relationships with suppliers.

- Raw materials are held for an average of 79 days. Since it is the company's policy to use raw materials within 75 days of purchase, these inventories are too high. The company's policy is being breached, which could lead to substandard drugs being manufactured.

- Overall, the working capital cycle is too long. At 146 days, it is 56 days longer than comparative companies. This is costing the company money in terms of cash tied up in working capital and lost opportunities elsewhere.

11 Choc Co

Helping hand. Remember to relate your answers to (c) and (d) to the company in the scenario. Although part (d) asks for some general comments on JIT, it also requires you to discuss whether the technique would be suitable for Choc Co.

(a) **Cost of current ordering policy**

Current order size = 5,000 kg

Average number of orders per year = demand/order size = 100,000/5,00 = 20 per year

Annual ordering cost = 20 × $35 = $700

Average inventory = 5,000/2 = 2,500 kg

Annual holding cost = 2,500 × $0.20 = $500

Total annual cost = $700+ $500 = $1,200

(b) **Cost if EOQ is used.**

$$EOQ = \sqrt{\frac{2C_0D}{C_H}}$$

$$EOQ = \sqrt{\frac{2 \times 356 \times 100,000}{0.2}} = 5,916 \text{ kg per order.}$$

Average number of orders per year = 100,000/5,916 = 16.9
Annual ordering cost = 16.9 × $35 = $591.50
Average inventory held = 5,916/2= 2,958
Annual holding cost = 2,958 × $0.20 = $591.60
Total annual cost using EOQ = $591.50 + $591.60 = $1,183.10

(c) **Costs associated with running out of sugar**

- Sales will be lost, therefore Choc Co would lose any contribution made from each lost sale.

- If emergency deliveries are required, there will be an additional cost for these.

- If production ceases altogether and staff and machines sit idle, there will be costs of lost production.
- Loss of customer goodwill will arise if orders cannot be met. This may lead to loss of sales to this customer in the future.

Note. Only three were required.

12 Bulb Co

> **Helping hand.** Don't forget that you are trying to calculate the working capital requirement in part (a) rather than the working capital cycle. You will still make use of the inventory, receivables and payables ratios however. In order to calculate the amounts required, make use of the information in the question regarding materials, labour and overheads (as percentages of turnover) – don't forget to show your workings. We have used a tabular approach to this question and you are advised to use a similar approach – it makes your workings easier to see and also makes it easier to mark.
>
> Part (b) should be quite straightforward if you remember the mnemonic CAMPARI. If you can't remember what all of the letters stand for, remember that you are only required to describe three factors which makes it easier! Don't be tempted to show the examining team that you remember them all – you will only get marks for the number required in the question.

(a) **Working capital requirement**

		$	$
Current assets			
Raw materials	(8/52) × $13 million		2,000,000
Finished goods:			
Raw material	(6/52) × $13 million	1,500,000	
Labour	(6/52) × $16.25 million	1,875,000	
Variable overhead	(6/52) × $9.75 million	1,125,000	
			4,500,000
Work in progress:			
Raw material	(2/52) × $13 million × 75%	375,000	
Labour	(2/52) × $16.25 million × 50%	312,000	
Variable overhead	(2/52) × $9.75 million × 50%	187,500	
			875,000
Receivables	(9/52) × $65 million		11,250,000
Total current assets			18,625,000
Less current liabilities			
Payables	(4/52) × $53.95 million		(4,150,000)
Working capital requirement			14,475,000

Working – annual costs

		$
Turnover	$65,000,000	
Direct materials	20% of $65 million	13,000,000
Direct labour	25% of $65 million	16,250,000
Variable overheads	15% of $65 million	9,750,000
Fixed and selling overheads	23% of $65 million	14,950,000
Total annual costs		53,950,000

(b) **Factors to be considered when deciding whether to grant a loan** (choose any three)

Remember CAMPARI!

Character of the customer

Bulb Co is a company therefore the bank may wish to look at the experience and integrity of Bulb Co's directors. It can do so by having personal interviews with some or all of the directors. Bulb Co's past record with the bank will also be assessed and the bank may wish to look at key ratios that indicate how well the company is performing.

ANSWERS

Ability to borrow and repay

The bank will look at Bulb Co's financial performance as an indication of future trends. Re-investment of retained profits is a sign of the owner's or directors' faith in the business. The bank will examine the company's financial statements for signs of low/declining profitability, increased dependence on borrowing and inadequate control over working capital (amongst other things). However the bank will not rely solely on published and management accounts – it will also check the viability of the loan and whether the company has the legal capacity to borrow (by examining the constitution of the company).

Margin of profit

Banks want to lend money to make money. Decisions on interest are therefore important.

Fixed rates
The lending policies of most banks stipulate different rates for different purposes to customers.

Discretionary rates
The bank will decide on the return which it requires from the lending. A loan for a risky venture (such as a new business) will be offered at a higher rate of interest, so as to compensate the bank for the risk it takes that the lending will not be repaid, than a loan perceived to be of low risk.

Purpose of the borrowing

The customer must specify the **purpose of the borrowing**. Loans for certain purposes will normally not be granted at all. Some will be granted only on certain conditions. Loans will normally be granted to finance working capital, as long as Bulb Co's liquidity position is still manageable. This can be assessed by looking at Bulb Co's key financial ratios.

Amount of the borrowing

The lending proposition must state exactly how much the company wishes to borrow. The bank will wish to check that the company is not asking for too much (or more than is needed) for the particular purpose. This is particularly important as it might affect the ability to repay the loan.

In addition the bank must check that the company has not asked for less than is required, otherwise it may have to lend more, purely to safeguard the original advance.

Repayment terms

The bank will pay close attention to the repayment terms of the loan. A bank should not lend money to Bulb Co if the company does not have the resources to repay it with interest (even if it has security for the loan). The repayment terms need to be clearly agreed, documented and realistic, given the borrower's financial position.

Insurance against the possibility of non-payment

If the bank feels it necessary to take out insurance against the possibility of non-repayment of the loan, then the loan should not be made. Security is only a safety net to be called upon only in the event of an unfortunate or unexpected inability to repay. Bulb Co might want to take out payment protection insurance to safeguard against the inability to pay.

13 All Weather Windows Co

Helping hand. This question looks harder than it is. Do not let costs appearing as percentages and the working capital statistics put you off. The first job is to calculate what the costs are in numerical terms, to do this all you need to do is multiply the sales revenue by the relevant percentage.

Working capital requirements consist of current assets less current liabilities. From the statistics you should see that the current assets include raw materials, WIP, finished goods and receivables. Raw material is a stand alone figure but WIP and finished goods are made up of raw materials, labour and variable/fixed production costs. To calculate them all you need to do is work out the proportion of the years' total cost that appears as working capital using the number of weeks given in the statistics. The calculation of current liabilities uses the same principle.

Working capital requirements

	$'000
Sales revenue for the year:	7,600
Raw materials costs $7,600,000 × 22%	1,672
Direct labour costs $7,600,000 × 18%	1,368
Variable production overheads $7,600,000 × 7%	532
Fixed production overheads $7,600,000 × 12%	912
Other costs $7,600,000 × 5%	380
	4,864

Current assets:

		$'000	$'000
Inventory			
Raw materials	6/52 × $1.672m		193
WIP			
Materials	3/52 × $1.672m × 80%	77	
Direct labour	3/52 × $1.368m × 75%	59	
Variable and fixed production overheads	3/52 × ($532k + $912k) × 50%	42	
			178
Finished goods			
Materials and direct labour	5/52 × ($1.672m + $1.368m)	292	
Variable and fixed production overheads	5/52 × ($532k + $912k)	139	
			431
Total inventory value			802
Trade receivables	2.5/52 × $7,600,000		365
Total value of current assets			1,167

		$'000	$'000
Current liabilities			
Accounts payable:			
Materials	8/52 × $1.672m	(257)	
Labour	2/52 × $1.368m	(53)	
Variable production overheads	4/52 × $532k	(41)	
Fixed production overheads	6/52 × $912k	(105)	
Other costs	3/52 × $380k	(22)	
Total value of current liabilities			(478)
Working capital required			689

14 Z Company

Helping hand. To answer part (a), you can use your general knowledge. When a business grows, the number of payments increases and payment by cheque can become an administrative burden.

For part (b), there are four types of expenditure and three methods of payment are mentioned in the question. Can you match the method of payment to the type of expenditure? Remember to give your reason for choosing a particular method of expenditure for each expenditure item.

Part (c) is worth just 2 marks, so a single well-explained point in your answer should be sufficient.

(a) Cheques can take a long time to write and record in the accounts. When a company grows in size, the number of payments becomes much larger, and the task of writing cheques becomes a bigger administrative burden. The task of signing cheques also takes up more management time, especially when cheques are for a large amount and require two signatures.

Documents prepared by hand are also more likely to contain errors, and there may be a need to cancel cheques that have been prepared incorrectly.

Cheques may also get lost in the post. When this happens, the lost cheque must be cancelled at the bank at a new cheque issued. This too can be time-consuming and inconvenient.

Bank reconciliations are more time consuming as uncashed cheques may be outstanding for some time if the recipient's banking arrangements are inefficient.

In extreme cases, there may be a risk of fraud. An individual may steal a cheque book and forge a signature in order to obtain a fraudulent payment.

However, the main reason for using alternative methods of payment is to reduce the administrative burden.

(b) (i) Payments of monthly salaries can be made using BACS (sometimes called BACS Direct Credit).

This involves sending an instruction to the bank in digital form, containing a list of salary payments to be made and the identity and bank details of the employees. The payment is then credited to the bank account of the employee.

A paper copy of the list of payments is provided to the bank, with the signature of one or two authorised signatories, to confirm to the bank that the payments have been properly authorised.

With BACs payments, the creation of the payment instructions is automated, and employees should receive their salary payments on time at the end of each month.

(ii) Utility bills involve regular payments to the utility companies, typically every three months. The amount of each payment varies according to the use of electricity, gas, water or communications services during the period, and the amounts of the payments therefore vary.

Utility companies are generally considered to be reliable suppliers, and the amount payable can be checked from invoices received. So, in view of the reliability of these suppliers, it may be appropriate for Z Company to arrange for payment by direct debit. By this method of payment, Z Company would allow the utility company to take payments for utility bills at the appropriate time, by giving a payment instruction direct to Z Company's bank. Z Company would authorise the direct debit payments just once, at the outset, when the direct debit payment method is first set up.

Payments by direct debit would be made without the need for any action by Z Company (except to check the amount of each bill and record the amount of payments in the accounting system). When the supplier is reliable and payments are variable but regular, direct debit is possibly the most convenient payment method.

(iii) Payments to most suppliers are often made at the same time, at the end of each month. When the number of payments is quite large, BACS provides a convenient method of payment, for the same reasons that BACS payments for employee salaries would be convenient. Suppliers would need to agree to payment by this method, and provide their banking details to Z Company.

However, since payment by BACS is automated, suppliers would benefit from prompt and reliable payments if they agree to BACS.

(iv) Payments of rental occur every six months and the amount of the rent charge is probably revised every few years. Rental payments are for a known amount and paid on a set payment cycle.

A suitable method of payment may therefore be standing order. With direct debit, the supplier sends the payment instruction to the bank. With a standing order, Z Company would control payments. Any changes to the amount payable (on dates specified to the bank by letter) would be initiated by Z Company. Since rental increases occur only infrequently, the requirement to submit a new payment instruction to the bank should not be a serious administrative problem.

(c) CHAPS is a real time payments system. Payments are made so that the funds are made available to the recipient (payee) during the same day. Bank charges for CHAPS payments are quite high, and this

15 Drab Company

> **Helping hand.** This question has two separate parts. To answer the first part, you need to demonstrate your understanding of the working capital cycle, and how the average payments periods from credit customers and to suppliers affect the working capital cycle. You can then go on to suggest how better management of payables and receivables may affect the length of the working capital cycle, and so the length of time that the company must wait until it receives cash from its trading activities.
>
> Part (b) calls for some thought, but the answer can be based largely on common sense. A company credit card means that a large number of small expenses can be included in a single monthly bill. One potential problem, however, is that with credit cards it may be difficult to control the total amount of spending – a common problem with personal credit cards for individuals, not just for company cards! Also, unless expenses are very high, it does not address the issue of supplier payments, and credit card interest is much higher than other forms of credit.

(a) The working capital cycle (or cash cycle) is an approximate measure of how long it takes on average for a business to receive cash from its business transactions from the time that it makes the payments for expenditures for the cost of sales. It may be calculated as:

(i) The average length of time that a business holds its inventory before the inventory is used or sold (as a separate product or within a manufactured product)

(ii) Plus the average length of time that it takes customers to pay for goods they have bought

(iii) Minus the average length of time that the business takes to pay for materials (and labour and other expenses) after incurring their cost of purchase.

A short average working capital cycle means that the business generates cash from its operations fairly quickly. A long cycle means that the business has to wait a long time for its cash from the time it pays for its raw materials. A business with a short working cash cycle should have fewer problems with cash flow and the availability of cash.

Trade receivables are relevant to the working capital cycle because they represent the amount of money that the business is owed. For a given amount of sales, a larger amount of trade receivables means that customers are taking longer to pay.

Trade payables are relevant to the working capital cycle because they represent the amount of money that the business owes to its suppliers. A large amount of trade payables, for a given amount of annual costs, means that the business is taking longer to pay its suppliers. As a result, the working capital cycle is shorter, and the business holds on to its cash for longer.

Within an industry, there are often established or 'normal' terms of credit for customers and suppliers. If a business is allowing its customers too long to pay, or if the business pays its suppliers sooner than it needs to, given the credit terms available, management is inefficient. Measures to speed up payment from customers and measures to take the available period of credit from suppliers will reduce the amount of receivables, increase the amount of payables, shorten the working cash cycle and so improve the company's cash position.

However, refusing to give customers a 'normal' period of credit or delaying payments to suppliers can be bad for business, and would not be 'efficient' management.

(b) A company may incur a large number of expenses through its senior management and sales representatives who travel extensively to meet customers, such as travelling expenses, hotel accommodation and subsistence. Many of these expenses cannot be paid for out of petty cash. An employer may require employees to pay expenses from their own resources, and claim back later, but this can be unfair on the employees – especially those with limited credit on their credit card and not much money in the bank. Giving credit cards to certain employees will mean that they can use the company's credit when paying for expenses on the company's business.

A company credit card can also be convenient for the company, because a large number of expense items are consolidated into a single credit card statement each month. Only a single payment is required to pay the liability.

One problem with a company credit card may be to control total spending. Employees may be more inclined to pay for items on their company credit card than they would be if they had to pay the cost themselves and then claim it back later. Careful monitoring of spending would be necessary to ensure that costs are kept to acceptable levels.

In addition, unless the credit card liabilities are paid off in full every month, the interest charges will be much higher than, for example, a bank overdraft. If the payment is made in full every month, there is no cash freed up to pay the suppliers.

Also, unless the expenses of the company are extremely high, paying for these on credit will not release enough funds to cover the suppliers invoices.

16 MCQ Answer Bank 2

16.1 The answer is Items which relate to the long-term running of the business.

Capital items relate to the long-term running of the business, such as the purchase of non-current assets.

Items that relate to the day-to-day running of the business or which are included in the business' working capital are revenue items. Unusual items are correctly known as exceptional items.

16.2 The answer is No, the total cash flow should be $248,000

The technician has made two errors.

Firstly, opening receivables is cash received during the year and closing receivables is cash owing at the end of the year. Therefore the opening figure should be added to, and the closing figure deducted from, cash in.

Secondly, depreciation is not a cash item and should be ignored from the calculation.

The correct calculation for cash in is therefore (325,000 + 23,500 – 17,500 + 125,000) = $456,000.

The correct calculation for cash out is therefore (193,500 + 27,000 – 12,500) = $208,000.

Total cash flow is therefore (456,000 – 208,000) = $248,000.

16.3 The answer is cash budget.

Cash budgets are prepared on the basis of cash accounting, while the others are prepared based on the accruals or matching principle.

16.4 The answer is tax payments.

Tax payments must be paid to the government and are therefore classed as priority cash flows. The other options are examples of operational cash flows.

16.5 The answer is a cleared funds forecast.

Only a cleared funds forecast shows the amount of available funds in a company's bank account.

16.6 The answer is All of them.

They could all cause differences between forecasted and actual cash flows.

16.7 The answer is Purchases figures which do not change over a number of months.

Figures which do not change from month to month, or which are not based on assumptions, indicate a weak forecasting system. Such figures will fluctuate in real life.

16.8 The answer is 37%

Margin is profit/selling price. Profit on each JigJog is (150 − 95) = $55. Margin = $\frac{55}{150}$ = 37%

16.9 The answer is depreciation.

Depreciation is not a cash item and is therefore not included in a cash forecast.

16.10 The answer is $4,275

	$
Assets held at 20X8	10,275
Add back non-cash 20X8 depreciation charge	1,500
Less assets held at 20X7	(7,500)
Total cash paid in respect of non-current assets	4,275

17 MCQ Answer Bank 3

17.1 The answer is (i), (ii) and (iv) only

Only depreciation is a non-cash item.

17.2 The answer is Discretionary cash flow

Purchase of new machinery is a discretionary cash flow. The company has the choice whether to make the purchase or not.

17.3 The answer is 10 days.

The cash cycle is the length of time raw materials and finished goods are held in inventory, plus the length of time the company takes to collect payment from customers, less the credit period it receives from its suppliers. In Tosh Co's case it is (5 + 10 + 20 − 25) = 10 days.

17.4 The answer is a bank loan

A bank loan is not classed as a current asset or liability and is therefore not a working capital item.

17.5 The answer is The effects of transactions and other events are recognised when they occur

This is the definition as described in the IASB's Framework for the Preparation and Presentation of Financial Statements. 'The effects of transactions and other events are recognised when the related cash payment is made or cash receipt is received' describes cash accounting. 'Financial statements must take into account future transactions and events if they are likely to occur' is nonsense. 'Financial statements must reflect all transactions and events in a manner which is true and fair', whilst being a correct description of financial statements, is not a definition of accruals accounting.

17.6 The answer is Leading and lagging

Delaying payments to suppliers whilst speeding up payment collection from customers is known as leading and lagging.

17.7 The answer is 18%

Mark up is $\frac{Profit}{Cost}$

Profit on Product YTW is (65 − 55) = $10. Therefore mark up = $\frac{10}{55}$ = 18%

17.8 The answer is The amount of money tied up between the time a payment is initiated and the cleared funds being available in a business's bank account.

ANSWERS

Float is the amount of money tied up between the time a payment is initiated and the cleared funds being available in a business's bank account. It includes cheques but other types of payment as well.

17.9 The answer is $4,625.

Cash receipts in April 20X9
75% of April sales ((10,000 + (3 × 1,500)) × 0.75 = $10,875
25% of March sales ((10,000 + (2 × 1,500)) × 0.25 = $3,250
Total = $14,125

Cash payments in April 20X9
February purchases (two months in arrears) = 8,000 + 500 = $8,500
Wages and salaries (fixed) = $1,000
Total = $9,500
Net cash flow (14,125 − 9,500) = $4,625

17.10 The answer is a cash surplus.

Where a forecast indicates an excess of equity and liabilities over assets, the business is expecting a cash surplus.

18 Coolshades Co

Budgeted cash flow for the three months to 30 September 20X1

	Working	July $'000	Aug $'000	Sept $'000
Receipts	1			
Cash sales revenue		25	25	25
From opening receivables		307	283	
Received in month 1			112	112
Received in month 2				104
Total receipts		332	420	241
Payments				
Trade payables	2	210	175	175
Expense payables	3	35	26	26
Admin expenses	4	18	18	18
Bank overdraft interest				9
Loan interest				5
Corporation tax				75
Dividends			125	
Loan repayment				20
Purchase of vans				80
Purchase of cars				100
Market research				
Total payments		263	344	508
Net cash flow		69	76	(267)
Opening cash balance		(200)	(131)	(55)
Closing cash balance		(131)	(55)	(322)

Workings

1

	$
Six monthly sales revenue	1,500,000
Monthly sales revenue = 1,500,000/6	250,000
Cash sales revenue per month = 250,000 × 10%	25,000
Credit sales revenue per month = 250,000 × 90%	225,000
Paid 1st month = 225,000 × 50%	112,500
Bad debts = 225,000 × 4%	9,000
Paid 2nd month = 225,000 − 112,500 − 9,000	103,500

It is assumed that all bad debts relate to accounts settled after one month.

2   Trade purchases are 70% of sales revenue. Purchases are made in the month prior to sale, and settled in the following month.

Monthly sales revenue is $250,000, and therefore:

Monthly purchases = 250,000 × 70% = $175,000

3   Monthly distribution expense payables = 33,000 − 7,000 = $26,000

These are paid one month in arrears. Depreciation is a non-cash item and is therefore excluded.

4   Monthly admin expenses excluding the Christmas bonus = (120,000 − 12,000)/6 = $18,000

December expenses = 18,000 + 12,000 = $30,000

It is assumed that expenses are paid in the month in which they are incurred.

19 Chocoholics Co

Cash budget for the three months ended 30 September 20X4

	July $'000	August $'000	September $'000
Cash inflows			
Sales receipts	173	255	271
	173	255	271
Cash outflows			
Payments to suppliers	60	125	133
Admin. Expenses	55	60	62
Delivery costs	3	3	3
Packaging	1	1	2
Misc. expenses	6	6	7
Loan repayments	50		
Overdraft interest	2	2	1
	177	197	208
Net cash flow	(4)	58	63
Opening balance	(155)	(159)	(101)
Closing balance	(159)	(101)	(38)

Working: Sales receipts

	July $'000	August $'000	September $'000
Cash: 30% × $250	75		
Credit: 70% × $140	98		
	173		
Cash: 30% × $266		80	
Credit: 70% ×$250		175	
		255	
Cash: 30% × $282			85
Credit: 70% × $266			186
			271

20 Health Foods Co

> **Helping hand.** The key to cash flow statements is to remember that you are explaining the movement from one statement of financial position to the next and that every item on the statement of financial position and statement of profit or loss affects, or is affected by, cash.
>
> If you ever forget the format of the cash flow do not panic. Start with operating profit and work down the statement of profit or loss and statement of financial position headings. You will still gain marks for your calculations even if you get them out in an incorrect order.

> As operating profit includes non-cash depreciation, you should add it back. Don't forget increasing assets such as inventory reduces cash as cash has been spent to purchase them. Decreasing liabilities such as trade payables reduces cash as cash has been spent to settle the debts.

Projected cash flow for Health Foods Co

	$'000
Operating profit	8,085
Depreciation	200
Finance costs	(785)
Tax paid (W1)	(1,836)
Dividends paid (W2)	(1,577)
Non-current asset purchases (W3)	(500)
Increase in inventory (W4)	(1,078)
Increase in trade receivables (W5)	(775)
Decrease in trade payables (W6)	(14)
Projected increase in cash	1,720

Reconciliation of cash

	$'000
Cash balance at 30.6.X6	1,264
Add increase in cash during year (above)	1,720
Cash balance at 30.6.X7 per statement of financial position	2,984

Workings

1 Tax paid

	$'000
Tax liability at 30.6.X6	(1,895)
Tax charge for year to 30.6.X7	(2,230)
	(4,125)
Less actual liability at 30.6.X7	2,289
Therefore cash paid during year	(1,836)

2 Dividends paid

	$'000
Dividend liability at 30.6.X6	(1,542)
Dividend payable for year to 30.6.X7	(2,270)
	(3,812)
Less actual liability at 30.6.X7	2,235
Therefore cash paid during year	(1,577)

3 Non-current asset purchases

	$'000
Non-current assets at 30.6.X7	(8,300)
Depreciation for year to 30.6.X7	(200)
Non-current assets at 30.6.X6	8000
Therefore cash paid during year	(500)

4 Increase in inventory

	$'000
Inventory at 30.6.X7	(3,245)
Inventory at 30.6.X6	2,167
Therefore increase in inventory during year	(1,078)

5 Increase in trade receivables

	$'000
Trade receivables at 30.6.X7	(3,318)
Trade receivables at 30.6.X6	2,543
Therefore increase in trade receivables during year	(775)

6　Decrease in trade payables

	$'000
Trade payables at 30.6.X7	1,723
Trade payables at 30.6.X6	(1,737)
Therefore decrease in trade payables during year	(14)

21 Tots Co

Monthly cash budget for Tots Co

	Jan $'000	Feb $'000	Mar $'000
Receipts			
Sales receipts (W1)	1,274	1,414	1,610
Play centre income	7	7	7
	1,281	1,421	1,617
Payments			
Purchases (W2)	650	750	850
Permanent staff	150	150	150
Temporary staff (W3)	45	51	57
Delivery costs (W4)	30	34	38
Admin costs (W5)	30	34	38
Conference	2		
Computer system			
	907	1,019	1,133
Net receipts/payments	374	402	484
Opening balance	1,200	1,574	1,976
Closing balance	1,574	1,976	2,460

Workings

		Nov $'000	Dec $'000	Jan $'000	Feb $'000	Mar $'000
	Sales figures	1,300	1,300	1,500	1,700	1,900
1	Sales receipts					
	70% one month later			910	1,050	1,190
	28% two months later			364	364	420
				1,274	1,414	1,610
2	Purchases					
	@ 50% of next month Sales	650	750	850	950	700
	Payment delayed by 2 months			650	750	850
3	Temporary staff = 3% of sales			45	51	57
4	Delivery costs = 2% of sales = 1% of sales			30	34	38
5	Admin costs = 30/1500 = 2% = 2% of sales			30	34	38

ANSWERS

22 Risky Co

> **Helping hand.** The key to answering this question is to set out to a proforma using the information in the question. You could have used a separate working for sales revenue if you wanted.
>
> When filling in the numbers always take care to ensure that you use the correct month's data. Questions such as this will always try to trip you up by changing the month where a cash flow appears – for example the two months' credit given by suppliers – this means the January payment is for November purchases.

	Jan $'000	Feb $'000	Mar $'000
Cash inflows			
Sales revenue: non-members	325	375	175
Sales revenue: members (5% discount)	309	356	166
Cash inflows	634	731	341
Cash outflows			
Purchases (W1)	38	180	260
Staff costs	45	60	70
Packaging costs	7	10	12
Distribution costs	50	58	28
Other costs excl. rent (W2)	33	43	13
Rent (3 × $30k)			90
Cash outflows	173	351	473
Net cash flows	461	380	(132)
Opening balance	(500)	(42)	338
Overdraft interest	(3)	–	–
Closing balance	(42)	338	206

Workings

	Nov $'000	Dec $'000	Jan $'000
1 Purchases			
Gross sales revenue	95	450	650
Purchases at 40%	38	180	260

2 Other costs   Each month

	Jan $'000	Feb $'000	Mar $'000
Per question	75	85	55
Less deprecation	(12)	(12)	(12)
Less rental costs	(30)	(30)	(30)
	33	43	13

23 Sporty Co

Venture capitalists

Factors that a venture capitalist organisation will take into account are as follows (choose any three – this is more than you will need for full marks):

(i) **Level of expertise of Cool Ski Co's management**

Venture capitalists will believe that the success of Cool Ski Co's business is dependant on the quality of the management. They will expect the three directors/shareholders to show a high level of commitment to the business. As all of the existing owners of the business are all involved in the running of the company, this should be proof of their commitment.

The venture capitalists will also look at the amount of money that the owners themselves have invested in the project in assessing their level of commitment. The venture capitalists will expect a place on Cool Ski Co's Board of Directors so that they can have a say in future business strategy.

(ii) **Level of expertise in the area of service**

The venture capitalists will seek assurance that the directors have the necessary know-how and technical support to be able to run the business properly. The fact that the business has been supplying the public direct through its website for the last three years is evidence of the ability of the directors/shareholders to run the company. However, running a manufacturing business is going to be different from simply being a retailer, and dealing with wholesale customers is different from dealing with the public direct. The directors have a lot to prove.

(iii) **The nature of Cool Ski Co's product**

In order to succeed in manufacturing and selling their own brand of skiwear, the directors need to show that they have excellent designs for a range of skiwear that people will want to buy and wear. The business already has a customer base with members buying skiwear at reduced prices. This should help the directors in persuading the venture capitalists that they have a likeable brand.

(iv) **The market and competition**

They will seek assurance that there is actually a market for the ski wear, as there are already some similar memberships available in the market place. They will ask to see the market research that has already been carried out. The venture capitalists will also look at the threat posed by new entrants in the market, and current rival membership schemes.

(v) **Future prospects**

Since the risk involved in investing in a new or expanding company is fairly high, the venture capitalists will seek to ensure that the prospects for future profits compensate for the risk. They will therefore want to see the business plan setting out the future business strategy.

(vi) **Exit routes**

The venture capitalists will consider potential exit routes before they invest in the venture. They will not invest money in a share of the business unless they are confident that it can be sold at some point in the future.

24 Print Co

> **Helping hand.** There is a considerable amount of information to process in order to produce the forecast. However it is not particularly difficult, so work through it methodically and slot the numbers into the proforma as you go.

Working: Uncleared funds – Receipts

	$
Anchor (Nov. sales)	16,000
Beauty Co (Dec. sales)	18,000
Light Co (Jan. sales)	4,500
Debit (DR) card receipts 19 Jan	170
Uncleared receipts 19 Jan	38,670
Less cleared DR card receipts from 19 Jan	(170)
Add debit card receipts from 20 Jan	210
Uncleared receipts 20 Jan	38,710
Less cleared DR card receipts 20 Jan	(210)
Uncleared receipts 21 and 22 Jan	38,500
Less cleared cheques from 19 Jan	(38,500)
Add uncleared credit card receipts	3,500
Uncleared receipts 23 Jan	3,500

ANSWERS

Cleared Funds Forecast

	19 Jan $	20 Jan $	21 Jan $	22 Jan $	23 Jan $
Receipts (W1)					
Anchor Co					16,000
Beauty Co					18,000
Kent Co	18,000				
Hut Co	2,200				
Light Co					4,500
Non-commercial customers – method:					
Cash		220	350		430
Debit card		170	210		
Credit card					
	20,200	390	560	0	38,930
Payments					
Ink Co					5,500
Toner Co					10,600
Paper Co					10,500
Other cheques					
Salaries				9,600	
Petty cash	150				
	150	0	0	9,600	26,600
Cleared excess receipts over payments	20,050	390	560	(9,600)	12,330
Cleared balance b/f	35,000	55,050	55,440	56,000	46,400
Cleared balance c/f	55,050	55,440	56,000	46,400	58,730
Uncleared funds float					
Receipts	38,670	38,710	38,500	38,500	3,500
Payments					(8,200)
	38,670	38,710	38,500	38,500	(4,700)
Total book balance c/f	93,720	94,150	94,500	84,900	54,030

25 Rich Co

(a) **Cash forecast**

	Q1	Q2
Cash inflows	2,000	2,500
Cash out flows	(4,000)	(5,500)
Net cash flows	(2,000)	(3,000)
Cash balance b/f	5,000	3,000
Cash balance c/f	3,000	0

(b) **Deposit options**

There are two alternative options for investing the cash. Option 1 is to make two three-month deposits; option 2 is to make one six-month deposit and one three-month deposit.

Option 1

Now, invest $5 million immediately on three-month deposit.
Return = ($5m × 9.4%) × 3/12 = $117,500.

AND

In three months time, invest $3 million on three-month deposit.
Return = ($3m × 9.6%) × 3/12 = $72,000.
Total income = $189,500.

Option 2

Now, invest $2m on three-month deposit and $3m on six-month deposit.
Return for $2m = ($2m × 9.4%) × 3/12 = $47,000
Return on $3m = ($3m × 9.7%) = $145,500
Total income = $192,500.

Therefore, option 2 should be chosen as it yields the higher return.

26 Porkys Co

Helping hand. You must read this question carefully and use all the information provided.

As cash from customers is received two months in arrears, the cash collected in Sept, Oct and Nov will be for sales made in July, Aug and Sept. A similar principle should be followed when calculating purchases.

As depreciation is an accounting entry it is not included in the cash flow and therefore must be added into the figures for the profit forecast. Note that the capital payments for the purchase of machinery and the loan repayments are ignored.

Profit forecast for the three months ending 30 September 20X7

	$'000
Sales (W1)	5,700
Purchases (W2)	(1,140)
Labour	(1,425)
Depreciation	(13)
Profit on disposal (W3)	3
Interest receivable	30
Sundry expenses	(260)
Net profit	2,895

Workings

1. Sales = receipts from Sept, Oct and Nov since the cash is received two months in arrears.
   $1,800,000 + $2,200,000 + $1,700,000 = $5,700,000.

2. Purchases – paid one month in arrears so use CFF figures from Aug, Sep, Oct.
   Ingredients:
   ($360,000 + $440,000 + $340,000) = $1,140,000.

3. Profit on disposal – it is this revenue figure that is relevant for the profit and loss forecast, rather than the actual sale proceeds of $45,000 since this is a capital disposal.

Notes for items excluded from the profit forecast

1. Purchase of machinery – these are capital payments and are only relevant in so far as they are used to calculate depreciation.

2. Loan repayments – ignored since these are capital in nature, not revenue.

ANSWERS

27 Cleared funds

> **Helping hand.** Cleared funds cash forecasts are possibly a bit more complicated that 'normal' cash budgets, and it may help to set out your workings and your answer clearly, preparing a blank table to structure your answer before you start to fill in the table with the figures for cleared funds or float. Tick off items from the question as you use them.
>
> You should also remember that part (b) is worth 8 marks, and you should not focus your efforts entirely on getting the numbers correct in part (a). It is important to understand that cleared funds in a bank account are the only funds available to make payments. 'Float' is not yet available, even though the receipts or payments have been recorded in the cash book of the business. In the short term, a business may need to monitor its cleared fund carefully: for these businesses (which include banks themselves) cleared funds forecasting may be essential.

(a)

(i)

	Monday $	Tuesday $	Wednesday $	Thursday $	Friday $
Cleared receipts					
Cheques	8,400	0	6,000	6,000	6,000
Cash	2,000	2,000	2,000	2,000	2,000
	10,400	2,000	8,000	8,000	8,000
Cleared payments	0	(500)	(15,900)	(12,300)	0
	10,400	1,500	(7,900)	(4,300)	8,000
Opening cleared funds	1,200	11,600	13,100	5,200	900
Closing cleared funds	11,600	13,100	5,200	900	8,900

(ii)
Float

	Monday $	Tuesday $	Wednesday $	Thursday $	Friday $
Receipts not cleared	6,000	6,000			
		6,000	6,000		
			6,000	6,000	
				9,000	9,000
					1,000
Total receipts not cleared	6,000	12,000	12,000	15,000	10,000
Payments not cleared	(12,300)	(12,300)	(12,300)	0	0
	(15,900)	(15,900)			
Total payments not cleared	(28,200)	(28,200)	(12,300)	0	0
Float	(22,200)	(16,200)	(300)	15,000	10,000

(b) The purpose of a cleared cash funds forecast is to assess whether the business will have enough cleared funds in its account to meet payment obligations, allowing for any overdraft facility that the business may have. Only cleared funds are available for payments, because receipts or payments that have not yet been cleared ('float') do not affect the available account balance.

If a forecast shows that there will be insufficient cleared funds and that the account will have a negative balance in cleared funds, it may be possible to take measures in advance to deal with the problem, without the risk that the bank may refuse a payment so that a cheque payment would be dishonoured. Measures that may be taken in advance include negotiating a sufficient temporary overdraft facility with the bank, or possibly deferring planned payments for a day or so until expected receipts have been cleared.

A cleared funds forecast will also enable a business to assess whether it will have sufficient cash to pay for an unexpected 'emergency' expense that may arise.

BPP LEARNING MEDIA

143

When a business is 'cash rich', a cleared funds forecast may help with decisions about transferring the surplus to an interest-earning account.

A cleared funds forecast is a short-term forecast because it is difficult to predict what receipts and payments will be for more than a few days in advance. The purpose of a cleared funds forecast is to manage the cleared funds in the bank account, and management action is generally short-term in nature – involving decisions to delay payments or bank receipts more quickly, and avoiding dishonoured payments to suppliers or employees. For longer term cash forecasting and planning, a standard cash flow forecast or cash budget should be sufficient for cash management purposes.

28 Larcher Co

> **Helping hand.** Make sure your spreadsheets are clear for the marker to follow, and feature a separate column for each day.

Marking scheme

			Marks
(a)	Sales		1
	Split 0.5 for cash sales and 0.5 for cc		
	Supplier payments		2
	Calc supplies at 40% of OFR sales value = 1 mark		
	(If use 60%, award 0.5 mark)		
	For inserting OFR into each of the five days = 1 mark		
	Rent – must be shown on Monday		0.5
	Wages – must be shown on Friday		0.5
	Utilities – award if simply ignored but only if the question has been attempted and some cash flows applied		0.5
	Opening balance		1
	Closing balance OFR		0.5
			6
(b)	Cash sales		1
	Credit card		1
	Cheque		1
	Rent		1
	Wages		1
	Opening balance		0.5
	Closing balance		0.5
			6
(c)	Change explained (2 each)		4
(d)	1 mark per point – and up to 3 marks per value discussed		4
Total marks			**20**

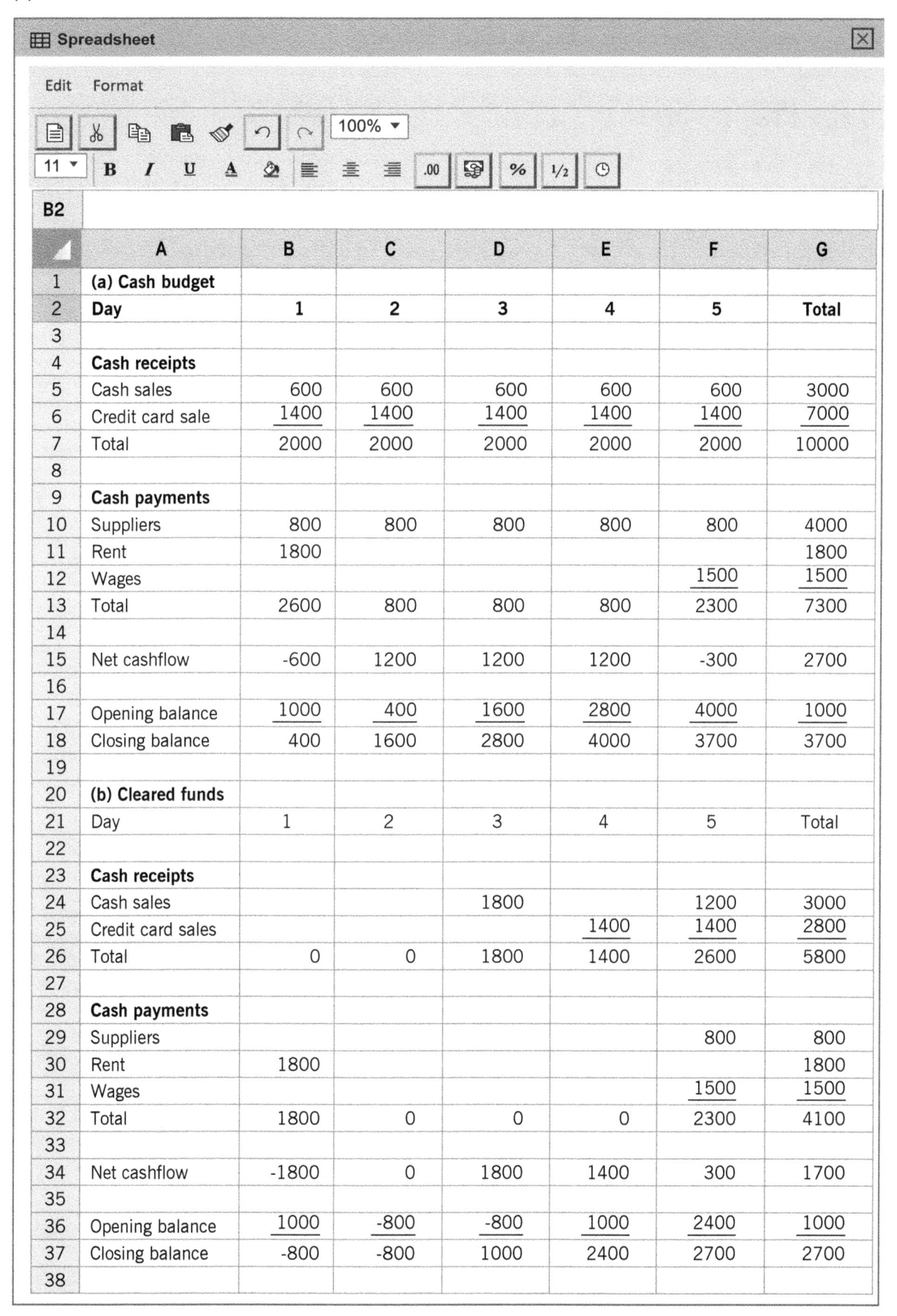

(a)

(a) Cash budget

Day	1	2	3	4	5	Total
Cash receipts						
Cash sales	600	600	600	600	600	3000
Credit card sale	1400	1400	1400	1400	1400	7000
Total	2000	2000	2000	2000	2000	10000
Cash payments						
Suppliers	800	800	800	800	800	4000
Rent	1800					1800
Wages					1500	1500
Total	2600	800	800	800	2300	7300
Net cashflow	-600	1200	1200	1200	-300	2700
Opening balance	1000	400	1600	2800	4000	1000
Closing balance	400	1600	2800	4000	3700	3700

(b) Cleared funds

Day	1	2	3	4	5	Total
Cash receipts						
Cash sales			1800		1200	3000
Credit card sales				1400	1400	2800
Total	0	0	1800	1400	2600	5800
Cash payments						
Suppliers					800	800
Rent	1800					1800
Wages					1500	1500
Total	1800	0	0	0	2300	4100
Net cashflow	-1800	0	1800	1400	300	1700
Opening balance	1000	-800	-800	1000	2400	1000
Closing balance	-800	-800	1000	2400	2700	2700

Tutorial note. The workings here are simple enough to be embedded in the cells of the spreadsheet. The following table shows the formulae that have been used to generate these values and is shown here as a student aid, it would not be produced as a part of your answer.

(b)

	A	B	C	D	E	F	G	H
1								
2		**(a) Cash budget**						
3								
4		Day	1	2	3	4	5	Total
5								
6		**Cash receipts**						
7		Cash sales	=2000*0.3	=2000*0.3	=2000*0.3	=2000*0.3	=2000*0.3	=SUM(C7:G7)
8		Credit card sales	=2000*0.7	=2000*0.7	=2000*0.7	=2000*0.7	=2000*0.7	=SUM(C8:G8)
9		Total	=C7+C8	=D7+D8	=E7+E8	=F7+F8	=G7+G8	=H7+H8
10								
11		**Cash payments**						
12		Suppliers	=0.4*C9	=0.4*D9	=0.4*E9	=0.4*F9	=0.4*G9	=SUM(C12:G12)
13		Rent	1800					=SUM(C13:G13)
14		Wages					1500	=SUM(C14:G14)
15		Total	=SUM(C12:C14)	=SUM(D12:D14)	=SUM(E12:E14)	=SUM(F12:14)	=SUM(G12:G14)	=SUM(H12:H14)
16								
17		Net cashflow	=C9-C15	=D9-D15	=E9-E15	=F9-F15	=G9-G15	=H9-H15
18								
19		Opening balance	1000	=C20	=D20	=E20	=F20	=C19
20		Closing balance	=C17+C19	=D17+D19	=E17+E19	=F17+19	=G17+G19	=G20
21								
22		**(b) Cleared fund**						
23								
24		Day	1	2	3	4	5	Total
25								
26		**Cash receipts**						
27		Cash sales			=E7+D7+C7		=G7+F7	=SUM(C27:G27)
28		Credit card sales				=C8	=D8	=SUM(C28:G28)
29		Total	=C27+C28	=D27+D28	=E27+E28	=F27+F28	=G27+G28	=H27+H28
30								
31		**Cash payments**						
32		Suppliers					=C12	=SUM(C32:G32
33		Rent	=C13					=SUM(C33:G33
34		Wages					=G14	=SUM(C34:G34)
35		Total	=SUM(C32:C34)	=SUM(D32:D34)	=SUM(E32:E34)	=SUM(F32:F34)	=SUM(G32:G34)	=SUM(H32:H34
36								
37		Net cashflow	=C29-C5	=D29-D35	=E29-E35	=F29-F35	=G29-G35	=H29-H35
38								
39		Opening balance	1000	=C40	=D40	=E40	=F40	=C39
40		Closing balance	=C37+C39	=D37+D39	=E37+E39	=F37+F39	=G37+G39	=G40

(c)

(i) If cash receipts were banked each day, there would be no change to the end of week cleared balance because the total cash banked in the week would remain the same. It would, however, improve the cleared cash balance at the end of Monday, Tuesday and Thursday.

(ii) If payments to suppliers cleared in three days by the end of week, the cleared funds balance would worsen by $800 to $1,900 because one extra payment would clear in the week.

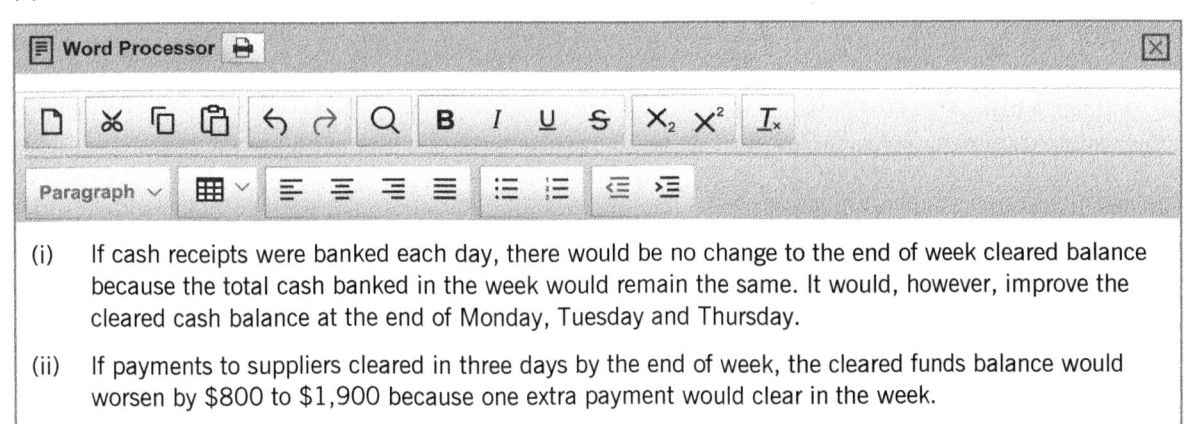

(d)

Definition

Sensitivity analysis (sometimes known as 'what if' analysis) is used to assess the responsiveness of model outputs (the dependent variable) to changes in input data (the independent variable).

Forecasts of future cash balances rely heavily on assumptions about the future (for example, future sales levels, customer payment behaviour, cheque clearing times). Any error in these assumptions will alter the value of the forecast.

Purpose

Sensitivity analysis helps identify the assumptions which have the most significant effect on forecasts. Once identified, these should become the focus of management attention.

Sensitivity calculations are simple and quick to perform using financial modelling and spreadsheet packages.

Problems

A major problem of sensitivity analysis is that it assumes that only one variable will change at a time. In practice, this is unlikely. For example, if we were testing the sensitivity of future cash balances to an increase in sales price, we could not sensibly do this without considering the knock-on effect of sales price on sales volume.

A second problem of sensitivity analysis is that it does not consider the probability of assumptions being wrong. A one-week extension on the rent payment date would have a major effect on cash flow, but in practice, it is very unlikely to happen.

29 GES Co

> **Helping hand.** As with all cash budgeting questions, there is a lot of information that requires methodical handling. Have a clearly labelled working for complicated items (such as direct materials) to make it as easy as possible for both you and the marker to follow your calculations.

Marking scheme

		Marks
(a)	Sales budget $ (for × $8)	1
	Production budget OFR sales units × 40% (0.5 mark) timing (0.5 mark)	
	OFR sales units ×60% (0.5 mark) timing (0.5 mark)	2
	Cash receipts OFR 30% of sales budget (1 mark)	1
	Credit receipts OFR 70% of sales budget (1 mark) timing (1 mark)	2
	Opening receivables	0.5
	Material purchases (this month 1 mark) prior month (1 mark) × $3.64 (1 mark)	3
	Conversion costs (OFR production × OFR cost (1 mark))	1
	Fixed overhead include (0.5 mark) deduct depreciation (0.5 mark)	1
	Machinery	1
	Cash opening balance	0.5
	Cash C/F OFR	1
		14
(b)	Up to 3 marks per benefit	6
Total marks		**20**

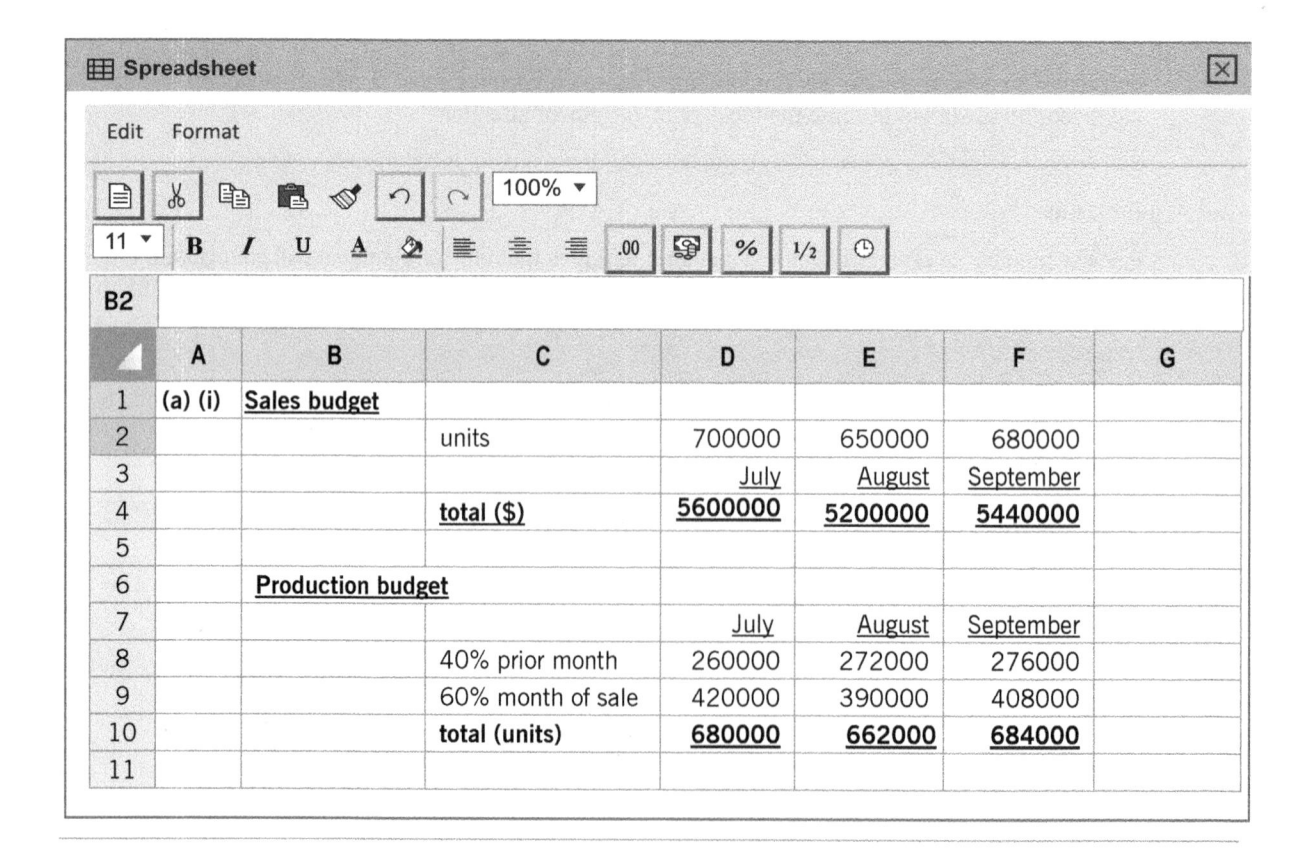

	A	B	C	D	E	F	G
1	(a) (i)	**Sales budget**					
2			units	700000	650000	680000	
3				July	August	September	
4			total ($)	**5600000**	**5200000**	**5440000**	
5							
6		**Production budget**					
7				July	August	September	
8			40% prior month	260000	272000	276000	
9			60% month of sale	420000	390000	408000	
10			total (units)	**680000**	**662000**	**684000**	
11							

ANSWERS

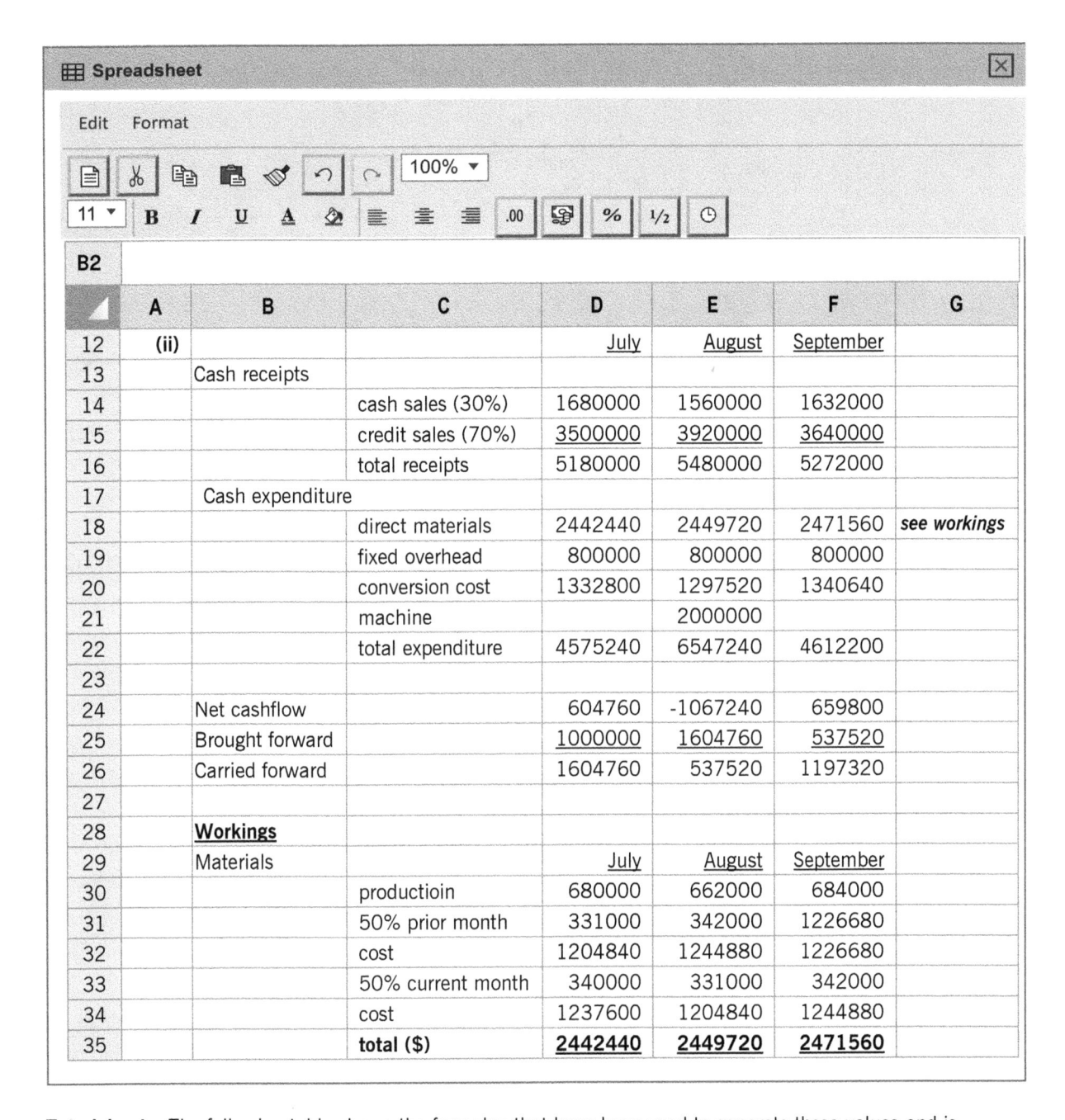

	A	B	C	D	E	F	G
12	(ii)			July	August	September	
13		Cash receipts					
14			cash sales (30%)	1680000	1560000	1632000	
15			credit sales (70%)	3500000	3920000	3640000	
16			total receipts	5180000	5480000	5272000	
17		Cash expenditure					
18			direct materials	2442440	2449720	2471560	see workings
19			fixed overhead	800000	800000	800000	
20			conversion cost	1332800	1297520	1340640	
21			machine		2000000		
22			total expenditure	4575240	6547240	4612200	
23							
24		Net cashflow		604760	-1067240	659800	
25		Brought forward		1000000	1604760	537520	
26		Carried forward		1604760	537520	1197320	
27							
28		**Workings**					
29		Materials		July	August	September	
30			productioin	680000	662000	684000	
31			50% prior month	331000	342000	1226680	
32			cost	1204840	1244880	1226680	
33			50% current month	340000	331000	342000	
34			cost	1237600	1204840	1244880	
35			**total ($)**	2442440	2449720	2471560	

Tutorial note. The following table shows the formulae that have been used to generate these values and is shown here as a student aid, it would not be produced as a part of your answer.

	A	B	C	D	E	F
1	(a) (i)	**Sales budget**				
2			units	700000	650000	680000
3				July	August	September
4			total ($)	=D2*8	=E2*8	=F2*8
5						
6		**Production budget**				
7				July	August	September
8			40% prior month	=E2*0.4	=F2*0.4	=0.4*690000
9			60% month of sale	=D2*0.6	=E2*0.6	=F2*0.6
10			total (units)	=D8+d9	=E8+E9	=F8+F9
11						
12	(ii)			July	August	September
13		Cash receipts				
14			cash sales (30%)	=D4*0.3	=E4*0.3	=F4*0.3
15			credit sales (70%)	3500000	=D4*0.7	=E4*0.7
16			total receipts	=D14+D15	=E14+E15	=F14+F15
17		Cash expenditure				
18			direct materials	=D35	=E35	=F35
19			fixed overhead	=1000000-200000	=1000000-200000	=1000000-200000
20			conversion cost	=D10*1.96	=E10*1.96	=F10*1.96
21			machine		2000000	
22			total expenditure	=SUM(D18:D21)	=SUM(E18:E21)	=SUM(F18:F21)
23						
24		Net cashflow		=D16-D22	=E16-E22	=F16-F22
25		Brought forward		=1000000	=D26	=E26
26		Carried forward		=D24+D25	=E24+E25	=F24+F25
27						
28		**Workings**				
29		Materials		July	August	September
30			productioin	=D10	=E10	=F10
31			50% prior month	=E30*0.5	=F30*0.5	=1226680
32			cost	=D31*3.64	=E31*3.64	=1226680
33			50% current month	=D30*0.5	=E30*0.5	=F30*0.5
34			cost	=D33*3.64	=E33*3.64	=F33*3.64
35			total ($)	=D32+D34	=E32+E34	=F32+F34
36						

(b)

> A cash budget will help to identify where a company is likely to have cash shortages and enable a company to fund any forecast deficits. A cash budget will predict the amount of funding needed and the amount of time it is needed for. This information will enable the company to arrange the best form of funding. This could be done by borrowing money, selling any short-term investments or simply delaying payment to suppliers.
>
> A cash budget will also help to identify where a company has cash surpluses which need investing. Cash surpluses held in business current accounts usually earn very low interest, if any at all. Depending on the size of the surplus and the time when it is likely to be available, a company can receive good returns by investing in a deposit account or in the money markets.
>
> A cash budget is a plan for the future and therefore it can act as a control mechanism. When actual cash balances are compared against budgets and a difference is identified, the company can investigate the cause of the difference and rectify it. For example, lower cash receipts than budgeted could indicate poor credit control, which could be improved by structured training in the credit control department.

30 MCQ Answer Bank 4

30.1 The answer is 4%

Return on bond/bond valuation = required return

$4.25/$106.5 = 4%

30.2 The answer is lodgement delay.

Lodgement delay refers to the delay in banking payments received.

30.3 The answer is the opportunity cost of keeping money in the form of cash

A variable cost is the opportunity cost of keeping the money in the form of cash. It is usually represented by the interest rate. The other options are all examples of fixed costs.

30.4 The answer is customers' deposits

The other options are assets of the bank.

30.5 The answer is the department is likely to be more responsive to meet the needs of individual operating units.

Decentralised treasury departments are likely to be more responsive in meeting the needs of operating units as they are closer to them. The other options are advantages of centralised treasury departments.

30.6 The answer is (i), (iii) and (iv) only

A business should base its cash management policy on profitability, liquidity and safety. Exposure may be taken into account in terms of safety, but it is not a principle in its own right.

30.7 The answer is unsystematic risk

Risk which is specific to a market sector is known as unsystematic risk.

FFM FOUNDATIONS IN FINANCIAL MANAGEMENT

30.8 The answer is Increases or falls to $100

Fixed interest stocks have a nominal value of $100 which is also their redemption value. On maturity, the market price will therefore increase or fall to reflect this redemption value. This is known as the pull to maturity.

30.9 The answer is the transactions motive.

The motive for a business to hold cash in order to meet its regular commitments such as paying employees is known as the transactions motive.

30.10 The answer is the purchaser is entitled to the next dividend payment

Cum Div means the purchaser of a share is entitled to the next dividend payment. Ex Div means the purchaser is not entitled to the next dividend payment.

31 MCQ Answer Bank 5

31.1 The answer is 16.67%

Gross redemption yield = (interest to maturity + par value at maturity)/cost of bond

= ($5 + $100)/$90

= 16.67%

31.2 The answer is Ensuring the business has investments which are easily convertible into cash

Liquidity means ensuring the business has sufficient cash to pay its suppliers on time. This can be achieved by ensuring the business has investments which are easily convertible into cash. The other options are an example of profitability or examples of safety.

31.3 The answer is office buildings.

Office buildings are the least liquid as they may take some time to sell. Shares and inventories have markets where they can be sold quickly.

31.4 The answer is: scrip dividends increase the issued share capital of a company as new shares are issued

31.5 The answer is Transmission delay.

Transmission delay refers to the delay incurred between posting a payment and it reaching the payee.

31.6 The answer is interest cost

Interest cost is represented by i in Baumol's model of cash management.

31.7 The answer is Caitlin.

Caitlin has made the same profit as the others but has done so using fewer net assets. The others may have been more profitable if they had used their surplus cash more effectively and made greater returns on it.

31.8 The answer is Super Saver

The compound annual rate of interest of the Super Saver account is 6.80%. This compares to 6.77% of the Easy Saver account and 6.65% of the Gold Saver account.

Super Saver account

If 0.0660% interest is paid n times per year, then the compound annual rate of interest is given by the following.

$$\left(\left(1+\frac{0.0660}{12}\right)^{12}-1\right) \times 100 = 6.80\%$$

Easy Saver account

If 0.0655% interest is paid n times per year, then the compound annual rate of interest is given by the following.

$$\left(\left(1+\frac{0.0655}{365}\right)^{365}-1\right)\times 100 = 6.77\%$$

31.9 The answer is 3.45%

$$\text{Interest yield} = \frac{\text{Coupon rate}}{\text{Market price}} \times 100\%$$

$$= \frac{5}{145} \times 100\% = 3.45\%$$

31.10 The answer is longs.

Longs are gilts that have a life of over 15 years.

32 MCQ Answer Bank 6

32.1 The answer is a deposit of any currency made outside that currency's country of origin

A Eurocurrency deposit is a deposit of any currency made outside of that currency's country of origin.

32.2 The answer is all of them

They are all roles of a central bank.

32.3 The answer is retail banking

High street banking is also known as retail banking.

32.4 The answer is loans between companies with surplus cash and those who need to borrow

On the inter-company market, deals are made between companies with surplus cash and those who need to borrow.

32.5 The answer is (ii), (iii) and (iv) only

Customer deposits are liabilities as banks are liable to pay the customers back their deposits.

32.6 The answer is the avoidance of using financial intermediaries when arranging lending or borrowing

Disintermediation is the avoidance of using financial intermediaries when arranging lending or borrowing.

32.7 The answer is all of them

Financial intermediaries pool money from savers and lend it in large amounts to borrowers. This means the risk of default is lower for savers as it is spread among them. As large numbers of customers are involved over a long period of time, the short and long-term needs of all can be met.

32.8 The answer is gilts

Government bonds are otherwise known as gilts or gilt-edged securities.

32.9 The answer is Speculative motive

According to Keynes, only the speculative motive will alter the demand for money as a result of changes to interest rates.

32.10 The answer is A secondary bank

A secondary bank deals in the wholesale money markets.

FFM FOUNDATIONS IN FINANCIAL MANAGEMENT

33 Treasury function

Advantages of a centralised treasury department

- Foreign currency management becomes easier, since the foreign currency expenditure in one company can be matched with receipts in the same currency in another group company.
- Higher interest rates may be attainable on investments because the department has larger amounts of cash available for investment.
- The treasury department may be a profit centre in its own right, resulting in an increased likelihood of a profit being made.
- Lower interest rates may be sought for borrowing, since borrowing can be arranged for the group as a whole.
- The level of cash held for precautionary purposes can be minimised since only one amount will be required for the whole group.
- Experts can be employed with specialised knowledge, more qualified to manage risk and make better investment decisions.

Note. Only two advantages were required.

34 Cleanly Co

Helping hand. It is unusual for a cash flow question to involve cleared funds but it is covered in your BPP text and the principle is much the same as a 'normal' cash flow forecast. Revise the layout from your text if you have problems.

Cleanly Co cash flow forecast for the period 2/1/X6 to 6/1/X6

	2/1 $	3/1 $	4/1 $	5/1 $	6/1 $
Receipts					
W Co	130,000				
X Co	180,000				
	310,000	0	0	0	0
Payments					
Supplier A Co	45,000				
Supplier B Co	75,000				
Supplier C Co	95,000				
Wages and salaries	56,000				12,000
Other payments	200	300		6,500	
	271,200	300	0	6,500	12,000
Excess of receipts over payments	38,800	(300)	0	(6,500)	(12,000)
Balance b/fwd	200,000	238,800	238,500	238,500	232,000
Balance c/fwd	238,800	238,500	238,500	232,000	220,000

Cleanly Co cleared funds forecast for the period 2/1/X6 to 6/1/X6

	2/1	3/1	4/1	5/1	6/1
Receipts					
W Co	130,000				
X Co				180,000	
	130,000	0	0	180,000	0
Payments					
Supplier A Co	45,000				

ANSWERS

	2/1	3/1	4/1	5/1	6/1
Supplier B Co			75,000		
Supplier C Co			95,000		
Wages and salaries	56,000				12,000
Other payments	200		300		
	101,200	0	170,300	0	12,000
Cleared excess receipts over					
Payments	28,800	0	(170,300)	180,000	(12,000)
Cleared balance b/fwd	200,000	228,800	228,800	58,500	238,500
Cleared balance c/fwd	228,800	228,800	58,500	238,500	226,500
Uncleared funds float					
Receipts	180,000	180,000	180,000		
Payments	(170,000)	(170,300)		(6,500)	(6,500)
	10,000	9,700	180,000	(6,500)	(6,500)
Total book balance c/fwd	238,800	238,500	238,500	232,000	220,000

35 Waslet Co

Roles of a treasury department

(i) Banking
(ii) Cash management
(iii) Funding management
(iv) Foreign currency management
(v) Corporate finance
(vi) Risk management
(vii) Insurance

Note. Only five were required.

36 KM Co

Definition

Treasurership has been defined as 'the function concerned with the provision and use of finance. It includes provision of capital, short-term borrowing, foreign currency management, banking, collections and money market investment'.

Responsibilities of treasury function

The main responsibilities of the treasury function include:

(i) **Liquidity management**

- Working capital and money transmission management
- Banking relationships and arrangements
- Money management

This involves making sure that the organisation has the **liquid funds** it needs and invests any surplus funds, even for very short terms. The treasurer should maintain a good relationship with one or more banks to ensure that negotiations are as swift as possible, and that rates are reasonable.

FFM FOUNDATIONS IN FINANCIAL MANAGEMENT

(ii) **Funding management**

- Funding policies and procedures
- Sources of funds
- Types of funds

Funding management is concerned with all forms of borrowing, and alternative sources of funds, such as leasing and factoring.

(iii) **Currency management**

- Exposure policies and procedures
- Exchange dealing, including futures and options
- International monetary economics and exchange regulations

(iv) **Corporate finance**

- Equity capital management
- Business acquisitions and disposals
- Project finance and joint ventures

(v) **Corporate taxation**

(vi) **Risk management and insurance**

(vii) **Pension fund investment management**

The financial control function is concerned with **determining whether** the **various activities** of the organisation are meeting their **financial objectives**. This function will therefore be interested in a **wide variety** of **stakeholder relationships**, for example, with customers, suppliers and employees. By contrast, the treasury function is mainly concerned with the relationship of the company to the **providers of finance**. In a geographically dispersed company such as KM Co, it is likely that financial control functions will exist at a variety of local levels, while the **treasury department** will be centralised at the head office.

37 Interest rates (1)

> **Helping hand.** (a) is a good test of your knowledge of financial instruments; you would not need to go into any more depth for the exam. (b) brings out the implications of interest rate changes not just for loan finance, but for share finance, investments and demand for products.

(a) **Nature of instruments**

(i) **Sterling certificates of deposits (CDs)**

These are securities issued by a bank, acknowledging that a certain amount of **sterling** has been deposited with it for a **certain period of time** (usually, a short term). The CD is issued to the depositor, and attracts interest. The depositor will be another bank or a large commercial organisation. CDs are traded on the money market and so if a CD holder wishes to obtain immediate cash, they can sell the CD on the market at any time. This second-hand market in CDs makes them attractive, flexible investments for organisations with excess cash.

(ii) **Local authority bonds**

These are **short-term securities** issued by local authorities to raise cash. They carry **interest**, and are **repayable on maturity**. They are traded second-hand in the money market, and so, like CDs, are a flexible investment for organisations with excess cash.

(iii) **Finance house deposits**

These are **non-negotiable time deposits** with finance houses (usually subsidiaries of banks). Finance houses specialise in lending money, and have to raise the funds (much of them from the money market) for re-lending.

(iv) **Treasury bills**

These are short-term debt instruments issued by the Bank of England, to raise **cash** for the **government's spending needs.** The bills are **sold by tender**, each week, at a price which is at a discount to their nominal value. They are **redeemable at their nominal value**, and so there is an implied rate of interest on the bill.

Treasury bills are **bought initially** by **money market organisations** with which the Bank of England has a special relationship, mainly the discount houses. The discount houses then carry out second-hand trading in Treasury bills (and other bills) on the discount market. Treasury bills are therefore negotiable.

(b) **Differences in interest rates between instruments**

Some money market instruments carry a higher interest rate than others. The main reasons for this are differences in their **relative marketability and risk**.

(i) **Treasury bills**

As **government debt**, these are therefore the most secure form of short-term debt available. **Interest rates** on Treasury bills should therefore be **lower** than on other money market instruments. Interest rates at which the Bank of England deals in bills in the money market usually set the level of interest rates for all other money market instruments.

(ii) **Finance house deposits**

As these are **not negotiable**, they are **less marketable** than the other money market instruments in the list. For this reason, **interest rates** on them are slightly **higher**. Similarly, CDs are more marketable than ordinary money market bank deposits, which are for a given (short) term; thus CD interest rates will be slightly lower than LIBID (the London inter-bank bid rate).

Differences in interest rates over time

Interest rates over time are affected by the **supply and demand of funds**, and by **expectations of future changes** in interest rates. Broadly speaking, interest rates on longer-term investments will be higher. In the data given, we see that interest rates are increased with the term of the deposit/bond/bill.

38 Interest rates (2)

Implications of a fall in interest rates for a typical company – note only 3 were required

(a) The **cost of floating rate borrowing will fall**, making it more attractive than fixed rate borrowing. For most companies with borrowings, interest charges will be reduced, resulting in higher profitability and earnings per share.

(b) The **value of the company's shares will rise,** both because of the higher level of company profitability and also because of the lower alternative returns that investors could earn from banks and deposits, if interest rates are expected to remain low in the longer term.

(c) The **higher share value results in a lower cost of share capital**, and hence a lower overall cost of capital for the company. Investment opportunities that were previously rejected may now become viable.

(d) As interest rates fall, consumers have **more disposable income.** This may increase demand for the company's products. Falling returns on deposits may, however, encourage many people to save more, rather than spend.

39 Financial intermediaries (1)

Financial intermediation is the process by which **providers** and **users** of finance are brought together. The organisations that promote this process are known as financial intermediaries.

Examples of financial intermediaries include:

- Clearing banks
- Building societies

- Investment banks
- Finance houses
- Insurance companies
- Pension funds
- Unit trust companies
- Investment trust companies
- Venture capital houses
- Bank of England

40 Money market instruments

Money market instruments

The main financial instruments in the money markets are as follows (choose any three).

(i) **Deposits**

These are simple deposits of money in bank accounts (both current and deposit accounts) and deposits with other financial intermediaries. In the inter-bank money market, for example, banks lend to other banks by placing money on deposit (overnight, at call, for seven days, or three months, etc).

(ii) **Bills**

Bills are short-term financial assets which can be converted into cash at very short notice, by selling them in the discount market.

(iii) **Commercial paper**

This represents short-term IOUs issued by large companies which can be held until maturity or sold to others.

(iv) **Certificates of deposit (CDs)**

These are available to customers who deposit £50,000 or more for fixed terms. Should the customer wish to obtain cash before the term is up, the CD can be sold on the CD market.

41 Banks and money markets

> **Helping hand.** Set out written answers carefully using short paragraphs and headers as this will help the marker identify and award you marks.

Central banks:

Act as banker to the central government

By providing a facility to collect taxes and distribute expenditure.

Are responsible for issuing currency

By printing and minting bank notes and coins.

Intervene in the foreign exchange markets

A currency's exchange rate by be affected a central banks that buy or sell it in large quantities.

Act as banker to the commercial banks

By providing the transactions system for transfers between banks.

Are the lender of last resort to the banking system

Central banks are the ultimate source of funds in the banking system.

Act as advisor to the government on monetary economic policy

Central banks are often involved in setting interest rates and providing economic advice to the government.

Act as agent for the government in carrying out its monetary policies

Central banks are often involved in carrying out government policy, for example to control inflation.

Participate in international economic institutions

Central banks often participate in international banking and economic institutions.

Note. Only three roles were required.

42 Banks and their customers (1)

Types of contractual relationship between bank and customer include the following (pick any three):

(i) **Debtor/creditor relationship**

When a customer deposits money with the bank it will enter their account and be available for withdrawal at any time. The bank is therefore the debtor (from the customer's point of view as the bank owes them money) and the customer is the creditor (from the bank's point of view as the customer is owed the money deposited).

The bank undertakes to receive money from the customer (effectively borrowing money from the customer) which it undertakes to repay on demand. In addition the bank will not cease to do business with the customer except on reasonable notice. The customer undertakes to exercise reasonable care so as not to mislead the bank or to facilitate forgery.

(ii) **Principal/agent relationship**

The bank may act as an agent for its customers or may employ other agents (such as stockbrokers, solicitors or other types of specialist) who are qualified to deal with certain transactions. An agent acts for another person (the principal), usually for the purpose of making a contract between the principal and a third party.

For example, where a bank arranges insurance such as buildings insurance for a customer, the bank is acting as an insurance broker and therefore the agent of the customer in question.

(iii) **Bailor/bailee relationship**

Banks may offer a safe deposit service to its customers – the bailor is the party which delivers personal property to the other party (the bailee). The bank has an obligation to take reasonable care to safeguard the property against damage or loss and also to redeliver the property only to the customer or a person authorised by the customer.

(iv) **Fiduciary relationship**

If a party in a relationship based on trust is in an influential position then that person could exert undue influence over the other party to enter into a contract. For example a bank often offers advice on different types of accounts, insurance policies and mortgages. The law expects banks to act in good faith when they are advising customers.

(v) **Mortgagor/mortgagee relationship**

This occurs when a customer (the mortgagor) is asked by the bank (the mortgagee) to secure a loan by a charge or mortgage over such assets as property. If the customer does not repay the loan, the bank has the right to sell the asset on which the mortgage is secured to pay off or reduce the outstanding loan.

43 Banks and their customers (2)

Any three from the following.

(i) **Confidentiality**

Banks have a duty to keep customers' information confidential except in the following circumstances.

- Where the bank is required by law to disclose
- Where there is a public duty to disclose the information
- Where the interests of the bank require disclosure
- Where the customer has given express or implied consent

(ii) **Comply with customers' instructions**

Banks must comply with instructions given by the customer to pay funds through direct debit or standing order (provided that the customer has sufficient funds in the relevant account).

(iii) **Provide a bank statement**

Banks have a duty to provide customers, within a reasonable time, with statements showing transactions on their accounts. They are also required to provide the customer with details of the balance on the account on request.

(iv) **Honour customers' cheques**

If the following conditions are met, the bank has a duty to honour (pay) a customer's cheques:

- Cheques are correctly made out and properly drawn.
- There are sufficient funds in the customer's account or payment will not lead to the account exceeding an agreed overdraft limit.
- There is no legal reason why the cheques should not be paid.

(v) **Receipt of customer's funds**

Banks are legally required to credit cash or cheques paid into a customer's account.

(vi) **Repayment on demand**

The bank must repay a customer's funds on demand provided there is a written request from the customer, the transaction takes place during the bank's opening hours and either at the customer's home branch or an agreed branch or bank.

(vii) **Closure of accounts**

Banks must give reasonable notice to customers if they intend to close their accounts, to allow the customers to make other financial arrangements.

(viii) **Advice of forgery**

Banks must advise customers if cheques bearing a forgery of the customer's signature are being drawn on their accounts.

(ix) **Care and skill**

Banks are required to use care and skill in their actions, not just for professional reasons but also to ensure that they receive certain legal protections.

44 Treasury management

Helping hand. This is a straightforward descriptive question. You are required to give two advantages which means there are 2.5 marks for each one you describe. You will therefore have to elaborate slightly on each advantage to give yourself the best chance of gaining all the marks available.

ANSWERS

Advantages of a centralised treasury department (choose any two):

(a) **Centralised liquidity management**

    (i) Avoids having a mix of cash surpluses and overdrafts in different localised bank accounts
    (ii) Facilitates bulk cash flows, so that lower bank charges can be negotiated

(b) Larger volumes of cash are available to invest, giving better **short-term investment opportunities**.

(c) Any borrowing can be arranged in bulk, at lower interest rates than for smaller borrowings, and perhaps on the eurocurrency markets.

(d) **Foreign exchange risk management** is likely to be improved in a group of companies. A central treasury department can match foreign currency income earned by one subsidiary with expenditure in the same currency by another subsidiary.

(e) A specialist treasury department can employ **experts** with knowledge of dealing in forward contracts, futures, options, eurocurrency markets, swaps and so on. Localised departments could not have such expertise.

(f) The centralised pool of **funds required for precautionary purposes** will be smaller than the sum of separate precautionary balances required if the department was decentralised.

(g) Having a separate **profit centre**, focuses attention on the contribution to group profit performance that can be achieved by good cash, funding, investment and foreign currency management.

45 Curtain Co

Helping hand. Don't be intimidated by the length of the scenario in this question. Look at the requirements to see what you have been asked to do and pick out the information you require. You are asked for the total finance costs (cheques and interest). However if you read the scenario you will find that the new system does not involve cheques so state this in your answer. That will indicate to the examining team that you are aware that there are no costs for cheques.

New system finance costs

As payments will be made by standing order or direct debit there will be no costs incurred from banking cheques. The only cost will be the interest.

	$
Interest costs $600,000 × (30 days/365 days) × 8%	3,945

46 Trade credit

Helping hand. To answer this, you may choose to give a brief definition of trade credit, but remember that the question asks about the merits and limitations of trade credit. You may recognise that the main benefit is that it has no cost: it can also be obtained fairly easily from many suppliers, provided that the suppliers are paid within the agreed credit period. The main limitations are that there is a limit to the amount of trade credit obtainable to finance business operations, and it is short term in nature.

A small business needs finance, and as it grows it needs additional finance for its operations. A large proportion of the finance for a small business is in the form of owner's capital. In addition, a small business relies on short-term finance, and in particular credit from its suppliers.

A major advantage of trade credit is that it is often **readily available**. Suppliers are often prepared to allow a business customer a period of credit before payment. Without trade credit, a small business would have to be much smaller, or would have to obtain additional capital. This is because trade credit, as a short-term liability, reduces the amount of the working capital of a business.

Another important advantage of trade credit is that it **does not have a cost**. Suppliers do not charge interest on unpaid invoices. Whereas a business may be expected to provide a return on equity capital to the owner or owners, and bank overdrafts will incur fees and interest, suppliers do not demand any payment in excess of the invoiced amount.

Trade finance has limitations as a source of finance. There is a **limit to the amount of credit** that suppliers are prepared to give. If a business is too slow with payment of invoices, and fails to pay invoices on time, there is a risk that suppliers will refuse further credit. Suppliers may even ask for payment in advance.

Creditors must also be managed efficiently, so that **invoices are paid at the correct time**. This may increase the administrative work for a business. Unlike long-term finance, short-term trade finance must continually be renewed. A business needs to continue obtaining credit from suppliers for new purchases.

47 Bills and securities

Marking scheme

	Marks
Instrument max 3 each. Award 1 mark per point	5
Total marks	**5**

Government securities

Government securities are issued by the government to finance government spending. In the UK, they are known as gilts (short for gilt edged securities). They have a nominal value of £100 and the coupon rate of interest is applied to this figure to calculate interest payments. Different types of gilts are issued covering periods up to 15 years or longer. Some gilts are 'undated' and offer no guaranteed repayment date. They are regarded as a very safe investment, being backed by the government.

Bill of exchange

A bill of exchange is an unconditional order in writing from one party to another requiring the party to whom it is addressed to pay a specified sum of money on demand or at some future date. The party to whom it is addressed recognises the obligation to pay by 'accepting' it. The holder of the bill can hold it to maturity and present it to the specified bank, or the bill can be sold for an amount below its payment value (at a discount). The level of discount depends upon the time to maturity and the credit standing of the party accepting the bill. Bills of exchange are commonly used to finance domestic and international trade.

48 Surplus funds

> **Helping hand.** This is a factual question, and tests your ability to explain the various terms in the question. If you cannot provide a definition or explanation, you need to go back to your study material and learn them.

(a) When funds are invested, the investor has expectations of the size of the return that will be obtained from the investment. However, there is often some risk that returns will be less than expected (and some

ANSWERS

possibility of high-than-expected returns). This is investment risk. Investment risk can be measured by the variability (or 'volatility') with different types of investment.

With low-risk investments, the variability in returns is low and actual returns will be equal to or close to the expected returns. Low-risk investments include savings deposits with a bank or investing in government securities. With high-risk investments, actual returns may differ from expected returns by a substantial amount but expected returns should be higher than with lower-risk investments. For investors, there is a choice between greater investment risk in the hope of earning a bigger financial return and lower investment risk but for lower expected returns. This is the risk-return trade-off.

(b) Default risk is the risk that someone will fail to pay money that is owed under some form of contractual agreement. Failure to pay may be caused by insolvency of the person or organisation owing the money. It is sometimes called credit risk. For an investor, default risk is the risk that expected returns on investments representing debt, such as a savings deposit with a bank or bonds or other debt securities, will not be paid. A bank may become insolvent and unable to pay interest on the debt and to redeem the debt at maturity. Similarly, a company may become insolvent and unable to pay the obligations on bonds that it has issued.

(c) The risk-return trade-off is particularly important when considering the investment of surplus cash, because any high-risk decision that does not result in a favourable outcome could threaten the solvency of the entire business. Therefore, care must be taken to ensure that sufficient cash contingency remains available to the business after approved investments had been financed, to enable ongoing cash commitments and any unforeseen events to be adequately covered.

Businesses generally do not fail because they can't make a profit in a given period, but because they run out of cash. Therefore, the risks associated with cash management have a more significant impact on the business than other aspects of business risk that can be more easily mitigated. This should be fully considered when determining an acceptable risk-return trade-off for the business and encourage a more prudent approach.

49 Appropriate liquidity

Helping hand. You may have come across differences in the working capital of different types of company in your studies. If not, this question may need some careful thought.

The key to an answer is to consider the elements of the working capital cycle (inventory turnover period, average credit period allowed to customer sand average credit period from suppliers). You can also comment on the current ratio and quick ratio in your answer.

One feature of supermarkets is that many of the goods that they sell have a short 'shelf life' and are sold fairly quickly after they have been received into store. A second feature of supermarkets is that most goods are paid for in cash or by credit card, so that the supermarket company receives cash from its sales very quickly – on or very soon after the time of sale. It would be relatively rare for a supermarket to have a trade receivable.

On the other hand, supermarkets expect to obtain normal credit terms from its suppliers, which may typically be up to 30 or even 60 days' credit from the time of delivery and invoicing.

As a consequence, the cash cycle or working capital cycle of a supermarket business is very short. It could even be negative, which means that the company receives payments for goods that it sells before it pays its suppliers for the goods.

The liquidity of a supermarket company can be monitored by measuring the average length of the working capital cycle, or by measuring the current ratio and quick ratio. All these will be low values, but changes in liquidity can be monitored by changes in these measures.

50 MCQ Answer Bank 7

50.1 Liquidity preference is the desire to hold onto wealth as cash rather than to invest it.

50.2 $1 + \text{Real rate of interest} = \dfrac{1 + \text{nominal rate}}{1 + \text{inflation rate}}$

$$1.06 = \dfrac{1 + \text{nominal rate}}{1.04}$$

$1 + \text{nominal rate} = 1.06 \times 1.04$
$\phantom{1 + \text{nominal rate}} = 1.1024$

Nominal rate = 10%

50.3 Changing taxation is a fiscal policy.

50.4 Money supply is increased by the government spending money in the economy.

Reducing the PSBR (public sector borrowing requirement) means the government is borrowing less money to spend in the economy, therefore reducing the money it feeds into the money supply.

Increasing the PSDR (public sector debt repayment) means the government is using more of the money it collects to repay its debts rather than to spend in the economy, therefore reducing the money it feeds into the money supply.

50.5 If an economy has high inflation, the cost of producing goods will rise and therefore its exports become relatively more expensive than its trading partners. It also means that its trading partners can produce their exports relatively cheaply and therefore the cost of the economy's imports will be relatively cheaper.

50.6

> **ACCA examining team's comments**
>
> In a question such as this, if candidates cannot see the answer straight away, they may find it easier to create a small scenario and substitute figures in.
>
> Let us say that Company Y is selling widgets to Company Z. To set the price for the sale, Company Y takes the actual cost of the widget and adds on 5% (we are told in the scenario that the price is set by actual cost plus a fixed percentage mark up). What happens if the cost to Company Y is $4, $5 or $6?
>
> | Cost of widget to Company Y | $4.00 | $5.00 | $6.00 |
> |---|---|---|---|
> | 5% mark up | $0.20 | $0.25 | $0.30 |
> | Sales price to Company Z | $4.20 | $5.25 | $6.30 |
>
> We can now see from the figures that whatever the cost of the widget to Company A, they will always recover the cost they have paid and receive the required profit of 5%. Company A therefore does not suffer the inflation risk, but it is Company B (the customer) who suffers the risk, and the answer is option A.
>
> The technique of creating a small scenario and substituting figures in can be useful in other Section A questions, for example if candidates are asked what the effect on say the quick ratio is of selling inventory, where it can clarify thinking.

50.7 $\text{Real rate of interest} = \dfrac{1 + \text{nominal rate}}{1 + \text{inflation rate}} - 1$

$\phantom{\text{Real rate of interest}} = \dfrac{1.07}{1.03} - 1$

$\phantom{\text{Real rate of interest}} = 0.039$ rounded up to 4%

ANSWERS

50.8 Whilst central banks are involved in setting interest rates, they do so in accordance with government monetary policy, to control inflation rates and with concern for the overall demand for borrowing in the economy. They do not seek to make a return for themselves.

50.9 All of the policies mentioned will affect the volume of bank lending.

50.10 False. Loan stock is an example of long-term finance.

51 MCQ Answer Bank 8

51.1 Banks are more likely to approve an overdraft if it is to cover a temporary cash shortfall and would rather offer long-term loans for more permanent or long-term investments.

51.2 Under a bullet repayment scheme the borrower repays the full amount of the loan at the end of the loan period.

51.3 They are all charges that may have to be paid in connection with a loan.

51.4 A rights issue is an offer to existing shareholders to purchase a company's shares at a reduced rate. The last option describes a scrip dividend. The other options are nonsense.

51.5 As with ordinary share dividends, preference share dividends cannot be paid if the company does not have sufficient distributable profit.

51.6 This is the description of a placing.

51.7 Under the Enterprise Finance Guarantee Scheme, the UK government provides guarantees for qualifying loans.

51.8 The main drawback of business angel finance is that there is no ready market for it. Business angels often invest in small and medium-sized enterprises and leave the day-to-day running of the business in the hands of the existing owners. The repayment schedule is unlikely to be demanding as that may affect the success of the enterprise.

51.9 Floating the company and issuing its shares onto a recognised stock exchange is not appropriate for a new business.

51.10 They are all reasons why small and medium-sized enterprises find it difficult to obtain finance.

52 MCQ Answer Bank 9

52.1 The first two options are examples of positive covenants, the third option is an example of a quantitative covenant.

52.2 Short-term loans are subject to a loan agreement giving the bank security and a definite repayment schedule. This lowers the risk from their perspective, hence the interest rate charged is lower.

52.3 Legal ownership of an asset which is the subject of a hire purchase arrangement passes once the final repayment instalment has been paid.

52.4 Overdrafts should not be regarded as a long-term source of finance.

52.5 Eurobonds are bonds which are sold on an international basis, not just within the European Union.

52.6 Private companies may not offer their shares to the general public and dividends must be paid out of post-tax profits.

52.7 A scrip dividend is a dividend which is paid by the issue of new shares.

52.8 Zero coupon bonds are issued at a discount to their redemption value and do not pay any interest.

52.9 The Enterprise Investment Scheme gives a qualifying investor tax relief on their investment.

52.10 Owner finance is the usual initial source of finance. Lenders and investors are unlikely to provide finance to a business unless the owner has a personal stake in it.

53 Question with help: Money supply

The **money supply** in an economy is the total stock of money in that economy.

There are different ways of defining the total stock of money in an economy. **Money** may be defined 'narrowly', meaning that financial assets have to be very liquid to be counted in the definition.

Broad money definitions of the money supply embrace forms of money held for **transaction purposes** and also money held as a form of **saving**. Such definitions provide an indicator of the private sector's holdings of relatively liquid assets, ie those which can be converted with relative ease and without capital loss into spending on goods and services.

The **commercial banks** are **agents** in the **creation of money** because money is created through the expansion of bank deposits. As a result, measures to limit or to reduce the growth of the money supply need to take account of the importance of the liquidity of the banks, which provides the means by which money is created.

In recent years, the UK government has rejected reliance upon most methods of seeking to control the supply of money and has instead sought to influence its demand through the policy instrument of the interest rate. Since 1997, **interest rate decisions** have been made by the Bank of England, in line with the government's inflation target.

54 Question with help: Commercial banks

A **commercial bank** operates with a widely varying pattern of **interest rates** for the following reasons (only three were required).

(i) Banks will lend money at a lower rate of interest to lower **risk** customers. This is apparent in short-term lending, where very low interest rates are charged on lending in the interbank market to leading banks, whereas higher interest rates are charged on similar short-term lending to even large and well-established companies. Higher interest rates will also be charged on personal loans to customers in a higher risk category.

(ii) Interest rates vary with the **duration of a loan or deposit**. Saving schemes requiring some notice of withdrawal will attract a higher yield than an ordinary deposit account. With an ordinary current account, where customers can withdraw funds on demand, no interest at all is paid.

(iii) Banks' interest rates vary with the **size of loans and deposits**. Generally, a lower interest rate will be charged for larger 'wholesale' loans and a higher interest rate offered for larger 'wholesale' deposits.

(iv) The need to make a **profit** on re-lending is clearly evident in the banks' rate of interest. For example, retail loans to customers will be at an interest rate higher than the bank's base rate, whereas low or nil interest is paid on current accounts, and the rate paid on deposit accounts is less than the bank's base rate.

(v) A substantial proportion of a bank's business is conducted in **foreign currencies**. The interest rate in which a bank deals, in the eurocurrency markets, will vary according to the currency, and the general level of interest rates in that country.

… ANSWERS

55 Trob Co

> **Helping hand.** Make sure your spreadsheets are clear for the marker to follow, and that key numbers are clearly labelled.

Marking scheme

	Marks
1 mark per ratio	5
Total marks	**5**

Spreadsheet

	A	B	C	D	E	F	G	H	I
1									
2			$		Operating margin				
3		Revenue	500,000			200,000	x 100	=	**40.0%**
4		Gross profit	275,000			500,000			
5		Operating Profit	200,000		Return on capital employed				
6		Non-current assets	800,000			200,000	x 100	=	**23.3%**
7		Inventory	50,000			857,000			
8		Receivables	100,000		Net asset turnover				
9		Cash at bank	7,000			500,000		=	**0.58**
10		Non-current liabilities	860,000			857,000			
11		Payables	100,000		Acid test				
12						107,000		=	**1.07**
13						100,000			
14					Payable days				
15						100,000	x 365	=	**162 days**
16						225,000			
17									

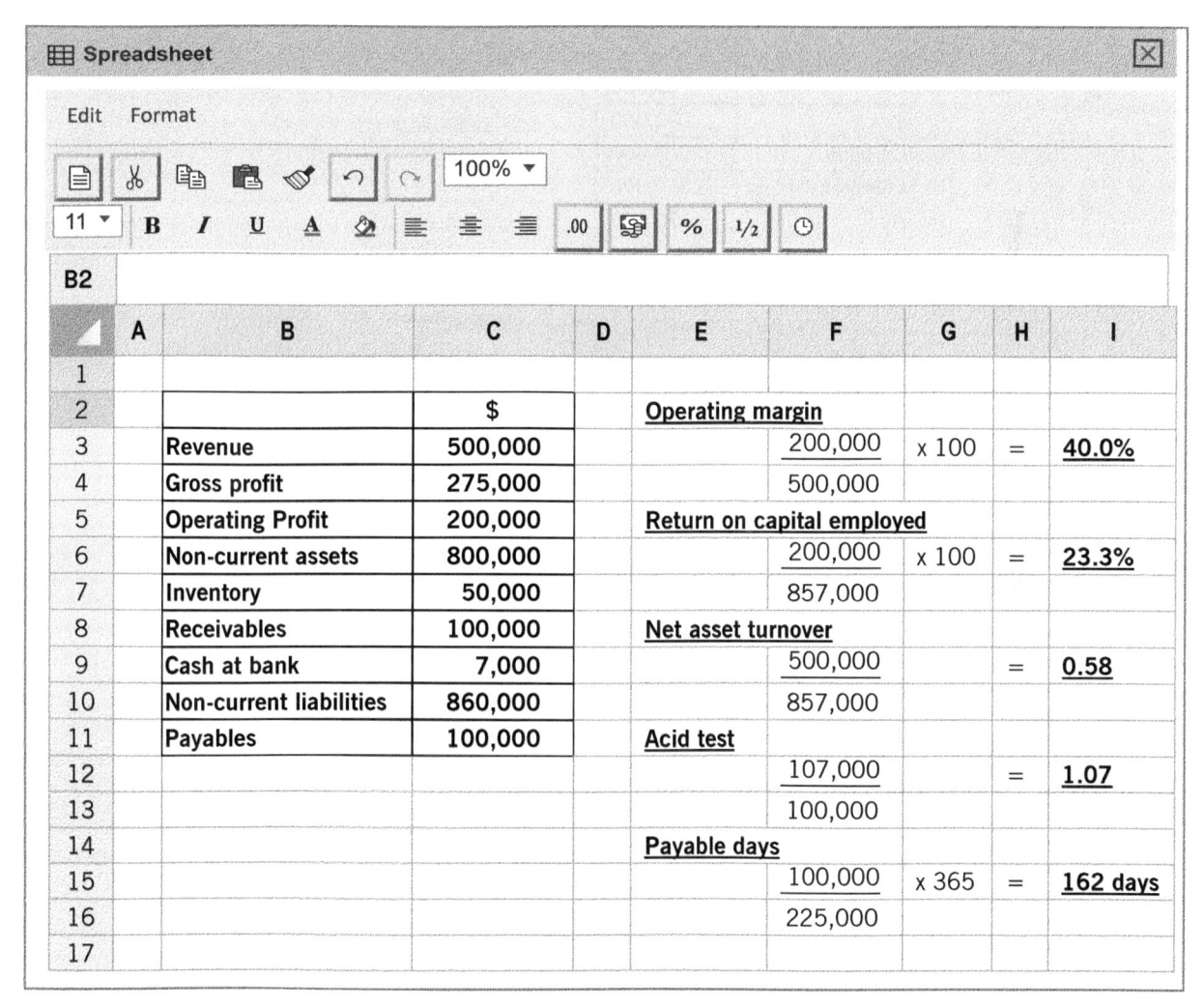

Tutorial note. The following table shows the formulae that have been used to generate these values and is shown here as a student aid, it would not be produced as a part of your answer.

Spreadsheet

	A	B	C	D	E	F	G	H	I
1									
2			$		<u>Operating margin</u>				
3		Revenue	500,000			=C5	x 100	=	=F13/F4
4		Gross profit	275,000			=C3			
5		Operating Profit	200,000		<u>Return on capital employed</u>				
6		Non-current assets	800,000			=C5	x 100	=	=F6/F7
7		Inventory	50,000			=C6+C7+C8+C9-C11			
8		Receivables	100,000		<u>Net asset turnover</u>				
9		Cash at bank	7,000			=C6		=	=F9/10
10		Non-current liabilities	860,000			=F7			
11		Payables	100,000		<u>Acid test</u>				
12						=C8+C9		=	F12/F13
13						=C11			
14					<u>Payable days</u>				
15						=C11	x 365	=	=F15/F16*365
16						=C3-C4			
17									

56 Retailer Co

Helping hand. 11 out of 20 marks are available for calculations, indicating that you only have time to make a brief comment on each ratio. However you should say more than just the ratio has risen or fallen; you can indicate why the movement has taken place or what the movement may demonstrate about Retailer's performance and position.

In the written parts, as with other questions, we have given more examples than you were required to provide.

			Retailer		Industry	
		20X2		20X1	20X2	20X1

(1) **Return on capital employed**

$$\frac{\text{Profit before interest and tax}}{\text{Shareholders' funds + medium and long-term liabilities}}$$

$\frac{275}{730+300} = 27\%$ $\frac{300}{550+400} = 32\%$ 29%   30%

(2) **Return on shareholders' funds**

$$\frac{\text{Profit after tax}}{\text{Shareholders' funds}}$$

$\frac{180}{730} = 25\%$ $\frac{188}{550} = 34\%$ 28%   28%

ically *ANSWERS*

		Retailer 20X2	Retailer 20X1	Industry 20X2	Industry 20X1
(3)	**Operating profit margin** $\dfrac{\text{Profit before interest and tax}}{\text{Sales revenue}}$	$\dfrac{275}{2{,}500} = 11\%$	$\dfrac{300}{3{,}000} = 10\%$	10%	10%
(4)	**Asset turnover ratio** $\dfrac{\text{Sales}}{\text{Shareholders' funds + Medium and long-term liabilities}}$	$\dfrac{2{,}500}{1{,}030} = 2.4$	$\dfrac{3{,}000}{950} = 3.2$	2.8	2.8
(5)	**Current ratio** $\dfrac{\text{Current assets}}{\text{Current liabilities}}$	$\dfrac{390}{220} = 1.77{:}1$	$\dfrac{450}{362} = 1.24{:}1$	1:1	1:1
(6)	**Quick ratio** $\dfrac{\text{Current assets excluding inventory}}{\text{Current liabilities}}$	$\dfrac{140}{220} = 0.64{:}1$	$\dfrac{150}{362} = 0.41{:}1$	0.7:1	0.7:1
(7)	**Receivables days** $\dfrac{\text{Receivables}}{\text{Trade sales}} \times 365$	$\dfrac{100}{2{,}500} \times 365 = 15 \text{ days}$	$\dfrac{150}{3{,}000} \times 365 = 18 \text{ days}$	12 days	12 days
(8)	**Gearing ratio** $\dfrac{\text{Medium and long-term debt}}{\text{Equity}}$	$\dfrac{300}{730} = 41\%$	$\dfrac{400}{550} = 73\%$	60%	50%
(9)	**Interest cover** $\dfrac{\text{Profit before interest (finance cost) and tax}}{\text{Interest (finance cost)}}$	$\dfrac{275}{35} = 7.9 \text{ times}$	$\dfrac{300}{50} = 6 \text{ times}$	4 times	5 times

(1) **Return on capital employed**

The withdrawal policy appears to have **lowered the return**, and it is now below the **industry average**.

(2) **Return on shareholders' funds**

Again the withdrawal policy has **lowered the return on funds** and the shareholders may be disappointed as the return is now **below** the industry average. A return based on market values may provide better information than a return based on book values.

(3) **Operating profit margin**

The withdrawal appears to have **improved the margin** so that it now exceeds industry levels.

(4) **Asset turnover ratio**

The fall in the ratio indicates that Retailer is **generating less** sales from assets owned and it is now less effective at using its assets than the rest of the industry.

(5) **Current ratio**

The policy of withdrawal from certain sectors has **improved Retailer's current ratio** so that it now is in excess of the industry average and is now above 1:1, which is sometimes considered a safe level.

(6) **Quick ratio**

Again **withdrawal has increased this ratio**, although it is still low compared with industry levels, and may indicate possible liquidity problems.

(7) **Receivables days**

Although this ratio **exceeds industry levels**, it has **fallen** since the strategic withdrawal began, and does not appear high. However it is likely that a significant proportion of the company's retail sales are for cash, and it would be more useful to calculate receivables days using credit sales rather than total sales.

(8) **Gearing ratio**

The redemption of the secured debenture has **reduced gearing** to a point significantly below the industry average, indicating Retailer is not at great financial risk.

(9) **Interest cover**

Again the redemption of the debenture has **increased interest cover** significantly, and Retailer has no problems in meeting its interest burden. Perhaps therefore Retailer could make more use of debt finance which is low cost and tax deductible.

57 Clean Lens Co

Mix of debt and equity finance

The factors that need to be taken into account by Clean Lens are as follows (only three were required).

(i) **Control of the business**

Unlike the issue of shares to new shareholders, there is **no dilution of ownership** (and hence voting power) if debt is issued. This will be an important consideration for the current owners if they wish to retain their voting control.

(ii) **Cost and availability**

Debt has a lower direct cost than equity finance, for two reasons: it is **less risky** to the investor, and **interest** (unlike dividends) is a tax allowable expense. **Equity funding** (assuming that it is available for Clean Lens as a private limited company) is **more expensive**, as the investor is subject to both the risk of business failure, and finance risk. As a result, they will demand a **higher return**.

(iii) **Current level/maturity of borrowings**

Unlike equity, **debt normally has to be repaid** at the end of its term. This may cause problems, especially if lenders are unwilling to renew the facility. It is also important not to be overcommitted to future debt repayments, so the current level of borrowing must be taken into account.

(iv) **Effect on gearing**

When comparing the amount of debt to the amount of equity (that is, the level of gearing), finance providers will regard a company that is **highly geared** as a **higher risk investment**. They will expect a **higher return** to compensate them for that increased level of risk. Assets of the company (or even personal assets of the owners) may need to be pledged as further security, or other restrictive loan covenants introduced.

(v) **Taxation**

As already mentioned, the **interest payable** on debt (unlike dividends) is a **tax allowable expense**. This factor contributes towards debt being cheaper.

58 Caterer Co

Helping hand. Your answer to (a) should not just have considered operating profits. Extra funding does mean extra interest cost.

In (b) you need more specific information about the present value of the project, but also need to consider the wider issues of variability of returns and non-financial factors.

Your answer to (c) should have identified that much depends on the attitudes of borrowers and lenders. Do the directors want to bear a heavy interest burden, and risk the consequences of not being able to pay what they owe. What can the company offer to lenders (security)? What is the attitude of lenders to the possibility of default?

ANSWERS

(a) PROJECTED STATEMENT OF PROFIT OR LOSS FOR THE YEAR ENDED 31 MAY 20X2

	Note	$m
Revenue (2.4m meals at $2)		4.80
Less variable costs	1	(1.92)
		2.88
Less fixed costs	2	(1.20)
Profit before finance cost and tax		1.68
Less finance cost	3	(0.40)
Profit before tax		1.28
Less income tax expense at 25%		(0.32)
Profit after tax		0.96

Notes

1. Variable costs are currently 50% sales = $1 per meal. This will be reduced by 20% to $0.80 per meal. Total cost will therefore be 2.4m × $0.80 = $1.92m.
2. Fixed costs will increase by $200,000 to $1.2m.
3. Interest on existing debenture = $2m × 10% = $0.2m.

    Interest on new debenture = $2m × 10% = $0.2m.

(b) **Gearing ratio**

	20X1		20X2
Total debt	$2m	$2m + $2m =	$4m
Total equity	$5m	$5m + $0.96m =	$5.96m
Gearing	40%		67%

The gearing ratio has risen sharply over the year, based on book values. This will **restrict** the company's **ability** to **borrow further** in the future and may impact on the attractiveness of the shares. However, the calculations have been based on book values. Although we do not know the current share price, it is probable that the effect will be less marked if market values are used.

Interest cover

	20X1	20X2
Profit before finance cost and tax	$1.0m	$1.68m
Interest payable	$0.2m	$0.40
Interest cover	5 times	4.2 times

Although there has been a reduction in the level of interest cover, it has not fallen to what would normally be regarded as a **critical level**. An interest cover in excess of three times is generally regarded as acceptable.

(c) Practical factors that influence the level of gearing that can be achieved include (choose any two):

(i) **Stability of earnings**. If earnings are stable and consistent the company will be able to sustain a higher level of gearing since there will be less risk of its being able to service the debt.

(ii) **Security**. Companies with a good quality asset base will be able to raise more finance and sustain a higher level of gearing than will those with poorer quality assets.

(iii) **The nature of the industry**. The range of acceptable gearing tends to vary from industry to industry. Similarly, this will be affected by the growth prospects for the industry, companies in sectors with better prospects being able to achieve higher gearing in anticipation of future earnings growth.

(iv) **Attitude to risk**. The attitude of the directors and shareholders to risk will be significant in determining what is an acceptable level of gearing for the company to achieve.

(v) **Reputation of the company**. The trading history and reputation of the company will influence the ease with which it will be able to gain credit, and therefore the level of gearing that it will be able to achieve.

(vi) **Constitution of the company**. This may restrict the amount that the company is permitted to borrow, and therefore its maximum gearing level.

(vii) **Existing loan covenants**. There may be covenants on existing loans that restrict the company's ability to borrow further.

Only four factors were required.

59 Zimmer Co

(a) **Advantages:**

Control

Taking on equity finance means the existing shareholders (including the original owners) would **lose some control** over the business. Debt finance does not affect control of the organisation.

Issue costs

Issue costs of debt are **lower** than equity as less work is involved and no prospectus is needed.

Cost of debt

Interest rates paid are usually **cheaper** than dividends as there is less risk to the investor, and the business can claim tax relief on its interest payments.

Fewer rules

Debt issues are **not subject to the same lengthy legal and stock exchange rules** as equity issues. It should therefore be quicker and easier to raise the finance.

Disadvantages:

Debt payments

Unlike equity dividends that do not have to be paid if the business cannot afford to, and **interest debt repayments must continue** to be made despite any difficulties. Failure to do so could result in the business failing.

Covenants

Lenders may seek to **restrict the activities** of a business to which it has lent. For example, it may prevent it taking on future debt until its loan is repaid. This may cause the business future problems as it may not be able to raise future funds to take advantage of opportunities that it encounters.

Interest rates

If the interest rate is not fixed, the business would be exposed to the risk of higher debt repayments if interest rates rise.

Future loans

Taking on debt **increases a business gearing ratio**, potentially making it harder to obtain future finance as high gearing increases the risk to lenders.

(b) **Payment**

Unlike loan capital, preference share dividends **do not have to be paid** if the business cannot afford to do so. However, most preference shares require dividends to be paid on a **cumulative basis** – when the directors recommend a dividend the business will have to pay the dividends that it did not pay when times were hard.

Control

Preference shares **do not dilute the control** of existing shareholders as they do not normally carry voting rights.

Security

Preference shares are **not secured over a company's assets**, nor do they allow covenants that restrict its activities.

Gearing

Irredeemable preference shares are **not classed as debt** and do not increase a company's gearing ratio. However, redeemable preference shares are classed as debt and therefore do increase gearing.

ANSWERS

60 Gym Jam Co

(a) Advantages of a lease to Gym Jam Co:

(i) The lease will be at a fixed rate of interest therefore reducing the interest rate risk currently faced by Gym Jam. At present Gym Jam has a variable rate loan and interest rates have been increasing.

(ii) Given that Gym Jam has struggled to finance its treadmill purchases it might be able to access lease finance easier and at a lower rate than a bank loan. The lessor under a leasing agreement retains legal title of the asset which reduces their risk associated with the financing arrangement. This can often result in the lessor charging a lower rate of interest.

(b)

Weakness	Rectification
1 Customers are invoiced quarterly and invoices are raised manually.	Introduce a computerised, more efficient invoicing system so that customers can be invoiced monthly.
2 Customers pay by cheque sent in the post, which is a slow method of receiving payment.	Encourage customers to pay by standing order, direct debit or electronic funds transfer.
3 Accounts receivable ledger staff are not coping with the increased workload.	Employ and train more accounts receivable ledger staff.
4 Customers are taking longer to pay, perhaps because there are no penalties for doing so.	Stricter credit control procedures are needed, perhaps including the imposition of interest penalties on late payments.

(c) The interest charges on Gym Jam Co's loan kept increasing because the interest on the loan was **variable** and linked to the **bank's base rate**. This base rate will vary according to conditions in the money markets and presumably, during this time has increased.

61 Sources of finance

> **Helping hand.** If you ever forget the sources of finance in an exam, think back to a statement of financial position. Most credit entries are potential sources of finance (overdrafts, payables, bank loans and share capital). The statement of financial position divides the sources between short-term (current liabilities), medium and long-term (other liabilities and capital).
>
> When searching for limitations in part (b), think of situations that may cause ratios to be inaccurate, misleading or inappropriate.

(a) **Sources of finance for small and medium sized businesses (SMEs)**

Any four from the following.

Short-term sources

(i) An **overdraft** is a negative bank balance.

The borrower pays interest each month to the bank, the amount of which depends on how much and how long the borrower was overdrawn. The advantage of this source is that it is flexible and interest is paid only when the facility is used.

The interest rates charged tend to be expensive and this makes it unsuitable for financing long-term investments as overdrafts in theory are repayable on demand. This said, they are often used as a permanent source of finance.

(ii) **Trade payables**

Trade credit is used to finance the purchase of materials in the very short term. It is a cheap source of finance as a company's suppliers often give a number of days interest free credit.

However, it does come at a price. Trade discounts may not be given to customers on credit and failure to pay on time may strain supplier/customer relations.

Long-term sources

(i) **Bank loans**

The company borrows a fixed sum from the bank and agrees to repay it in full over a fixed period. The bank charges the company a rate of interest which may be given for the term of the loan or it may be varied from time to time. Normally the rate will be less than the overdraft rate and is more suitable for financing long-term investments as the cost is spread over a longer period.

Banks may suggest converting overdrafts into loans as it forces borrowers to start repaying the debt.

(ii) **Equity**

When a company is first formed it will have very few assets so finance is usually found by the owner and injected into the business in return for shares in the company.

Established companies can seek additional finance by selling more shares either privately (not through stock exchange), or publicly (through a stock exchange).

This disadvantages of this source is that investors have an input in the running of the company (through votes) so the original owner will lose some control.

(iii) **Business angels**

Business angels are individuals or groups with large personal wealth who are often known by an owner of a company (for example a wealthy friend or business contact).

The owner and business angel will make an informal arrangement between themselves in which the business angel supplies funds to the business.

The advantage of this source of finance is that the company is free from onerous legal obligations, but as there is no formal business angel market, access is limited to the contacts a business has.

(iv) **Venture capitalists**

Venture capitalists seek new businesses to invest in. The companies that attract them are likely to have high growth potential (to earn them profits), and be ready to list on the stock market in a relatively short time (to provide them an exit route).

Due to this, few SMEs will attract venture capitalists and SME owners may not welcome the level of involvement a venture capitalist would want in running their company.

(b) **Limitations of ratio analysis**

Any two from the following.

(i) **On their own they do not represent clear picture of the company's performance**

Ratios must be compared over time, to budgets, forecasts, prior year results, or against similar companies to be meaningful.

(ii) **There are many different methods of calculating certain ratios**

Care must be taken when comparing the same ratio between companies as the use of different formulas will cause misleading results.

(iii) **Ratios based on financial statements may not be directly comparable**

Different companies use different accounting policies (for example the depreciation method used) in their financial statements. Therefore misleading results may occur when comparing ratios if the accounts have not been prepared in exactly the same way.

(iv) **Ratios do not take inflation into account**

When analysing one company's performance over time, adjustments should be made to reflect how prices have changed over the period.

(v) **Ratio analysis relies on information being available**

Changes to accounting systems or other sources of information may mean directly comparable information is not available. In this case meaningful ratio analysis may not be able to be done.

(vi) **Ratios are based on historical information**

Accounts are often published many months after the accounting period, therefore ratios will be based on out of date information.

62 Slim Jim Co

> **Helping hand.** Ensure your answer reflects the mark allocation. You need to provide a source of finance and a sentence or two of explanation.

Sources of finance (only three were required)

(i) **Retained earnings**

This is the most obvious source of finance for at least part of the funds required. Slim Jim could use part of the $1.3 million for the investment. However, given that the loan is repayable in six months' time, the company must keep $0.5 million back for this. Also, there are often cost overruns on this sort of project so Slim Jim must keep some retained earnings back to cover these.

(ii) **Loan**

Slim Jim Co could take out a loan from the bank. It is unlikely to have access to any other source of debt provider (such as the international bond market) since it is not a large company.

(iii) **Rights issue of shares**

Presumably, since we know that Slim Jim's current owners are 'wealthy', they could inject more cash into the company in the form of shares. This will prevent any dilution of control by selling shares outside of the company.

(iv) **New share issue**

This would have to be to private investors, unless the company were to be floated on the stock exchange.

(v) **Venture capital**

Slim Jim could approach a venture capital company with a view to obtaining funds for the expansion of the business. However, venture capitalists would want to be closely involved with the new venture, even expecting a place on the board of directors.

63 Convertible loan notes

Marking scheme

	Marks
Allow up to 2 marks for each of the three requirements	5
Total marks	**5**

> Convertible loan notes are fixed return securities which give the holder the option to convert into a predetermined number of ordinary shares at predetermined dates.
>
> – A company would issue convertible loan notes when its ordinary share price is considered to be undervalued. The convertible loan notes are therefore a deferred sale of equity and the conversion will take place when share prices have increased and is less likely to dilute the earnings per share.
>
> – Due to the conversion option, the interest rate on the convertible loan notes is often lower than on a straight loan note. This makes it attractive to the company as it reduces debt service costs.
>
> – Providing the conversion terms are structured appropriately, it is expected that most investors will convert the loan notes. The advantage of this for the issuing company is that it will not have to find the cash to redeem the loan notes at maturity.
>
> **Note.** Only **TWO** reasons were required

64 Educate Co

Helping hand. Don't just list reasons why a company might seek a stock exchange listing – you are required to explain each reasons (remember there are 10 marks available). If you can't remember four, just explain the ones you can remember, rather than leaving the entire section blank.

You should hopefully be familiar with the term 'gearing' – if not, go back to your Interactive Text to revise this important topic. You can use your common sense for the second part of (b) – if you had a lot of debt do you think your bank would be willing to lend you more?

(a) **Reasons why a company might seek a stock exchange listing** (choose any four)

Access to a wider pool of finance

A company that is growing fast may need to raise larger sums than is possible as a private unlisted company. A stock market listing widens the number of potential investors. It may also improve the company's credit rating, making debt finance easier and cheaper to obtain.

Improved marketability of shares

Shares that are traded on the stock market can be bought and sold in relatively small quantities at any time. This means that it is easier for exiting investors to realise a part of their holding.

Transfer of capital to other uses

Founder owners may wish to liquidate the major part of their holding either for personal reasons or for investment in other new business opportunities.

Enhancement of the company image

Quoted companies are commonly believed to be more financially stable, and listing may improve the image of the company with its customers and suppliers, allowing it to gain additional business and to improve its buying power.

Facilitation of growth by acquisition

A listed company is in a better position to make an offer for a target company than an unlisted one.

(b) '**Gearing**' refers to a company's capital structure – how much of the company is funded by debt as compared to equity. '**Highly geared**' means that the company has more debt in its financing structure than equity.

The level of gearing is important when a company is trying to raise extra finance. If the company already has a lot of debt in its capital structure, lenders may be reluctant to advance further funds due to the greater risk of default. Debt means that the company has to pay interest and the more debt a company has, the greater the amount of interest that has to be paid in each period. The company will therefore be more vulnerable if sales revenue falls, as there will be fewer profits from which to pay interest.

65 Venture capital

Marking scheme

	Marks
1 mark per point – allow up to 3 marks per condition but only give full marks if three conditions are stated	5
Total marks	5

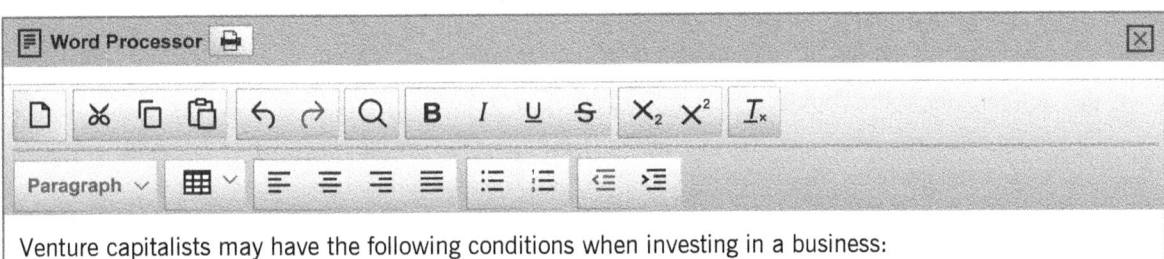

Venture capitalists may have the following conditions when investing in a business:

- They will want an equity stake in the business so that they can participate in its success.
- They will require the business's owners to bear a significant part of the risk of the venture. This is common in management buyout situations where the phrase 'enough so that it hurts' is commonly used.
- They will require a business plan which convinces them that the business can offer high future growth as a reward for the risks involved.
- They will require representation on the company's board so that they protect their investment.
- They will require an exit route, normally within five years, so that they can realise their investment. This could be a flotation, a trade sale or a sale to existing owners.

Note. Only **THREE** conditions were required

66 Skint Co

Helping hand. This is a general question rather than being specific to the scenario therefore you should be able to use information that you have read in the Interactive Text. Remember you only have to explain two general factors and the explanations will only be worth two and a half marks each so don't write too much.

Factors to be considered

In general, a bank wishes to ensure that the client will be able to make the scheduled repayments, in full and within the required period of time. A bank's decision whether to lend will be based on the following factors (choose any two).

(a) **The purpose of the borrowing**

The type of funds must be matched to the **purpose** for which they are required. For example, a **business expansion programme** is likely to **require finance** both for the purchase of additional non-current assets, and for an increase in the level of working capital. In general cheaper **short-term funds** should only be used to **finance short-term requirements**. Short-term debt, usually in the form of an overdraft, is repayable on demand, and it would therefore be risky to finance long-term capital investments in this way.

(b) **Ability to borrow and repay**

Lenders need to be convinced of the client's ability to service the debt and to repay it at the end of the term. The client may need to provide financial statements, and put together a **business plan** that shows, for example, how earnings will be sufficient to cover interest costs, and also how repayment at the end of the loan period will be funded. The client must also confirm that it has the **legal capacity** to borrow in the manner required, by checking the company's constitution, and making sure that there is no breach of any restrictive covenants on existing borrowings.

(c) **Repayment terms**

The **relative costs** of the alternative sources of finance must be considered. For example, short-term debt is usually cheaper than long-term debt, but will carry a higher level of risk. The **repayment terms** must also be **matched** to the pattern of expected cash flows. A bank should not lend money to a client which has not got the resources to repay it with interest. The timescale for repayment is also very important.

(d) **Character of the borrower**

To assess this, the bank may look at the **client's past record** with the bank (if relevant), or conduct a personal interview. Key performance ratios may also be examined.

(e) **Margin of profit**

The bank needs to decide what **level of interest** to charge, in order to make money. The lending policies of most banks stipulate different rates for different purposes to customers. The interest rate charged will also depend on the **perceived risk** of the investment to the lender, and this is another reason for putting together a comprehensive business plan.

(f) **Amount of the borrowing**

The bank must make sure of **exactly how much** the customer wishes to borrow, to be satisfied that it is lending neither too much nor too little for the purpose. This is especially important with requests for an overdraft facility. The bank's lending policy will indicate limits on the amount of certain loans, and the amount which must be paid up front by the client.

(g) **Security**

As insurance, the bank might ask for the amount to be secured, by **fixed** or **floating changes** over assets. If the borrower defaults on repayments, the bank can attempt to obtain its money by selling the assets secured.

67 Lease and hire purchase

Helping hand. This is a fairly straightforward question, but requires more than a simple description of these two forms of finance.

Marking scheme

	Marks
1 mark each point up to a maximum of 2 marks each explanation. To gain maximum marks candidates must attempt both similarities and differences.	5
Total marks	5

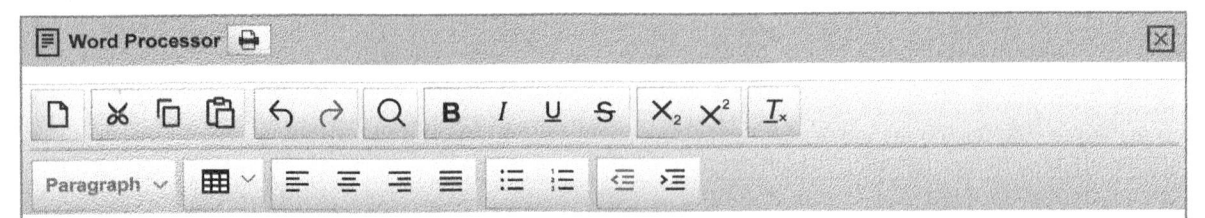

Similarities

- Both leasing and hire purchase allow a company to acquire the use and rewards of an asset by paying a fee which is usually set at regular intervals.

- Both hire purchase and leases are medium-term financing agreements which cannot be withdrawn as long as the agreed payments are made. Thus, both types of finance offer a degree of certainty for cash budgeting.

- Throughout the term of both hire purchase and lease agreements, legal title is retained by the finance company, therefore the asset itself provides some security against the loan.

Differences

- With a hire purchase agreement legal ownership passes automatically on final payment (or on payment of an option-to-purchase fee) whereas under a lease agreement legal title does not usually pass to the lessee.

- With a lease agreement the lessor claims the capital allowances against taxation whereas with a hire purchase agreement the user is treated as the owner of the equipment and benefits directly from the capital allowances.

68 Leasing and hire purchase

Helping hand. This question may need careful planning before you start to write an answer. The question asks about the benefits of leasing or hire purchase.

Many businesses try to finance their operations through a combination of equity capital and debt. It is risky to finance medium-term assets with short-term sources of finance, such as a bank overdraft. It is much less risky to finance medium term assets with a medium term source of funding.

Non-equity sources of medium term finance are often restricted to bank loans and either leasing or hire purchase arrangements, since many companies are unable to get access to the market for issuing corporate bonds. The choice available to a business, other than equity finance, is therefore restricted. A business may select a method of financing that minimises the cost or which is more readily available, and the choice between a medium term bank loan and a leasing or high purchase arrangement may vary according to circumstances.

There may be times when a bank loan may be the cheapest method of financing medium term non-current assets. On the other hand, there may be other cases when the after-tax cost of leasing or a hire purchase arrangement is cheaper.

FFM FOUNDATIONS IN FINANCIAL MANAGEMENT

Similarly, there may be occasions when a business finds it easier to obtain a bank loan to finance medium-term assets, especially if sufficient security can be provided. On the other hand, a business may find it easier to arrange a long-term lease or a hire purchase arrangement to obtain an asset.

69 Gearing and EPS

> **Helping hand.** This question tests your ability to calculate earnings per share from fairly simple data. It also tests your understanding of the link between gearing and earnings per share. You should be able to present earnings per share calculations is a neat and clear format: this will demonstrate your understanding of the topic to an exam marker.

(a) The earnings per share (EPS) of each company are calculated as follows:

	Company A $		Company B $
Before interest and tax	200,000		200,000
Interest	0	($1,000,000 × 6%)	60,000
Profit before taxation	200,000		140,000
Taxation (25%)	50,000		35,000
Profit after tax	150,000		105,000
Number of shares	2,000,000		1,000,000
EPS	$0.075		$0.105

(b) If the profits before interest and tax increase by 50% to $300,000. The change in EPS will be as follows:

	Company A $		Company B $
Before interest and tax	300,000		300,000
Interest	0	($1,000,000 × 6%)	60,000
Profit before taxation	300,000		240,000
Taxation (25%)	75,000		60,000
Profit after tax	225,000		180,000
Number of shares	2,000,000		1,000,000
EPS	$0.1125		$0.18

(c)

	Company A	Company B
Increase in EPS	50%	71.4%

The percentage change in the EPS in the geared company, Company B, is greater than the percentage change in EPS in the ungeared company, Company A. This illustrates the fact that the percentage change in EPS is larger for a company with higher gearing, for any percentage change in profit before interest and taxation.

The effect is the same for a reduction in operating profit as well as for an increase. If profit before interest and tax falls, the percentage fall in EPS will be larger for a higher-geared company than for a lower-geared company.

ANSWERS

70 Blimp Company

> **Helping hand.** This is another basic question on earnings per share and gearing. The key to a good answer is neat and clear presentation of the EPS calculations, and a good explanation of the link between gearing and earning per share.
>
> In this question, the solution to part (c) should recognise the nature of the solution to part (b), and your answer should make specific reference to the company in the question, instead of simply presenting the general principles about gearing and EPS.

(a) Earnings in the year to 31 December 20X5 = $15.6 million

Number of shares = 24 million

EPS = ($15.6/24) = $0.65

(b)

EPS for the year to 31 December 20X6

	All-equity financing $m		Mixed equity and debt financing $m
Profit before interest and taxation	26.8		26.80
Interest payable	2.0	(10% × $26 million)	2.60
Profit before taxation	24.8		24.20
Tax (25%)	6.2		6.05
Profit after taxation	18.6		18.15
Number of shares (million)	29		26
EPS	$0.641		$0.698
% change in EPS	(1.4)%		+ 7.4%

(c) With all-equity financing, the EPS would fall because the additional earnings would be $3 million ($4 million less tax of 25%) and there would be 5 million additional shares. The 'additional earnings per additional share' would therefore be $0.60 which is less than the current EPS for 20X5.

With mixed financing, part-equity and part-debt, there would be an increase in EPS of 7.4%. This is because the additional earnings would be $2.55 million (= $18.15 million – $15.6 million) and there would be additional shares of 2 million, giving an 'additional earnings per additional share' of $1.275. This is higher than the current EPS for 20X5. This explains why the EPS would be expected to increase.

This proposed investment illustrates the significance of capital structure and gearing for EPS.

71 Internally-generated funds

> **Helping hand.** The question is very short, so you have to structure the answer yourself. It is important to recognise that internally-generated funds relate largely to profitability, and are also important for liquidity. Your answer should discuss internally-generated funds as both a source of new equity and also a source of liquidity. The answer is longer than you would be expected to give for full marks.

Profit

The main source of internally-generated funds for a business is profit. Profits are either paid out to shareholders (as dividends or share repurchases) or reinvested in the business to finance growth.

Retained profits are a major source of long-term finance for many businesses. There are no issue costs or arrangement costs involved with this source of finance, unlike new issues of shares or arrangement of new debt finance.

They are also a convenient source of new funds, because a business acquires retained profits simply by operating profitably. Debt capital may be 'cheaper' and have a lower after-tax cost, but a business may be restricted in its ability to raise new debt finance, especially if it is already highly geared.

When a company needs additional finance to invest in growth of the business, it may be difficult to raise new finance from external sources, depending on the current state of the capital market and loans market. Retained profits may therefore be the only significant source of new finance.

Liquidity

Internally-generated funds are also important for liquidity as well as profitability. The main items in cash flows from operations (internally-generated funds) are usually profit before interest and tax plus depreciation charges.

Conclusion

In summary, internally-generated funds are important both because they are a source retained profits for investing in business growth and also a major source of cash flow and liquidity.

72 New company

Helping hand. If you are unfamiliar with some of the terminology in part (a) of the question, you may need to make an 'educated guess' about what they could mean. Parts (b) and (c) test your knowledge of sources of finance for small companies, but they also test your awareness of which sources of finance may be available in the particular case of a small start-up company. For example, a second-tier listing on a stock market is not a possibility for a one-year old company, and it is most unlikely that a venture capital organisation will want to concern itself with a small start-up business, until it has grown and developed a more established business.

(a) (i) A **funding gap** is the difference between the amount of funds that is available or obtainable for a business and the amount of funds that it needs for development and growth. The main source of funding for a small company is equity finance, and there should also be some trade credit and also possibly some bank funding. This is often insufficient to develop the business at the rate of growth that would be possible if more long-term funding were available. Start-up companies are often unable to grow mainly because they lack funding.

(ii) A **maturity gap** for a small company is the difference between the maturity of its assets and the maturity of its liabilities. In a well-financed business, long-term assets should be financed by long-term sources of funding, such as equity and long-term debt. Short-term assets should be financed partly by long-term funding and partly by short term credit. A maturity gap arises for a small company when it uses short-term funding for longer-term assets.

(iii) A business is often able to raise medium-term or longer-term finance provided that it can offer reasonable prospects of paying back the loan out of profits and in addition if it can provide sufficient security for the lender in case the primary source of repayment (from cash flows and profits) fails. If a borrower defaults on payments for a loan, the lender can make claim to the secured assets in order to obtain payment.

Small businesses are often unable to obtain bank loans because they cannot provide sufficient security. A small business owner may provide their personal assets, such as their home, as security for a business loan, but this involves high personal risk and many business owners are not prepared to do this.

(b) The company in this question has only been in existence for about one year, and unless it began with a large amount of equity capital, it is unlikely to be well funded. It may be making some profit, but the amount of cash flow generated from operations is unlikely to be sufficient to fund a major expansion of the business. The company should have access to short-term trade credit to finance some of its current assets, but short-term funding is inappropriate for financing long-term expansion.

At this stage of its development, the company may need to rely on new equity capital for expansion. Some equity will come from retained profits. The owner may be able to provide more equity from his own resources. It is possible that a 'business angel' could be interested in investing in the company, but any such investor would probably expect to have a voice in the management or strategic development of the company, a substantial share of the equity and an 'exit route' for the sale of his investment after

ANSWERS

perhaps three years or so. There are organisations that specialise in introducing small businesses to business angels.

As an alternative, or in addition to equity funding, the company may be able to obtain a bank loan for a part of its funding requirement. If it is unable to borrow, it may be able to acquire assets through a hire purchase or leasing arrangement.

(c) For a one-year old company, some sources of funding used by small and medium-sized enterprises will not be available. In particular, the company does not have a sufficient track record to consider a second tier stock market listing, and it is unlikely to be of sufficient size yet to interest a venture capital organisation. Venture capitalists normally prefer to invest in private companies with a history of successful trading and growth, rather than in start-up and very young companies.

It is possible that some government funding may be available, such as EU regional development funds. However government funding can take a long time to arrange, and is not easily obtained. When the national government is cutting back on public expenditure, public funds for start-up companies become even more difficult to obtain.

73 MCQ Answer Bank 10

73.1 The answer is a present value is the amount that could be invested now to obtain the future cash flow, given a return on investment equal to the discount rate.

Discounting allows for the time value of money. Money could be invested now to generate interest or profit.

73.2 The answer is $11,261.62

$10,000 \times (1.02)^6 = \$10,000 \times 1.126162 = \$11,261.62$

73.3 The answer is Lower

When the discount rate is higher, the PV factor is smaller and the present value of a future cash flow is lower.

73.4 The answer is Project X only

> **ACCA examining team's comments**
>
> In this question, the first thing candidates should note is that the projects are mutually exclusive. This means that either Project X, or Project Y, or neither project can be undertaken, but not both projects. This therefore discounts the first option (both projects) straight away. This was actually the option picked by the majority of candidates implying that candidates did not read the question with enough care.
>
> Candidates are now left to choose between the last three response options. To do this the method of project appraisal needs to be found, and in this case we are told that the company uses the net present value method to appraise projects with a cost of capital of 10%. The candidate therefore needs to calculate the net present value of both projects:
>
> NPV of X = ($15,000) + 2.487 × $8,000 = $4,896
> NPV of Y = ($15,000) + 0.751 × $26,000 = $4,526
>
> Note that in doing the calculation, I have used annuity factors, which are a valuable tool when answering questions under exam time pressure, and yet this is a technique few candidates generally use in Section B questions. This shows that both projects have a positive net present value, and so in an ideal world, the company would accept both projects. However, as the projects are mutually exclusive, only one project can be undertaken.
>
> Therefore selecting the project with the higher new present value, gives Project X, and hence the answer is Project X only.

73.5 The answer is PV of $30,000 at the end of Year 6

PV of $25,000 at the end of Year 4 = $25,000 × 0.708 = $17,700
PV of $30,000 at the end of Year 6 = $30,000 × 0.596 = $17,880
PV of $20,000 at the end of Year 2 = $20,000 × 0.842 = $16,840
PV of $50,000 at the end of Year 12 = $50,000 × 0.356 = $17,800

74 MCQ Answer Bank 11

74.1 The answer is (i), (ii) and (iv) only

Purchasing a building would be classed as capital expenditure. Expenditure on maintaining the earning capacity of non-current assets is classed as revenue expenditure.

74.2 The answer is $582

> **ACCA examining team's comments**
>
> Relevant costing techniques are regularly examined within both Section A and Section B questions, and the concept of having a scarce resource is an area which often causes candidates difficulty. In this question, skilled labour is the scarce resource as it is fully used within the business. Although more labour can be hired in, only 30 hours is available for hire, and 60 hours are needed for the project. To fulfil the remaining 30 hours, labour will have to be taken away from its existing activities in the business. This means that there are two elements to the calculation. Candidates need to calculate the cost of hiring in 30 hours of labour, and the cost of moving labour to the project from its existing activities. The cost of hiring in labour is fairly straightforward as we are told that labour that is hired, costs 25% more than the internal pay rate of $6.40. The cost of hiring in is therefore:
>
> 30 hours × $6.40 × 1.25 = $240
>
> We then move to the cost of moving labour from its current activities. The cost of moving the labour from its current activities is calculated as the hours required multiplied by (the cost per hour plus the contribution lost).
>
> This would give us:
>
> 30 hours × ($6.40 + $5.00) = $342
>
> Adding the two elements together gives $582 and the correct answer is 582
>
> The majority of candidates opted for $432 as their answer. These candidates correctly calculated the cost of hiring the labour as $240, but in calculating the cost of moving labour from its current activities, only took into account the cost per hour of $6.40. Their calculation was:
>
> $240 + $6.40 × 30 hours = $432
>
> Candidates need to remember to include the contribution that the organisation will lose from the current activities if labour is moved to work on the project in a calculation of this type.

74.3 The answer is Authorisation

Authorisation follows detailed evaluation in the decision making and control cycle.

74.4 The answer is 40%

$$\text{Accounting rate of return} = \frac{\text{Average Profit}}{\text{Average investment}}$$

$$\text{Average profit} = \frac{\$8,000}{4} = \$2,000$$

$$\text{Average investment} = \frac{\text{Initial investment} + \text{Residual value}}{2}$$

$$= \frac{\$7,500 + \$2,500}{2} = \$5,000$$

$$\text{Accounting rate of return} = \frac{\$2,000}{\$5,000} = 40\%$$

… ANSWERS

74.5 The answer is two years and ten months.

The net cash flows of the project are:

	$
Year 1	(89,500)
Year 2	(44,000)
Year 3	8,000

Therefore the machine pays back between Years 2 and 3.

Assuming the cash flows accrue evenly during the year, the machine will pay back

$(\frac{\$44,000}{\$52,000}) \times 12 = 10$ months into the year.

Therefore the payback period is two years and ten months.

74.6 The answer is three years and ten months

The net cash flows of the project are:

	$	PV Factor	Cumulative Present value $
Year 0	(85,000)	1	(85,000)
Year 1	15,000	0.909	(71,365)
Year 2	20,000	0.826	(54,845)
Year 3	45,000	0.751	(21,050)
Year 4	37,000	0.683	4,221

Therefore the machine pays back between Years 3 and 4.

Assuming the cash flows accrue evenly during the year, the machine will pay back

$\left(\frac{\$21,050}{\$37,000 \times 0.683}\right) \times 12 = 10$ months into the year.

Therefore the payback period is three years and ten months.

74.7 The answer is $2,802

Annuity rate for Years 4 to 6 is 4.355 – 2.487 = 1.868.

$1,500 × 1.868 = $2,802

74.8 The answer is 13.6%

$$\text{IRR} = 10 + \left[\frac{5,000}{5,000 - -2,000} \times (15 - 10)\right]$$

$= 10 + 3.57 = 13.6\%$

74.9 The answer is *Yearly costs* 5.868   *Yearly revenues* 3.658

> **ACCA examining team's comments**
>
> When answering this question, it is important to look carefully not only at the cost of capital (in this case 10%) but also at the time periods in which the cash flows arise.
>
> Considering the costs first, the cash flows arise at T0, T1, T2, T3, T4, T5, T6 and T7, so we need the annuity factor (AF) from T0–T7, ie AF0–7. The annuity factor tables given in the exam show the annuity factors when the first cash flow is at T1. Looking at our cash flows again, we can see that there are cash flows in T1–T7 inclusive, and then an extra cash flow at T0. The table can give us the AF1–7 @10% (it is 4.868), and the discount factor that is always applied to the cash flow at T0 is 1. When we add the two elements together:
>
> DF0 + AF1–7 = 1 + 4.868 = 5.868
>
> The mistake that many candidates made was to not add on the discount factor at T0, and give the answer as 4.868.

> Candidates struggled less with the revenues where the cash flows arise at T4, T5, T6, T7, T8, T9 and T10. To get the annuity factor that we need, AF4–10, one approach would be to use the discount factor tables provided in the exam and add up the discount factor at 10% for each of the time periods, and this would give the correct answer of 3.658.
>
> A quicker way though would be the subtraction method. The annuity factor tables give us AF1–10. We only want AF4–10, so we can take the AF1–10, and simply deduct the annuity factor for the years we do not want, in this case deduct the annuity factor for years 1–3 inclusive. In effect we are saying AF4–10 = AF1–10 – AF 1–3.
>
> Using the annuity factor tables AF4–10 = 6.145 - 2.487 = 3.658.
>
> So the answer is *Yearly costs* 5.868   *Yearly revenues* 3.658

74.10   The answer is they take into account social costs and social benefits

Public sector capital budgeting decisions take into account social costs and social benefits.

75 Financing concepts

> **Helping hand.** This question tests your basic understanding of financing and investment concepts, which is essential for a proper understanding of capital investment appraisal. You should use the numerical part of the question to gain familiarity with a present value table and annuity table.

(a) (i) With simple interest, the amount of interest is calculated as the initial principal sum multiplied by the interest rate per period and the number of interest periods.

Simple interest i = Prt

With compound interest, the amount of interest in a period is added to the principal sum, and interest in the following period is calculated on the original principal plus accumulated interest. In other words, with compound interest, interest is calculated on accumulated interest as well as the original principal amount. With simple interest, the amount of interest is calculated on the original principal amount only.

(ii) The present value of a future cash flow is equal to the future value of the cash flow, discounted at an appropriate cost of capital. This means that if the present value of the cash flow is invested at the cost of capital at the cost of capital, its value with interest will accumulate to equal the future value. The future value of a cash flow increases with each succeeding time period as additional interest is accumulated.

(b) Future value = $20,000 \times (1.04)^3 \times (1.02)^4 = \$24,352$

76 Question with help: Two capital projects

(a) Annual depreciation = $\dfrac{\$200,000 - \$40,000}{4}$

= $40,000 per annum

(i) **Payback period**

Year	Project X $'000	Project Y $'000
Cash flows 1	120	70
2	120	90
3	80	130
4	60	160
Project resale value	40	40
Payback period	1 + (80/120) years = 1.7 years	2 + (40/130) years = 2.3 years

ANSWERS

(ii) **Accounting rate of return**

The accounting profits are given in the question and we need to calculate the average over the four years. The average investment will be the same for both projects.

Average investment = $\dfrac{\$200,000 + \$40,000}{2}$ = $120,000

	Year	Project X $'000	Project Y $'000
Accounting profits	1	80	30
	2	80	50
	3	40	90
	4	20	120
		220	290
Average (÷ 4)		55	72.5
Average investment		120	120
∴ Average accounting rate of return		$\left(\dfrac{55}{120}\right)$ 45.8%	$\left(\dfrac{72.5}{120}\right)$ 60.4%

(iii) **Using the cash flows from (i)**

Year	Discount factor 16%	Cash flow $'000	Project X Present value $'000	Cash flow $'000	Project Y Present value $'000
1	0.862	120	103.44	70	60.34
2	0.743	120	89.16	90	66.87
3	0.641	80	51.28	130	83.33
4	0.552	100	55.20	200	110.40
			299.08		320.94
Initial capital cost			200.00		200.00
Net present value			99.08		120.94

(b) **Project Y** should be undertaken because it gives the highest **net present value**. This is a more important measure than the accounting rate of return because it takes account of the timing of cash flows and the time value of money. However the directors should bear in mind that project Y has a longer payback period which can lead to increased risk and reduced liquidity.

(c) There are a number of ways to take into account **risk** when making an investment decision (choose any three).

(1) **Set a short payback period.** If risk is deemed to increase with the length of time a company waits for its returns, then selecting only those projects with a short payback period will tend to reduce the risk.

(2) **Use a higher discount rate.** This is referred to as adding a 'risk premium' to the discount rate. If a project is considered to be fairly risky then, say, 2% could be added to the basic cost of capital. If it is considered to be very risky then, say, 5% could be added.

(3) **Use probabilities to assess the range of possible outcomes.** Managers could be asked to forecast a number of different values for sales, costs and so on, together with their associated probabilities.

(4) **Undertake a sensitivity analysis.** This involves asking a series of 'what if' questions and re-evaluating the project with different sets of assumptions. For example managers might ask, 'what if sales volume is 5% lower than expected?' The project would be re-evaluated to see how sensitive the final result is to this particular change. By carrying out a number of such sensitivity tests it is possible to highlight which particular forecasts are most important to the outcome of the project.

77 Taxi Co

(a)

	0	1	2	3	4	5
	$'000	$'000	$'000	$'000	$'000	$'000
Revenue (W)		800	1,150	1,528	1,934	2,371
Cost saving (1% of revenues)		110	116	121	127	134
		910	1,266	1,649	2,061	2,505
Implementation	700	700	700			
Training		425				
Wages (Additional costs, 5%)		120	200	210	221	232
Maintenance		75	75	75	75	75
	700	1,320	975	285	296	307
Net revenue/(cost)	(700)	(410)	291	1,364	1,765	2,198
10% discount factor	1	0.909	0.826	0.751	0.683	0.621
Discounted cash flows	(700)	(373)	240	1,024	1,205	1,365
Cumulative discounted cash flows	(700)	(1,073)	(833)	191	1,396	2,761

	Cumulative present value
	$'000
0	(700)
1	(1,110)
2	(819)
3	545
4	2,310
5	4,508

Working

Year	With Kwictrac	Without	Increment
	$'000	$'000	$'000
1	11,000	10,200	800
2	11,550	10,400	1,150
3	12,128	10,600	1,528
4	12,734	10,800	1,934
5	13,371	11,000	2,371

(b) The **discounted payback period** is the length of time required before the total present value of cash inflows received from the project is equal to the cash outlay.

This is 2 years + (833/1,024 × 12 months) = two years and ten months. This compares closely with the non-discounted payback period of two years and seven months. As with the basic payback method, the significant positive cash flows occurring after the end of the payback period tend to be ignored.

(c)

Year	Amount required	Discount factor	Present value to be invested now
	$	8%/9%	$
1	700,000	0.926	648,200
2	700,000	0.842	589,400
			1,237,600

ANSWERS

78 Quick Freeze Foods Co

> **Helping hand.** In (a) all you need to do for the Italian project is to identify that its IRR exceeds the other two's. The reasons discussed in (b) for preferring NPV are fundamental to this area of the syllabus.

(a) The projects will be discounted at both 10% and 15% for the purpose of calculating the IRR.

Indian range

	Year 0 $	Year 1 $	Year 2 $	Year 3 $	Year 4 $	Total $
Cash flow	(80,000)	26,500	26,500	26,500	26,500	
10% discount factors	1.000	0.909	0.826	0.751	0.683	
Discounted cash flow at 10%	(80,000)	24,089	21,889	19,902	18,100	3,980
15% discount factors	1.000	0.870	0.756	0.658	0.572	
Discounted cash flow at 15%	(80,000)	23,055	20,034	17,437	15,158	(4,316)

Net present value at 10% = $3,980

The IRR can be found by interpolation using the following formula:

$$\text{IRR} = A + \left[\frac{a}{a-b} \times (B - A) \right]$$

where A is the rate of return with a positive NPV
B is the rate of return with a negative NPV
a is the amount of the positive NPV
b is the amount of the negative NPV

In this case:

IRR = 10% + [(3,980/(3,980 − − 4,316) × (15% − 10%)]% = 12.4%

Alternatively using the spreadsheet function for IRR:

B5			fx	=IRR(B3:F3)	
	A	B	C	D	E	F
1		Year 0	Year 1	Year 2	Year 3	Year 4
2		$	$	$	$	$
3	Cash flow	-80,000	26,500	26,500	26,500	26,500
4						
5	IRR	12.3%				
6						

Chinese range

	Year 0 $	Year 1 $	Year 2 $	Year 3 $	Year 4 $	Total $
Cash flow	(20,000)	5,000	6,000	8,000	10,000	
10% discount factors	1.000	0.909	0.826	0.751	0.683	
Discounted cash flow at 10%	(20,000)	4,545	4,956	6,008	6,830	2,339
15% discount factors	1.000	0.870	0.756	0.658	0.572	
Discounted cash flow at 15%	(20,000)	4,350	4,536	5,264	5,720	(130)

Net present value at 10% = $2,339

The IRR can be found by interpolation as above:

IRR = 10% + [(2,339/(2,339 − − 130) × (15% − 10%)]% = 14.7%

189

Alternatively using the spreadsheet function for IRR:

	A	B	C	D	E	F
1		Year 0	Year 1	Year 2	Year 3	Year 4
2		$	$	$	$	$
3	Cash flow	-20,000	5,000	6,000	8,000	10,000
4						
5	IRR	14.7%				

B5 =IRR(B3:F3)

The results can be summarised and the projects ranked as follows:

	NPV	Ranking	IRR	Ranking
Indian range	$3,980	1st	12.4%	2nd
Chinese range	$2,339	2nd	14.7%	1st

(b) The IRR and NPV approaches are similar in that they are both based on the principle of **discounted cash flow** (DCF). The main advantage of the IRR method is that the information it provides is **more easily understood** by managers, especially non-financial managers. However, since the results are expressed in percentage terms, the method can be **confused** with the **accounting return on capital employed**. A fundamental drawback to the IRR method is that it **ignores the relative size of investments**. This is not the case with the NPV technique, which measures the amount by which the net worth of the firm will be increased by undertaking the project. This method is therefore superior for **ranking mutually exclusive projects**. A further advantage of the NPV approach is that when discount rates are expected to differ over the life of the project, such variations can be incorporated easily into NPV calculations, but not into IRR calculations.

79 Weavers Co

Helping hand. In (a) don't forget to exclude sunk and non-cash costs.

(a)
Option 1

Year	0	1	2	3	4	5
	$'000	$'000	$'000	$'000	$'000	$'000
Cost of loom	(800)					
Sales		1,000	1,000	1,000	1,000	1,000
Materials		(400)	(400)	(400)	(400)	(400)
Labour (2% inflation)		(100)	(102)	(104)	(106)	(108)
Machine time		(200)	(200)	(200)	(200)	(200)
Cash flows	(800)	300	298	296	294	292
10% discount factors	1.000	0.909	0.826	0.751	0.683	0.621
Discounted cash flow	(800)	273	246	222	201	181

Net present value = **$323,000**.

Alternatively using the spreadsheet function for NPV:

B5 =NPV(0.1,C3:G3)

	A	B	C	D	E	F	G
1	Year		1	2	3	4	5
2			$'000	$'000	$'000	$'000	$'000
3	Cash flows		300	298	296	294	292
4							
5	Present value of time 1-5	1,124					
6	less outlay	-800					
7	NPV	324					

Option 2

Year	0	1	2	3	4	5
	$'000	$'000	$'000	$'000	$'000	$'000
Sales		1,000	1,000	1,000	1,000	1,000
Subcontractor costs ($700 per carpet)		(700)	(700)	(700)	(700)	(700)
Annual fee (5% infl'n)		(150)	(158)	(165)	(174)	(182)
Cash flows	–	150	142	135	126	118
10% discount factors	1.000	0.909	0.826	0.751	0.683	0.621
Discounted cash flow	–	136	117	101	86	73

Net present value = **$513,000**.

Notes

1 **Depreciation** is not a cash flow and therefore has not been included in the NPV calculations.

2 The $100,000 costs of research into the subcontracting arrangement is a **sunk cost**, and is therefore not relevant.

3 Revenues and costs are assumed to arise at the end of each year.

Alternatively using the spreadsheet function for NPV:

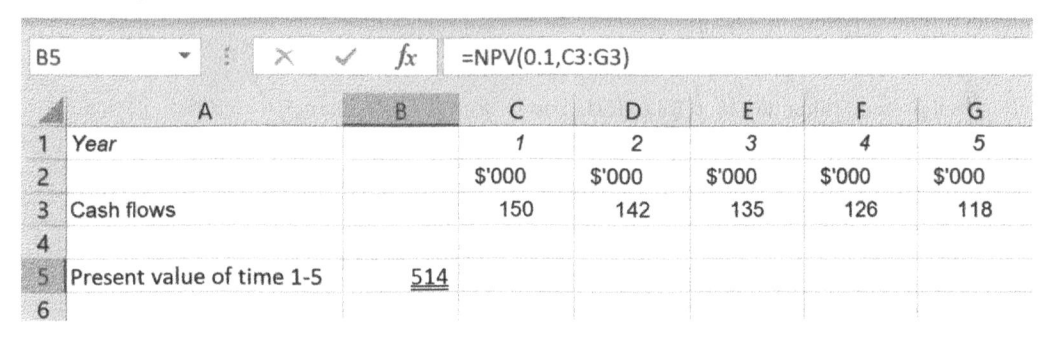

B5 | fx | =NPV(0.1,C3:G3)

	A	B	C	D	E	F	G
1	Year		1	2	3	4	5
2			$'000	$'000	$'000	$'000	$'000
3	Cash flows		150	142	135	126	118
4							
5	Present value of time 1-5	514					
6							

(b) The two options concerned are mutually exclusive. **Therefore, the option with the higher NPV, in this case Option 2, should be chosen.**

80 Rainbow Co

(a), (b)

	0 $'000	1 $'000	2 $'000	3 $'000	4 $'000	5 $'000	6 $'000
Sales		1,550	1,550	1,550	650	650	
Cost of sales (40% sales)		(620)	(620)	(620)	(260)	(260)	
Distribution costs (10% sales)		(155)	(155)	(155)	(65)	(65)	
Net profits		775	775	775	325	325	
Royalty to inventor (20% net profits)			(155)	(155)	(155)	(65)	(65)
Investment	(2,100)						
Net cash flows	(2,100)	775	620	620	170	260	(65)
Discount factor 5%	1.000	0.952	0.907	0.864	0.823	0.784	0.746
Present value	(2,100)	738	562	536	140	204	(48)
Discount factor 10%	1.000	0.909	0.826	0.751	0.683	0.621	0.564
Present value	(2,100)	704	512	466	116	161	(37)

Net present value at 5% is $32,000. The project is (just) financially viable.

Net present value at 10% is ($178,000)

$$\text{IRR} = A + \left[\frac{a}{a-b} \times (B-A)\right]$$

$$\text{IRR} = 5 + \left[\frac{32}{32-178} \times (10-5)\right] = 5.76\%, \text{ say } 6\%$$

81 Pills Co

> **Helping hand.** (a) and (b) require you to understand how to identify relevant costs in capital investment appraisal, and then to use this knowledge to disentangle the relevant costs in relation to a specific development project. The NPV calculations themselves are relatively simple since they only cover a two-year timescale. Don't, however, forget to take account of time factors when calculating the breakeven value in (b) (ii).

(a) A **relevant cost** is a future cash flow that arises as a direct consequence of the decision being considered. Non-cash items such as depreciation should be ignored. The main principles used to identify relevant costs are as follows (choose any two).

  (i) **Relevant costs are future costs**. A decision is about the future; it cannot alter what has been done already. A cost that has been incurred in the past is totally irrelevant to any decision that is being made now. Such costs are known as **sunk costs** and include payments that have been contractually committed (**committed costs**), even if payment has not yet been made. An example of a sunk cost in this case is the $250,000 that has already been invested in the development of Gravia.

  (ii) **Relevant costs are incremental costs**. A relevant cost is one that arises as a direct consequence of a decision. In this case, the cost of the lab technicians should be excluded, since they can be transferred to other work and they will continue to be employed whether or not the project goes ahead.

ANSWERS

(iii) **Opportunity costs**. These are the benefits which could have been earned, but which have been given up, by choosing one option instead of another, ie they are cash flows that are foregone as a result of the project being undertaken. In this case, the income that is foregone as a result of not scrapping material B is an opportunity cost.

It should be noted that the **costs of financing the investment project** is not included as relevant costs within the cash flow projections, even though they meet the above conditions. This is because they are accounted for in the process of discounting, and therefore to include them in the cash flows would be to double count them.

(b) (i)

	Note	Year 0 $	Year 1 $	Year 2 $
Sale of patent				1,000,000
Type A material			(150,000)	(150,000)
Type B material	1	(20,000)		
Specialist equipment	2	(100,000)		25,000
Chemist salaries	3		(40,000)	(40,000)
Chemist redundancies	3	40,000		(40,000)
Fixed overheads	4		(40,000)	(40,000)
Sale of formula foregone		(250,000)		
Net cash flow		(330,000)	(230,000)	755,000
10% discount factors		1.000	0.909	0.826
Discounted cash flow		(330,000)	(209,070)	623,630
Total net present value		**$84,560**	($85,000 to the nearest $'000)	

Notes

1. Neither the **original cost** of the material nor its **replacement cost** are relevant to the decision. However, Pills will forego the proceeds from the sale of the material as scrap, and this should therefore be included in the cash flow.

2. The specialist equipment would only be purchased if the **project is undertaken**, and therefore its cost is relevant to the decision.

3. The chemists will only continue to be employed if the **project is undertaken**, and therefore their salaries should be included. If the project does not go ahead, Pills would have to make them redundant now, and therefore this payment that is saved as a result of the project being undertaken should be included as a positive cash flow. However, since they will be made redundant at the end of the project, the cost of redundancy must be included in year 2.

4. Only that element of the overheads that are **specifically incurred** as a direct consequence of the project should be included.

(ii) Since the project has a positive NPV it should add to the net worth of the company. It is therefore recommended that, on the basis of the information provided, Pills should proceed with the Gravia development project.

82 Soke Co

Helping hand. In (a) your answer needs to bring out the phased nature – initial general investigation and then a more detailed overview. The other key aspect is control – authorisation, monitoring and the post-completion audit.

In (b) ideally the results should influence projects currently in progress as well as projects that will be started in the future. The suggested solution to (b) contains more points than are required by the question. Other sensible suggestions would be equally valid.

(a) **To:** Finance Director
From: Financial Assistant
Date: 16 October 20X2
Subject: Evaluating and controlling expenditure projects

The main stages involved in evaluating and controlling capital expenditure projects are as follows:

(1) **Initial investigation**

We need to consider whether the project is **technically and commercially feasible**, what are the **main risks** and whether it fits with the company's **long-term strategic objectives**.

(2) **Detailed evaluation**

Once the feasibility of the project has been established, a **detailed investigation** will examine expected cash flow arising from the project, using DCF and other appropriate techniques.

The effects of risk should be analysed using **sensitivity analysis**.

Sources of finance should be considered. If there are insufficient funds to undertake all the proposed projects, they should be ranked in order of priority.

(3) **Authorisation**

For capital projects that are significant relative to the size of the company, **authorisation rules** should require that the decision to go ahead be made by **senior management** or the board of directors. Those making the decision must be satisfied that an appropriately detailed evaluation has been carried out, that the proposal meets the necessary criteria to contribute to profitability, and that it is consistent with the overall strategy of the enterprise.

(4) **Implementation**

Once the decision has been made that the project will be undertaken, **responsibility** for the project should be **assigned** to a project manager or other responsible person. The **required resources** will need to be made available to this manager, who should be given specific targets to achieve.

(5) **Project monitoring**

After the start of the project, **progress** should be **monitored** and senior management should be informed regularly on the development of the project.

(6) **Post-completion audit**

At the end of the project, a **post-completion audit** should be undertaken in order to learn from the experience in the planning of future projects.

Signed: Financial Assistant

(b) Benefits of a post completion audit include the following (only two were required).

(1) **Better future investment decisions.** The audit can identify where mistakes have been made, so that similar mistakes can be avoided in the future. It might also identify areas of success that could be replicated in future projects.

(2) **Better current investment decisions.** Awareness that an audit will be carried out at a later date may encourage managers involved to be more realistic and not unduly optimistic in their judgements.

(3) **Contribution to performance evaluation.** A project audit can provide feedback to senior management which is of use in the process of management control and performance assessment.

ANSWERS

83 Silly Filly Co

(a)

> **Helping hand.** The key to NPV calculations is to get the timing of the cash flows correct. Note that all cash flows are assumed to occur at the end of the year. Watch out for sunk costs and finance costs that will not be included in the NPV calculation.

Net present value calculation

Reference in the question

					Year			
		0	1	2	3	4	5
		$'000	$'000	$'000	$'000	$'000	$'000
(i)	Market research (sunk cost)						
(ii)	Animation	(260)	(260)				
(iii)	Producers' salaries		(240)				
(iv)	Other production costs		(650)				
(v)	Director's salary		(160)				
(vi)	Revenues			1,200	2,200	1,600	
(v)	Royalties @ 5% of revenue				(60)	(110)	(80)
(viii)	Specialist equipment	(2,300)	1,700				
(ix)	Loan interest (irrelevant)						
	Net cash flow	(2,560)	390	1,200	2,140	1,490	(80)
	Discount factor @ 10%	× 1.000	× 0.909	× 0.836	× 0.751	× 0.683	× 0.621
	Present value cash flows	(2,560)	355	991	1,607	1,018	(50)

Net present value is $1,361,000 which is a positive NPV at a 10% discount rate. The company should therefore proceed with the project.

(b) **Costs associated** with a **new equity issue** (only four required):

    (i)   Accountants' fees
    (ii)   Issuing house fees
    (iii) Solicitors' fees
    (iv) Public relations consultants' fees
    (v)   Stock exchange listing fees
    (vi) Underwriting costs
    (vii) Prospectus costs
    (viii) Advertising costs

84 Mr Food

> **Helping hand.** The key to this question is to take it one step at a time and try to gain the easy marks first. Set up a proforma table for your final NPV calculations and fill in the gaps as you calculate the figures. Workings should be labelled clearly (as we have done below) to make it as easy as possible for both you and the marker to see where each figure comes from.
>
> Watch out for sunk costs (not relevant as they have already been incurred) and depreciation (not a cash flow). If you are not sure about how to calculate a particular figure, state an assumption and perform calculations on this basis. You might not get the correct answer but if your technique is correct you will gain marks for workings.
>
> Make sure you use the correct discount factors – you are given both the individual factors and the annuity factors. As the cash flows are different each year, you should use the individual factors. Part (a) specifically asked for a conclusion – make sure you give one to avoid throwing away marks unnecessarily.

Net Present Value Calculation

	0 $	1 $	2 $	3 $	4 $	5 $
Revenue						
Net income from diners (W3)			91,520	121,680	144,560	144,560
Costs						
Building costs (W4)	(50,000)	(150,000)				
Lost income (W5)		(20,000)	(10,000)	(10,000)	(10,000)	(10,000)
Cleaners			(8,000)	(8,000)	(8,000)	(8,000)
Chefs (W2)			(20,000)	(30,000)	(30,000)	(30,000)
Waiting staff (number required at $5,000)			(10,000)	(15,000)	(15,000)	(15,000)
Overheads (8% × 30,000)			(2,400)	(2,400)	(2,400)	(2,400)
Professional fees – sunk cost						
Depreciation – non-cash						
Net relevant cash flows	(50,000)	(170,000)	41,120	56,280	79,160	79,160
Discount Factor	1.000	0.909	0.826	0.751	0.683	0.621
	(50,000)	(154,530)	33,965	42,266	54,066	49,158

Net Present value is $(25,075) and the expansion should not proceed.

Workings

1   Number of diners

Year	2	3	4	5
Number of diners F–Su	120	150	180	180
Number of diners M–Th	80	120	140	140
Total number of diners per week	200	270	320	320
Per year (at 52 weeks per annum)	10,400	14,040	16,640	16,640

2   Cost of chefs

Year	2	3	4	5
Number of diners per week (w1)	200	270	320	320
Number of chefs required	2	3	3	3
Annual cost (at $10,000 per chef) $	20,000	30,000	30,000	30,000

3   Net income from diners

Year	2	3	4	5
Diners Friday–Sunday at $10 per person	1,200	1,500	1,800	1,800
Diners Monday–Thursday at $7 per person	560	840	980	980
Total weekly income $	1,760	2,340	2,780	2,780
Annual income (at 52 weeks per annum) $	91,520	121,680	144,560	144,560

4   Building costs

25% at beginning of the project 0.25 × $200,000 = $50,000

75% at the end of the building work 0.75 × $200,000 = $150,000

5   Lost income

Year	1	2	3	4	5
10% of $200,000	$20,000				
5% of $200,000		$10,000	$10,000	$10,000	$10,000

85 Nippers

(a) **Option 1 – No extension**

Mrs Dibble will receive six years' net cash flows of $98,000, and $500,000 in six years' time.

		$
98,000 × 4.355	=	426,790
500,000 × 0.564	=	282,000
NPV	=	708,790

Option 2 – Extension

Mrs Dibble will pay $45,000 now and $40,000 in one year's time for the extension.

She will receive net cash flows of $98,000 in year 1 and $135,000 in years 2 to 6, and $600,000 in year 6.

	Time			
	0	1	2–5	6
Building materials	(45,000)			
Building labour		(40,000)		
Net cash inflows		98,000	135,000	135,000
Sale price				600,000
Net cash flow	(45,000)	58,000	135,000	735,000
Discount/annuity factor (10%)	1	0.909	2.882 (W1)	0.564
Discounted cash flow	(45,000)	52,722	389,070	414,540

NPV = $811,332

Note. Planning permission is a sunk cost and irrelevant for the decision.

Working

Annuity factor for 5 years – Discount factor for 1 year
= 3.791 – 0.909
= 2.882

Option 3 – Sell to developer

Mrs Dibble would receive $850,000 now. There is no need to discount the amount.

Answer

Financially, Option 3 is the best option for Mrs Dibble as it produces the highest NPV. She should sell the nursery to the developer.

(b) **Non-financial factors**

Any two from the following:

(i) By selling to the developer, Mrs Dibble will be putting the **friends** and **relatives** she employs out of work. This may strain her relationships with them.

(ii) By continuing with or without the extension, Mrs Dibble will be able to continue to do the work she **enjoys** so much. Selling now would mean she would stop and have to find something else to do with her time.

(iii) Choosing her brother to do the work may prevent him from becoming **bankrupt**.

(iv) More children in the **local community** would benefit from nursery education if she builds the extension.

(v) There is already a **lack** of nursery education in the local area, selling to the developer would make the situation worse.

(vi) Building the extension and remaining open may create a **danger** to the children and interference from **noise** and **dust** may disrupt the nursery's activities.

86 Robo Clean Co

Helping hand. The following formulas will help you calculate the sales revenue and material, labour and variable costs.

Sales revenue

Sales volume × sales price

eg Year 1 = 5k × 1,000 = 5,000k

Material cost

Sales volume × material cost per unit

eg Year 1 = 5k × 125 = 625k

Labour cost

Sales volume × labour cost per unit

eg Year 1 = 5k × 100 = 500k

Variable cost

Sales volume × variable cost per unit

eg Year 1 = 5k × 50 = 250k

Don't forget to use annuity factors rather than discount factors where you are calculating a present value for a large number of consecutive periods that all have the same net cash flow.

NPV

	0 $'000	1 $'000	2 $'000	3 $'000	4 $'000	5 $'000	6–10 $'000
Market research costs (sunk)	–						
Development costs (sunk)	–						
Factory costs	(6,000)	(5,750)					
Project management company		(250)					
Machinery costs		(2,500)					
Deprecation (non-cash)	–	–	–	–	–	–	–
Maintenance			(250)	(250)	(250)	(250)	(250)
Production lines		(1,500)					
Sales revenue			5,000	8,000	21,000	21,000	25,000
Material costs			(625)	(1,250)	(3,750)	(3,750)	(6,250)
Labour			(500)	(1,000)	(3,000)	(3,000)	(5,000)
Fixed overhead (relevant as incremental)			(240)	(240)	(240)	(240)	(240)
Variable overheads			(250)	(500)	(1,500)	(1,500)	(2,500)
Head office costs (incremental element only)			(3,700)	(3,700)	(3,700)	(3,700)	(3,700)
Reduced Robovac contribution (W1)			(125)	(250)	(750)	(750)	(1,250)
Net cash flows	(6,000)	(10,000)	(690)	810	7,810	7,810	5,810
Discount factor (W2)	1	0.952	0.907	0.864	0.823	0.784	3.393
Discounted cash flows	(6,000)	(9,520)	(626)	700	6,428	6,123	19,713

The net present value of the project is $16,818 million. The company should therefore proceed with it.

Workings

1. Reduced Robovac contribution is calculated as: $\dfrac{\text{Robonum Sales Volume} \times \$50}{2}$

2. Annuity factor for periods 6–10 = 7.722 – 4.329 = 3.393

ANSWERS

87 Go Green Co

	Year					
	0	1	2	3	4	5
	$'000	$'000	$'000	$'000	$'000	$'000
Product development costs (sunk)						
Test marketing costs (sunk)						
Sales: soap ($1.75 × sales)		438	350	263	158	53
– washing up liquid ($1.60 × sales)		384	448	512	272	80
Direct materials: soap ($0.15 × sales)		(38)	(30)	(23)	(14)	(5)
– washing up liquid ($0.35 × sales)		(84)	(98)	(112)	(60)	(18)
Direct labour: soap (W)		(75)	(50)	(38)	(23)	(8)
– washing up liquid (W)		(34)	(34)	(38)	(20)	(6)
Variable overheads: soap ($0.5 × sales)		(125)	(100)	(75)	(45)	(15)
– washing up liquid ($0.24 × sales)		(58)	(67)	(77)	(41)	(12)
Fixed overheads (irrelevant)						
New machinery	(500)					
Modifications	(150)					
Lost top floor income		(125)	(125)	(125)	(125)	(125)
Net cash flow	(650)	283	294	287	102	(56)
Discount factors at 10%	1.000	0.909	0.826	0.751	0.683	0.621
Present value	(650)	257	243	216	70	(35)

The net present value of the project is approximately **$101,000**. The company should therefore proceed with the project.

Working: Direct labour

Soap: cost per unit in year 1 = $7.20 ÷ 60 × 2.5 = $0.30

	1	2	3	4	5
Sales in units	250	200	150	90	30
Cost per unit	0.3	0.25	0.25	0.25	0.25
	$'000	$'000	$'000	$'000	$'000
Annual cost	75	50	37.5	22.5	7.5

Liquid: cost per unit in year 1 = $7 ÷ 60 × 1.2 = $0.14

	1	2	3	4	5
Sales in units	240	280	320	170	50
Cost per unit	0.14	0.12	0.12	0.12	0.12
	$'000	$'000	$'000	$'000	$'000
Annual cost	33.6	33.6	38.4	20.4	6

88 Wicker Co

> **Helping hand.** Don't forget to apply relevant costing principles in your answer, in particular to wood and fabric costs. In both cases material has already been purchased but this cost is a past cost and therefore irrelevant. The relevant cost will be the opportunity cost.
>
> In Year 1 there is sufficient stock of Wood X so the opportunity cost is the higher of its value as a substitute or if sold ($13 per m^2). Once the stock is used up, the relevant cost is the purchase price ($14 per m^2).
>
> The same principle applies to fabric costs. The opportunity cost is the resale value of fabric held in stock ($10 per m^2). Once this is used up the relevant cost is the purchase price ($22 per m^2).

Net present value

	Year 0 $'000	Year 1 $'000	Year 2 $'000	Year 3 $'000
Sales (W1)	–	8,600	9,460	10,406
Machine modification (75 + 100)	(175)	–	–	–
Depreciation – ignore				
Wood (W2)	(2,080)	–	(2,464)	(2,710)
Fabric (W3)	(2,940)	–	–	(3,727)
Labour	–	(1,590)	(1,980)	(2,179)
Variable overheads	–	(900)	(990)	(1,089)
Fixed overheads	–	(180)	(180)	(180)
Net cash flows	(5,195)	5,930	3,846	521
Discount factors	1	0.901	0.826	0.751
Present value	(5,195)	5,343	3,177	391

The net present value of the contract is $3.716m. Since the net present value is positive, the contract should be entered into.

Workings

1 Sales

	Year 0	Year 1	Year 2	Year 3
Annual sales levels per question				
R:		20,000	22,000	24,200
S:		25,000	27,500	30,250
H:		30,000	33,000	36,300
Total sales levels		75,000	82,500	90,750

	Year 0	Year 1 $'000	Year 2 $'000	Year 3 $'000
Sales revenue				
R:		4,000	4,400	4,840
S:		2,500	2,750	3,025
H:		2,100	2,310	2,541
Total sales		8,600	9,460	10,406

2 Wood

	m^2	m^2	m^2
R: annual sales level x $1m^2$	20,000	22,000	24,200
S: annual sales level x $2m^2$	50,000	55,000	60,500
H: annual sales level x $3m^2$	90,000	99,000	108,900
Total m required per annum	160,000	176,000	193,600

	Year 0 $'000	Year 1 $'000	Year 2 $'000	Year 3 $'000
Total cost at $13 per m^2 Year 0	2,080	–	2,464	2,710
$14 per m^2 at T2 and 3 Years 2 and 3				

3 Fabric

	m	m	m
R: annual sales level x 3m	60,000	66,000	72,600
S: annual sales level x 2m	50,000	55,000	60,500
H: annual sales level x 1m	30,000	33,000	36,300
Total m required per annum	140,000	154,000	169,400
Less already in inventory	(140,000)	(154,000)	0
Purchase requirements	0	0	169,400

	$'000	$'000	$'000	$'000
Total cost at $10 for Year 0, $22 for Year 3	2,940	–	–	3,727

89 Painless Co

> **Helping hand.** This is a long question with only one requirement. Layout is always important in NPV questions so use a tabular format. Label all workings and cross-reference them to the NPV calculation. Non-relevant costs have been mentioned in the NPV table in the answer. Although you are not specifically required to do this, labelling these costs as non-relevant in your answer (rather than just leaving them out completely) will indicate to the marker that you understand why these costs should not be included.

	Time 0 $'000	1–4 $'000	5 $'000
Salary savings (W1)		3,260	3,260
Redundancy costs (W2)	(2,402)		
Warehouse lease lump sum – SUNK			
Warehouse rental costs – Not incremental			
Rental income			30
Factory sale (W3)	300		
Incremental cost (W4)		(783)	(783)
Net cash flow	(2,102)	2,507	2,477
Discount/annuity factors	1	3.17	0.621
Present value	(2,102)	7,947	1,538

The net present value of the proposal is $7.383 million. Since this is positive, the proposal should go ahead.

Workings

1. Salary savings (per annum)
   (130 × $16,000) + (20 × $19,000) + (15 × $32,000) + (5 × $64,000)
   = $2,080,000 + $380,000 + $480,000 + $320,000
   = $3,260,000.

2. Redundancy costs (per annum)
   A & B: ($2,080,000 + $380,000) × 70% = $1,722,000
   C & D ($480,000 + $320,000) × 85% = $680,000
   Total redundancy costs = $2,402,000.

3. Factory sale/lease
   Establish best alternative use – sell or lease.
   Present value of selling = $300,000.
   Present value of leasing:
   PV of first rental receipt at T0 = $55,000.
   PV of remaining 4 receipts = $55,000 × 3.17 = $174,350.
   PV at lease end = $65,000.
   Therefore, total value of leasing = $55,000 + $174,350 + $65,000
   = $294,350.

   Factory should therefore be sold immediately.

4. Incremental cost of buying boxes
   Paracetamol: 64,000 × $5.20 = $332,800.
   Ibuprofen: 67,200 × $6.70 = $450,240.
   Total incremental cost = $783,040.

90 Discounted payback period

> **Helping hand.**
>
> As with any NPV calculation, use a tabular approach as this makes it clear to the marker which figures you have used and which year they have been allocated to.

Marking scheme

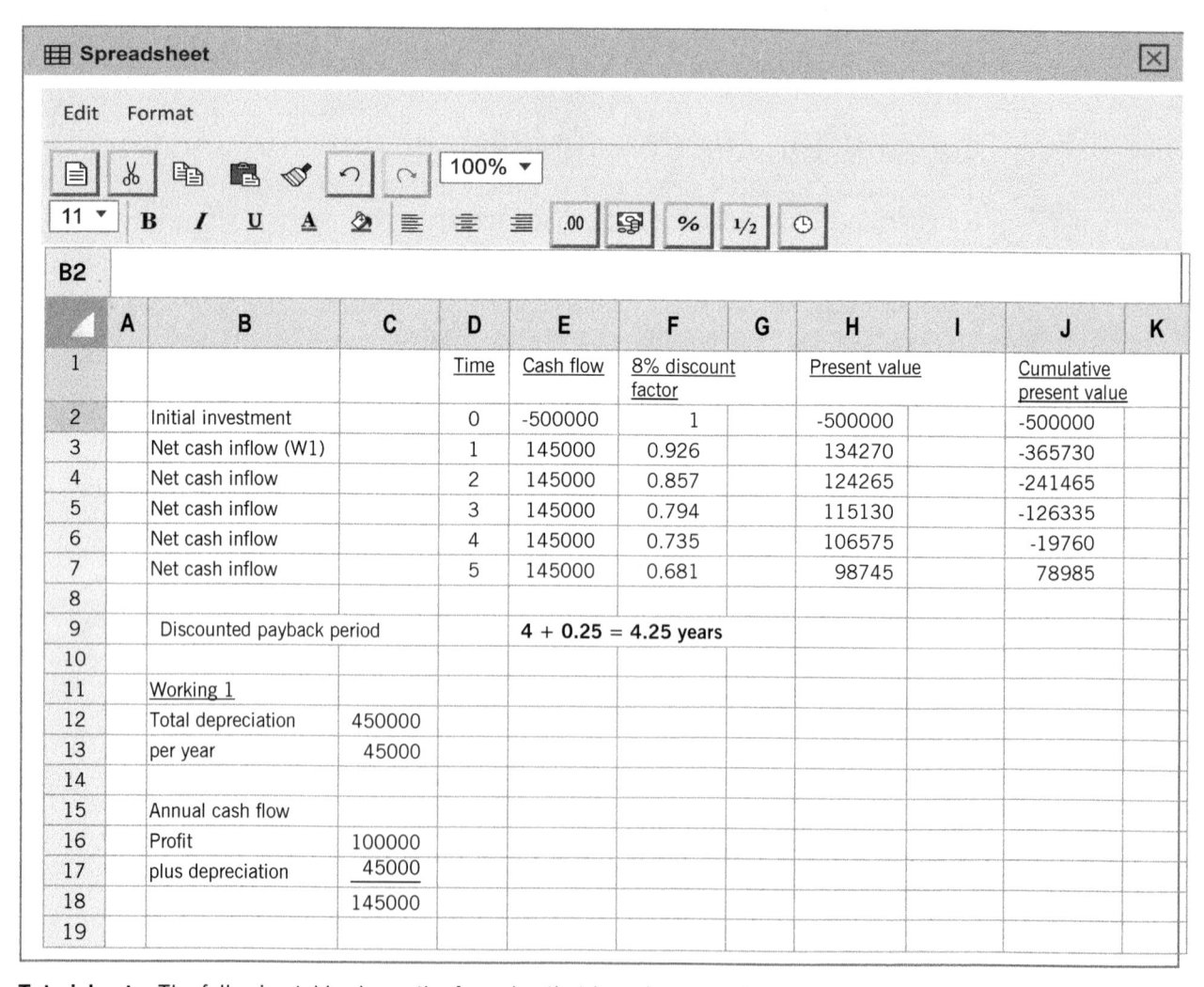

	Marks
Annual depreciation – award 0.5 if RV is omitted = ($500k/10)	1
Annual cash flow – award 0.5 for $100k – OFR dep'n (e.g. $55k)	1
Discounting	1
Cumulative cash flow (OFR)	1
Discounted payback period – award 0.5 for 4 years and 0.5 for 0.2 years	
If candidate states 5 years give 1 mark only if explained that cash flows occur at year end	1
Total marks	**5**

Spreadsheet

	A	B	C	D	E	F	G	H	I	J	K
1				Time	Cash flow	8% discount factor		Present value		Cumulative present value	
2		Initial investment		0	-500000	1		-500000		-500000	
3		Net cash inflow (W1)		1	145000	0.926		134270		-365730	
4		Net cash inflow		2	145000	0.857		124265		-241465	
5		Net cash inflow		3	145000	0.794		115130		-126335	
6		Net cash inflow		4	145000	0.735		106575		-19760	
7		Net cash inflow		5	145000	0.681		98745		78985	
8											
9		Discounted payback period			4 + 0.25 = 4.25 years						
10											
11		Working 1									
12		Total depreciation	450000								
13		per year	45000								
14											
15		Annual cash flow									
16		Profit	100000								
17		plus depreciation	45000								
18			145000								
19											

Tutorial note. The following table shows the formulae that have been used to generate these values and is shown here as a student aid, it would not be produced as a part of your answer.

ANSWERS

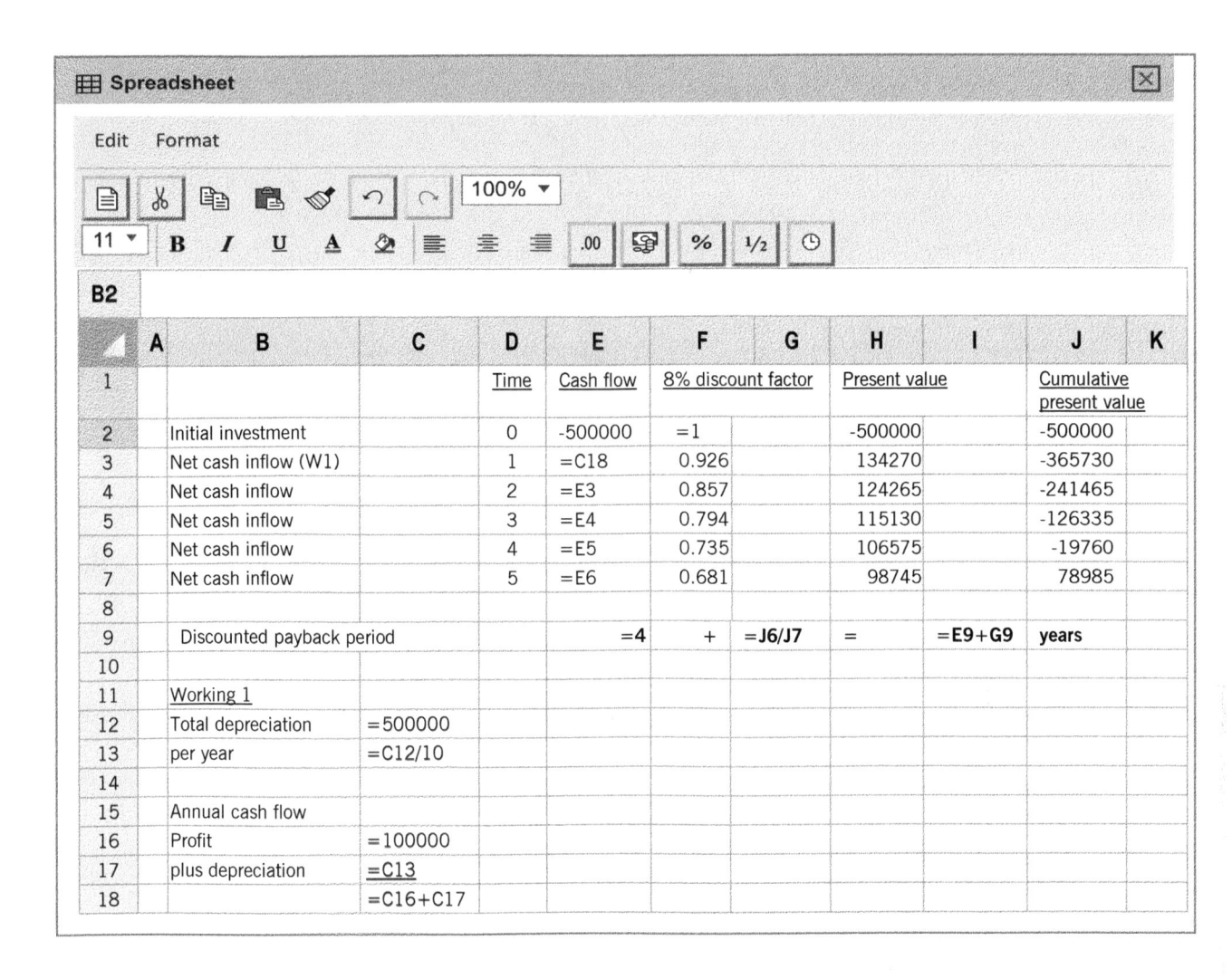

	A	B	C	D	E	F	G	H	I	J	K
1				Time	Cash flow	8% discount factor		Present value		Cumulative present value	
2		Initial investment		0	-500000	=1		-500000		-500000	
3		Net cash inflow (W1)		1	=C18	0.926		134270		-365730	
4		Net cash inflow		2	=E3	0.857		124265		-241465	
5		Net cash inflow		3	=E4	0.794		115130		-126335	
6		Net cash inflow		4	=E5	0.735		106575		-19760	
7		Net cash inflow		5	=E6	0.681		98745		78985	
8											
9		Discounted payback period			=4	+	=J6/J7	=	=E9+G9	years	
10											
11		Working 1									
12		Total depreciation	=500000								
13		per year	=C12/10								
14											
15		Annual cash flow									
16		Profit	=100000								
17		plus depreciation	=C13								
18			=C16+C17								

91 Edgely Co

Helping hand.

Remember that depreciation is a relevant cost in an ARR calculation as this is a profit based measure, not a cash based measure.

Marking scheme

		Marks
(a)	Sales – 1 mark for $20k in year 1 and mark 1 for inflating by 5%	2
	Materials – 30% of OFR sales value	1
	Labour – 0.5 for year 1 and 0.5 for 2% increase	1
	Depreciation – for correct inclusion	1
	Average profit – OFR profit 0.5 and divide by 4 0.5	1
	Residual value – 0.5 for 4 × 7 and 0.5 for deducting from $34K	1
	Average investment – 0.5 for adding the RV and 0.5 for dividing OFR by 2	1
	ARR	1
		9
(b)	Benefits NPV 1–3 each; only award full marks if three benefits are stated	6
Total marks		**15**

(a)

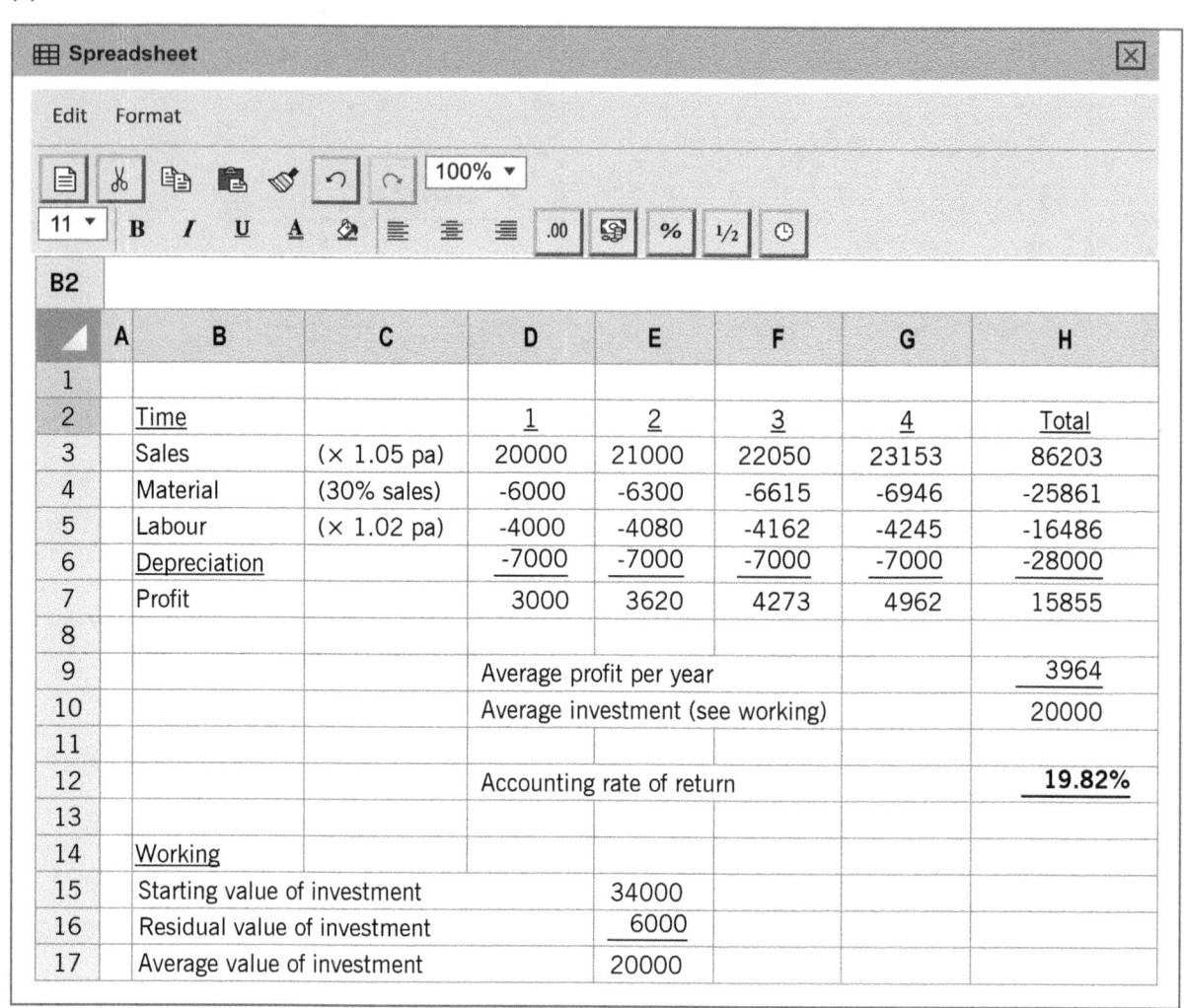

	A	B	C	D	E	F	G	H
1								
2		Time		1	2	3	4	Total
3		Sales	(× 1.05 pa)	20000	21000	22050	23153	86203
4		Material	(30% sales)	-6000	-6300	-6615	-6946	-25861
5		Labour	(× 1.02 pa)	-4000	-4080	-4162	-4245	-16486
6		Depreciation		-7000	-7000	-7000	-7000	-28000
7		Profit		3000	3620	4273	4962	15855
8								
9					Average profit per year			3964
10					Average investment (see working)			20000
11								
12					Accounting rate of return			**19.82%**
13								
14		Working						
15		Starting value of investment		34000				
16		Residual value of investment		6000				
17		Average value of investment		20000				

Tutorial note. The following table shows the formulae that have been used to generate these values and is shown here as a student aid, it would not be produced as a part of your answer.

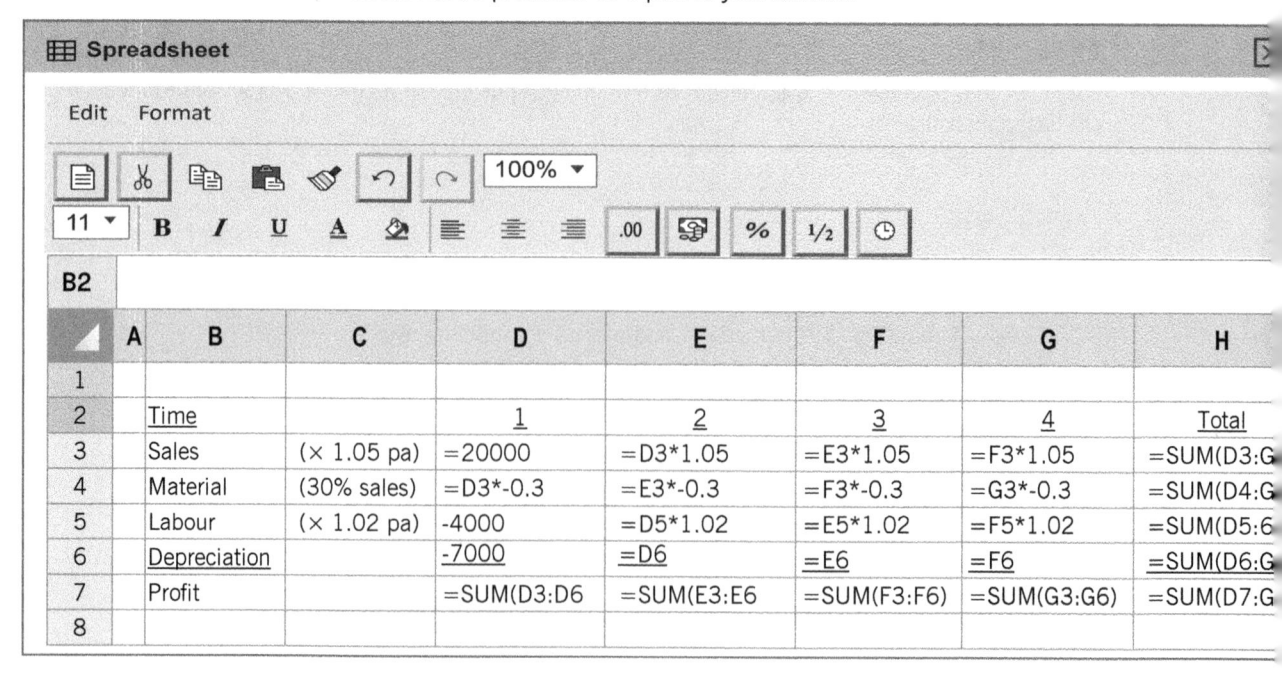

	A	B	C	D	E	F	G	H
1								
2		Time		1	2	3	4	Total
3		Sales	(× 1.05 pa)	=20000	=D3*1.05	=E3*1.05	=F3*1.05	=SUM(D3:G
4		Material	(30% sales)	=D3*-0.3	=E3*-0.3	=F3*-0.3	=G3*-0.3	=SUM(D4:
5		Labour	(× 1.02 pa)	-4000	=D5*1.02	=E5*1.02	=F5*1.02	=SUM(D5:6
6		Depreciation		-7000	=D6	=E6	=F6	=SUM(D6:G
7		Profit		=SUM(D3:D6)	=SUM(E3:E6)	=SUM(F3:F6)	=SUM(G3:G6)	=SUM(D7:G
8								

ANSWERS

	A	B	C	D	E	F	G	H
9				Average profit per year				=H7/4
10				Average investment (see working)				=E17
11								
12				Accounting rate of return				**=H9/H10**
13								
14		Working						
15		Starting value of investment			=34000			
16		Residual value of investment			=E15+H6			
17		Average value of investment			=(E15+E16)/2			

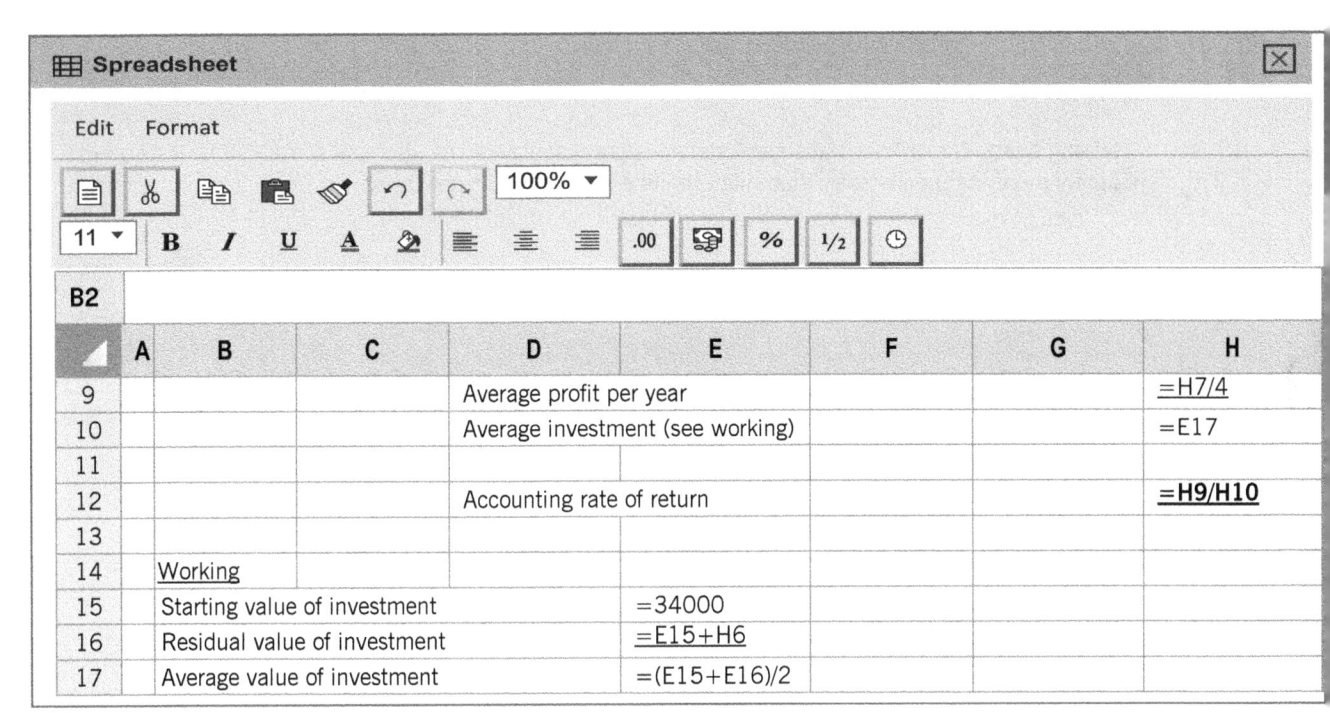

(b)

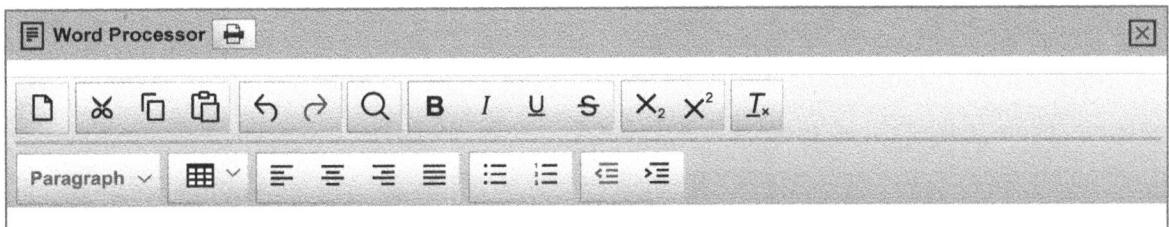

Benefits of using NPV instead of ARR

- Net present value is based upon cash flows rather than profit. Profit is based upon accounting conventions whilst cash is an objective measure. It is cash which pays dividends and wages, not profits.

- Net present value takes into account the time value of money. It recognises that a $ received in one year's time is worth less to the business than a $ received now. Accounting rate of return makes no distinction between the value of $1 of profit earned in early or later years.

- The net present value technique includes a clear decision rule. Projects with positive NPVs should be accepted, those with negative NPVs should be rejected. ARR has no clear-cut decision rule.

- NPV has a direct link to shareholder wealth. If a positive NPV is adopted, the value of shareholder wealth should increase by the expected NPV of the project.

- NPV is an absolute measure of project worth. ARR is a relative measure, making it difficult to compare returns on projects of different sizes.

Note. ONLY 3 BENEFITS ARE ASKED FOR

92 Mem Co

> **Helping hand.** The NPV spreadsheet function is a quick way of calculating a project NPV. It also produces a slightly more accurate answer than that obtained by using discount tables.

Marking scheme

		Marks
(a)	Replacement machine 0.5 mark each for purchase price and RV	1
	Scrap existing machine	1
	Foundation	0.5
	Survey – aware if this is absent from the computation	0.5
	Increase fixed costs	1
	Increase revenue	1
	Variable costs (1 mark for the incremental and 1 mark for the existing) Take care if candidate have combined in contribution. Also please be aware that comparing total old VC and new VC is also valid (1 mark) award full marks 1,650,000 – 1,500,000	2
	Discount	1
	NPV	1
	Conclusion	1
		10
(b)	Up to 3 marks each point	5
Total marks		**15**

(a)

	A	B	C	D	E	F	G	H	I	J
1										
2		Time				0	1	2	3	4	5
3		Incremental revenue					700000	700000	700000	700000	700000
4		Saved variable cost					400000	400000	400000	400000	400000
5		Incremental variable cost					-250000	-250000	-250000	-250000	-250000
6		Incremental fixed cost					-43000	-43000	-43000	-43000	-43000
7		Residual value									10000
8		Replacement machine			-25000000						
9		Scrap existing machine			48000						
10		Foundation			-15000						

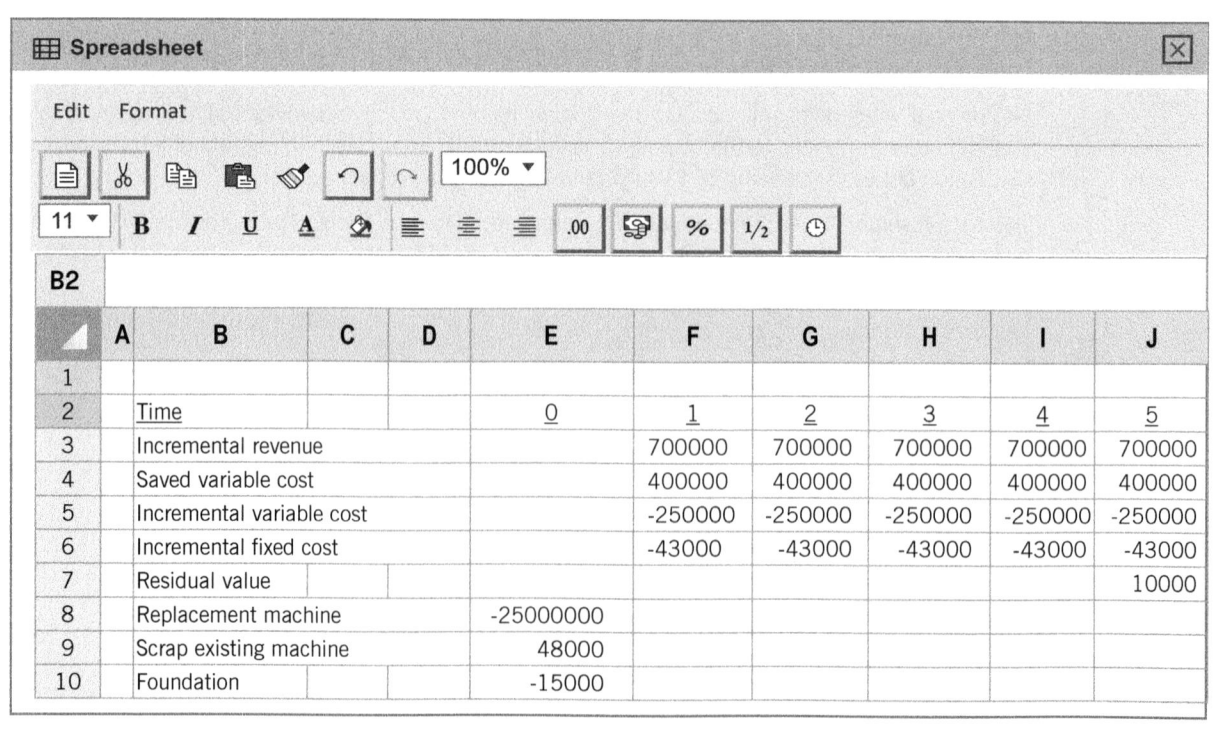

ANSWERS

Spreadsheet

	A	B	C	D	E	F	G	H	I	J
11		Surveyor			0					
12										
13		Net cash flow			-2467000	807000	807000	807000	807000	907000
14										
15		Net present value time 1 to 5			3,203,942					
16		Less time 0 outlay			-2,467,000					
17		Overall NPV			736,942					
18										
19		The NPV is positive so the project should be accepted.								

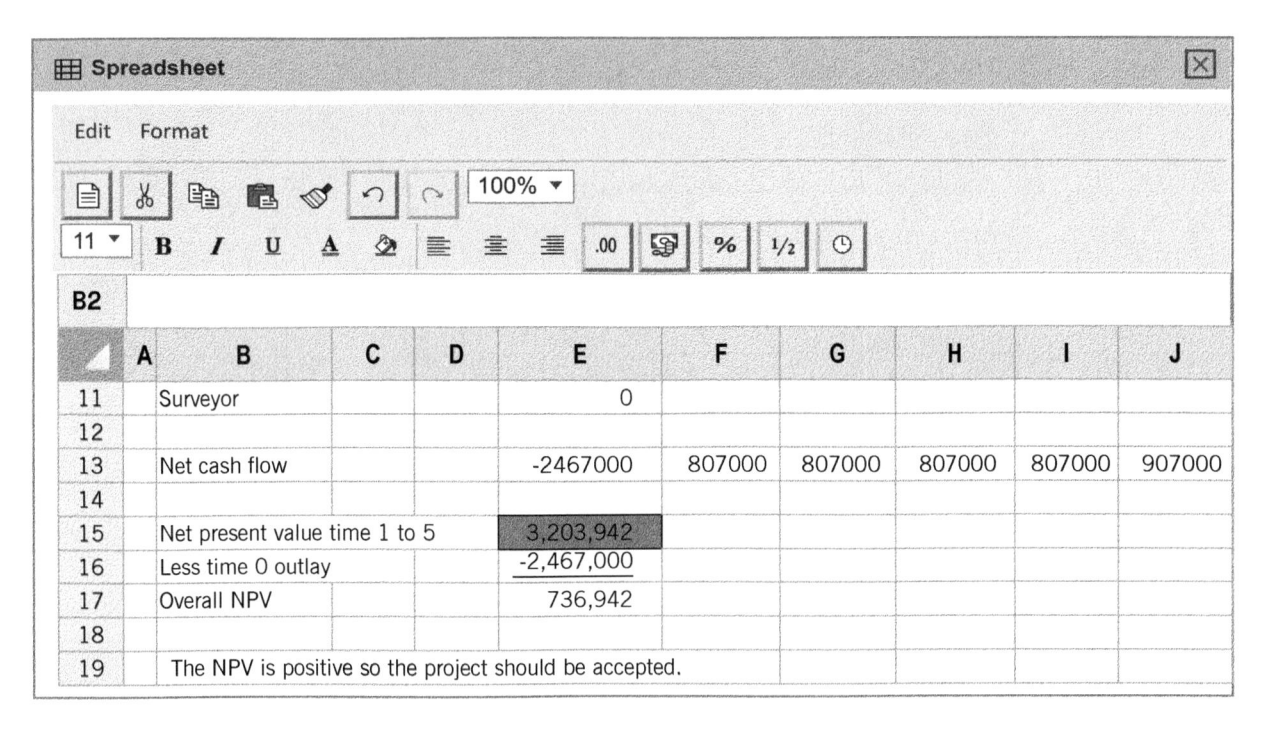

(b)

Word Processor

Benefits of NPV compared to ARR

NPV considers the time value of money whereas the accounting rate of return (ARR) does not. The timings of the cash flow are not recognised in the ARR calculation and thus a $1 received in 15 years' time is deemed to be of equal value to a $1 now. This is rarely the case and therefore is an inaccuracy inherent in the model.

NPV uses cash flow whereas the ARR uses accounting profit. Cash flow is considered to be more accurate and objective for investment appraisal as accounting profit can be calculated using different accounting policies which can result in different profit figures depending on which is used.

The NPV is an absolute measure of the benefit of the project which indicates the increase in shareholder wealth which will result from a project with a positive NPV. ARR on the other hand is a relative measure which makes comparison difficult between projects and the likely impact on shareholders.

The ARR can be calculated using different methods and assumptions which can make comparison difficult, whereas NPV is calculated using universally accepted methods

93 MCQ Answer Bank 12

93.1 The answer is *Quantum meruit*

Quantum meruit is a remedy for breach of contract.

93.2 The answer is Action for the price

Action for the price involves a party taking action against another to recover a sum owed to them.

93.3 The answer is 85c

The correct answer to this question should be
(Profit − Preference share dividend) / Number of shares
$(1{,}500{,}000 − (250{,}000 \times 8\%)) / 1{,}750{,}000 = 84.6c$ or 85c

93.4 The answer is an arrangement whereby a third party takes over the collection of trade debt and advances a proportion of the money it is due to collect. The other options describe invoice discounting, default or credit insurance and the government loan guarantee scheme.

93.5 The answer is The seller's right to hold onto goods that have been sold, if the purchaser does not pay for them and they are still in their possession.

Lien is the seller's right to hold onto goods that have been sold, if the purchaser does not pay for them and they are still in the seller's possession. "The seller's right to retain title for goods until they are paid for." describes retention of title clauses. These clauses differ from lien as they apply even if the goods have been delivered to the purchaser. Lien only applies where the seller still has the goods in their possession.

93.6 The answer is (i) and (ii) only

Only Sale of Land and Consumer Credit Agreements must be in writing. Legally, commercial contracts do not have to be in writing but in practice they are.

93.7 The answer is What each party brings to the contract. Usually it is a promise from one party in return for payment by the other.

Consideration is what each party brings to the contract and is usually a promise in exchange for a price.

93.8 The answer is 5.4

$$P/E = \frac{\text{Market value ex div}}{\text{EPS}}$$

Market value ex div = Market value cum div − dividend due = $(2.85 − 0.15) = $2.70

$$P/E = \frac{\$2.70}{\$0.50} = 5.4$$

93.9 The answer is Administration involves a moratorium over a company's debts while an insolvency practitioner seeks a good resolution for all creditors.

The other options describe receivership, liquidation and voluntary arrangements.

93.10 The answer is Personal visit

Out of all the options, personal visits are the most expensive method of chasing debts.

94 Collecting debts

> **Helping hand.** To answer part (a) fully, you need to explain the nature of these contract clauses and then explain why they may be difficult to apply in practice. If you are not sure about the practical difficulties, you should at least be able to explain the nature of the clauses, to earn some marks.
>
> Debt collection is mainly a commercial activity, not a legal process. However when a debt is unpaid and overdue, a supplier may take legal action to obtain payment of the debt. It is fairly common to use a specialist debt collection agency to do this work. A possible problem is that for personal customers, this may involve giving the debt collection agency some personal information about the customer and data protection issues may arise. Part (b) is only worth five marks; therefore there is a limit to the legal knowledge you are expected to show. Include as much as you can in your answer, and check the answer provided here.
>
> If you are not sure of the answer to part (c), study carefully the answer provided here.

(a) (i) A retention of title clause may be included in a contract to supply materials or components to a commercial customer. The clause states that in the event that the supplier remains the legal owner of the goods until payment has been received, and if the customer fails to pay for the goods within a reasonable time, the supplier has the right to take back possession of the goods.

The problem with this clause is that it is often impractical to enforce. The customer may use several different suppliers, and it may be difficult to identify which physical goods were bought from each supplier. In addition, the customer may have used the goods, or re-sold the goods, so that they are no longer in the customer's possession and the supplier cannot recover them.

(ii) An interest on late payments clause gives the supplier the right to add interest to the amount of the invoice if the customer is late with payment. This is intended to compensate the supplier for financing the customer with the unpaid trade credit.

This clause also has some practical problems. First, there is a problem of issuing one or more new invoices to include the penalty interest charge when the customer is late with payment. The customer may even receive several invoices, each for a different amount of interest.

Customers who are late with payments may eventually to agree to pay what they owe but without the interest penalty. In order to obtain this payment, a supplier may agree to waive the interest charge.

A further problem is that an interest penalty may create ill feeling between the supplier and the customer, and the customer may be reluctant to purchase from the supplier in the future, preferring to use a different supplier instead.

A more appropriate approach to collecting debts than an interest charge for late payments is probably more efficient debt collection procedures and the use of skilled staff in the accounts receivables collection department.

(b) When customers are very late with payments of invoices, a supplier may decide to take legal action to obtain payment. Depending on the amount of money owed, there are certain legal procedures to follow, and the supplier should make use of the services of a lawyer to ensure that the appropriate legal measures are taken correctly.

A supplier must ensure that any measure against a consumer for the collection of an unpaid debt in the UK may be affected by the provisions of the Consumer Credit Act. Letters to the customer asking for payment, for example, need to comply with the requirements of the Act.

Measures to obtain payment through the courts may begin with an application for a County Court judgement against the debtor. When a County Court judgement has been obtained, the supplier may need to use enforcement methods to obtain payment, such as the use of bailiffs.

The demand for payment may even lead eventually to a petition to the court for bankruptcy or insolvency procedures against a customer.

A business may not have the necessary expertise or legal knowledge for the collection of overdue payments by in-house staff, and it may choose to use the services of an external debt collection agency. To do this, the debt collection agency must be provided with sufficient details about the customer to enable it to collect the money, and there is a risk that the provision of information to the agency about personal customers may breach the provisions of the Data Protection Act.

To deal with this problem, the business may ask customers to sign credit agreements that permit it to transfer information about a customer to the debt collection agency.

(c) Insolvency means that an individual or business is unable to pay their debts. This may arise either from lack of cash or negative equity in the statement of financial position. When an individual or business becomes insolvent, legal measures can be taken. Bankruptcy is one legal measure that may be taken against an individual, and a court may be asked to declare an individual bankrupt. When this occurs, the legal provisions relating to bankruptcy are applied. An alternative legal solution to the insolvency of an individual is an Individual Voluntary Agreement between the individual and his creditors.

When a company becomes insolvent, legal measures may be taken for the winding up of the company and the liquidation of its assets to pay the unpaid creditors.

Bankruptcy is therefore a specific legal action in the event of insolvency, which is a more general term. Even so the two terms are often used in practice as if they mean the same thing.

95 Doha Co

(a) **Offer**

An **offer** is a key element in the formation of a **legally binding contract**, made orally or in writing by one party to a contract to the other (for example the offer of a certain price to buy a house). It can be accepted by anyone fulfilling the necessary conditions.

(b) **Acceptance**

Acceptance occurs when the other party makes it known that the **offer is unconditionally accepted**. When it occurs a binding contract is formed. A **request for information** does not constitute acceptance.

(c) **Consideration**

Broadly speaking, consideration is '**an act in return for a promise**'. At its simplest, it is the price to be paid by a buyer in return for the goods that are being supplied by a seller.

96 Receivables analysis

> **Helping hand.** The answer to part (a) requires some organisation, so that the information in the answer is presented in a logical order. Although much of the answer requires a simple list of items in accounts receivable records, it will be improved if you add a few words of explanation.
>
> Part (b) is largely a test of your ability to prepare an aged receivables analysis from a small amount of data in the question. An aged receivables report is of no value unless the information it contains is used. This is the purpose of part (ii) in question (b).

(a) The information in the accounts receivable record of a customer should contain both 'standing' data that does not change often, and transaction data that is continually updated.

The 'standing' data must contain details of the customer:

- Name
- Customer code
- Address
- Other contact details

The standing data should also include commercial data relevant to the customer's account:

- Credit limit
- Credit rating, if the business has a rating system for its customers
- Payment terms, including length of credit allowed and any early settlement discount terms
- Normal payment method (BACS or cheque)

ANSWERS

The record should also contain transaction details, including details of:

- Invoices sent to the customer
- Credit notes issued
- Settlement discounts allowed
- Payments received
- Current unpaid balance

There may also be details of the most recent monthly statement sent to the customer.

Where there have been problems with collecting payments from the customer in the past, there should be a record on file of the details of the problem and how payment was eventually obtained.

(b) (i)

Aged receivables report: 30 November

Customer	Less than 1 month (Nov) $	1 – 2 months (Oct) $	2 – 3 months (Sept) $	Over 3 months $	Total $
AB	500	250			750
CD	800		460		1,260
EF		720			720
GH		640			640
IJ		910		160	1,070
KL		225			225
MN	430				430
OP			370		370
QR	660				660
ST	–	–	–	880	880
Total	2,390	2,745	830	1,040	7,005

We do not know what normal credit terms are offered by this business, but it is normal business practice to offer 30 day credit, and possibly up to 60 days. Credit terms in excess of 60 days (two months) are unusual.

(ii) This report shows that a large amount of receivables have been unpaid for over three months, and there are also unpaid amounts from between two and three months previously. This may indicate poor collection procedures and practices, and urgent measures should be taken to collect the overdue payments.

97 Monitoring accounts receivable

Helping hand. You should quickly prepare a list of the items you intend to include. It is important to spot that there is a distinction between existing credit customers and new customers who are applying for credit for the first time. With existing customers there may be an extensive trading record with the customer that can provide internal information, whereas there is no such internal information for new applicants for credit.

Internal information can be used to monitor existing customers and their payment record.

An aged receivables report should be produced regularly, every month or possibly more frequently. The size and format of the report will depend on the number of credit customers with unpaid invoices. An aged receivables report can provide a list of each credit customer with one or more unpaid invoices, and the period of time for which the invoice has been unpaid. This report can be used for monitoring purposes, because customers who are late with payment scan be identified, and procedures set in process to chase them for payment. In addition, the report will also enable management to monitor the collection for receivables in general, and to assess whether collection processes seem to be operating effectively.

Receivables in general can be monitored by measuring the average time to collect payments, and changes in this average collection period. The actual average collection period can also be compared with the expected average collection period.

FFM FOUNDATIONS IN FINANCIAL MANAGEMENT

The efficiency of credit control and the management of receivables can also be monitored by checking the incidence of bad debts. A high level of bad debts and frequent incidents of bad debts, would be an indication of inefficient collection procedures.

98 VDO Co

Helping hand. In (a) there are only five pieces of information given for industry comparison. Since six marks are available for calculations and comments, you can therefore infer that a further calculation is required beyond those suggested by the comparative figures. The suggested solution includes two that you could choose – the quick ratio and the EPS – however, others could also be used.

In (b) the question asks for reasons for a manufacturing company such as VDO to experience cash shortages in spite of sales growth. It is not asking specifically for reasons for VDO's problems, although these may be relevant to parts of your answer.

(a) (All figures $'000)

Profitability

This is measured by the **return on capital employed** (ROCE).

$$\text{ROCE} = \frac{\text{Profit on ordinary activities before interest (finance cost) and tax (PBIT)}}{\text{Capital employed (equity and bank loan)}}$$

For VDO Co:

	20X1	20X0
PBIT	120	120
Capital employed	850	600
ROCE	14.1%	20%
Industry averages	20%	18%

While VDO's profitability compared favourably with industry averages in 20X0, it has fallen back in 20X1, while average profitability for the industry has increased. Capital employed has risen, reflecting a significant **investment** in both **non-current and current assets**. Although this investment has generated a doubling in the level of sales, this has been at the expense of profit margins, actual profits being unchanged at $120,000. This should be a major concern for the shareholders. The company needs to address its **sales and pricing policies**, and also its **product cost base**, as a matter of urgency.

Liquidity

This is measured by (i) The **current ratio** (current assets: current liabilities) and (ii) The **quick ratio** (current assets excluding inventory: current liabilities).

	20X1	20X0
Current assets	500	300
Inventory	250	100
Current assets excl inventory	250	200
Current liabilities	200	150
Quick ratio	1.25:1	1.33:1
Current ratio	2.5:1	2:1
Industry current ratio	2:1	2:1

At 31 May 20X0, the current ratio was in line with the industry average. By 31 May 20X1, it had risen above the industry average, while at the same time the quick ratio had decreased. This suggests that VDO may be holding an **excessive amount of inventory**. The deterioration in the quick ratio suggests a **reduction** in the **liquidity** of the company.

Working capital ratios

The only working capital ratio that can be compared with the industry averages is the **receivables days**. This measures the average length of time taken by customers to pay their bills. It is calculated as:

ANSWERS

$$\frac{\text{Trade receivables}}{\text{Revenue}} \times 365$$

Note. Credit sales is usually used in this formula, however as that information is not available, revenue is used instead.

	20X1	20X0
Trade receivables	250	120
Revenue	4,000	2,000
Receivables days	23 days	22 days
Industry average	35 days	33 days

Receivables days compare very favourably with the industry average, which suggests that VDO has tight control over its receivables. However, it must consider whether it is damaging its competitive position by imposing **tighter restrictions** on its receivables than does the rest of the industry.

Gearing ratio

This is measured by the debt : equity %.

	20X1	20X0
Long term (non-current) liabilities	200	0
Shareholders' funds	650	600
Debt: Equity %	30.8%	0%
Industry average	20%	20%

The gearing ratio has risen from zero to a level significantly above the industry average. This indicates that the **financial risk** faced by the shareholders has **increased**.

Stock market ratios

These include (i) **Earnings per share (EPS)** and (ii) **Price/earnings (P/E) ratio**. The P/E ratio is calculated as the market price of the share divided by the earnings per share. EPS is calculated as earnings available for dividend divided by the number of shares in issue.

	20X1	20X0
Number of shares	500	500
Earnings	80	96
EPS	16 c	19.2 c
Market price	240c	346c
P/E ratio	15 times	18 times
Industry average	20 times	18 times

Both the earnings per share and the share price have fallen significantly over the past year. The proportionately greater drop in the share price (a fall of 30%) has resulted in a drop in the P/E ratio. This ratio was previously in line with the industry average, indicating that at that time the market believed VDO's growth prospects to be in line with the rest of the industry. However, the position has now changed, and the market perception is that VDO's **earnings prospects** are **significantly below** those for the rest of the industry. These facts taken together should give the shareholders real cause for concern about their investment in the company.

(b) **Possible reasons for cash shortages include the following** (choose any two):

(i) **Lower profit margins** may cause a **fall** in the **level of cash** available in the business. In the case of VDO sales have doubled, but profits have remained unchanged. This could be due to pressure on prices, increases in direct costs, or to increased overheads. The amount of cash generated from operations is therefore unchanged, but the amount of cash required by the increases in working capital needed to generate the additional sales has increased significantly. This is reflected in the conversion of the $80,000 cash resources into a $200,000 term loan – a depletion of the cash level by $280,000.

(ii) Businesses with **long working capital cycles** will need large amounts of cash to finance high levels of inventory and receivables.

FFM FOUNDATIONS IN FINANCIAL MANAGEMENT

(iii) **Seasonal businesses** may have cash flow difficulties at certain times of the year when cash inflows are low but outflows are high, often because the company is producing at a high level ready for the **next period** of **high sales**. An example of this would be a company manufacturing fireworks; pressure on cash would be worst during the summer when fireworks are being produced ready for the increase in demand during the autumn.

(iv) **One-off large items of expenditure** such as the purchase of a freehold property may stretch the cash resources of a company for a long time to come.

(v) **Increased competition** may force a business to reduce prices just to retain its existing volume of sales. This will reduce profit margins and therefore the amount of cash generated by the business will fall.

(vi) **Inflation** means that a company may need **increasing amounts** of cash to **replace used up** and worn out assets. Thus a business that is profitable in historic cost terms may still not be making sufficient money to sustain itself in the long term.

99 Noise Co

Note. Using compound interest rate gives the same answer as the BPP method but using the simple method will give a different answer.

BPP Text method – cost of not taking the discount

$$\left(\frac{100}{98}\right)^{\frac{365}{46}} - 1 = 17.38\%$$

where:

(a) 98 is the discount offered

(b) 46 is the reduction in the payment period in days which would be necessary to obtain the early payment discount (60 – 14)

Noise **should take** the discount as the cost of not taking it (17.38%) exceeds the cost of taking it (12%).

Alternative method – annualised compound/simple effective interest rate

The effective interest rate (over 46 days)

$$\frac{2}{98} = 2.04\%$$

Annualised interest rate

Correct answers could either express the annualised interest rate using compound or simple interest.

Compound interest method

$(1.0204^{365/46} - 1) \times 100 = 17.38\%$

Simple interest method

$2.04\% \times \frac{365}{46} = 16.19\%$

Noise **should take** the discount as the annualised interest rate gained (17.38% or 16.19%) exceeds the benefit of the interest rate foregone (12%).

ANSWERS

100 Credit control

Two features of a credit control system to encourage on time payment. (Only two were required)

Timely and accurate dispatch of invoices

Invoices should be sent out to customers as **soon as possible**. Care must be taken to ensure all the **details**, such as customer name and address are **correct**, and that the invoice contains the correct goods, prices and quantities. The invoice should also be **correct arithmetically**.

This will enable swift delivery to the customer with few queries to delay payment being received.

Supplier terms

Customers should be **made aware of the terms** under which goods are supplied. This can be done at the time the customer's account is set up, when an order is placed and should be given in clear writing on the face of the invoice.

This will **minimise delays** caused by customers not knowing, or 'forgetting' when their payments are due.

Management procedures

Management **should ensure a clear procedure is set up** to manage debts. All customers should be sent a monthly statement of account detailing invoices, payments and a running balance. Overdue amounts should be investigated swiftly and suitable action taken to deal with them. Action may include resolving invoice queries, sending out letters and chasing with phone calls.

Management should also have **procedures in place to deal with non-payment of debts** and passing them over to debt collection agencies.

Customer awareness

Different organisations have **different systems** for making payments to suppliers. Some prefer to make regular payments by on dates, others are flexible to make payments when it suits them according to their cash flow.

A good credit control department should be **aware of the systems** adopted by its customers. This will improve the efficiency of collecting debts if those systems are acceptable. For example if a customer always pays on the last Friday of the month, there is no need to waste resources chasing them on the second Monday.

101 Trade references

Marking scheme

	Marks
Award 1 mark per point up to a maximum of 3 marks for each check	5
Total marks	**5**

Trade references

Here, the vendor asks the credit applicant for the names of its existing suppliers, usually two, whom it may approach and ask for comments on the customer's credit record. The vendor should specify the amount of credit involved and the payment terms it requires. Trade references provide a cheap source of information, but their value is limited as credit applicants are likely only to choose suppliers who will give a favourable reference.

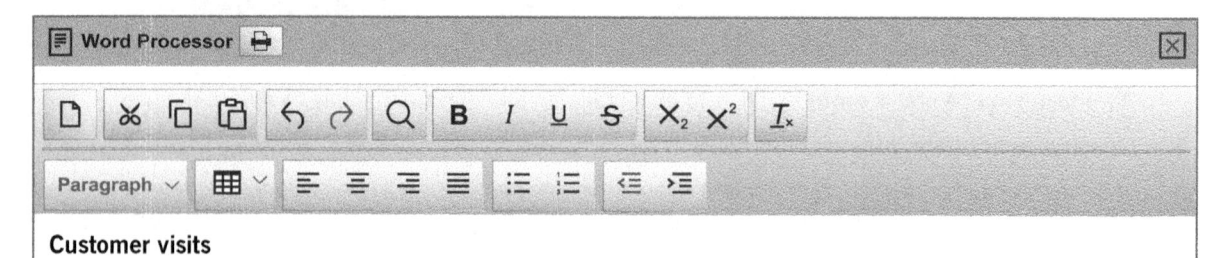

> **Customer visits**
>
> These involve visits to the customer's premises by credit control staff. They provide an opportunity to resolve queries arising from other credit reference data and give the credit controller an opportunity to get a detailed view of the customer's business. For example, the adequacy of the premises and the level of organisation in the accounts department. Customer visits can take up a lot of credit controller time and be expensive. They are only likely to be economic for large customers.

102 Expander Co

> **Helping hand.** Construction of the aged receivables schedules is easier if in your workings you tabulate the monthly sales and date of receipt for each of the customer types. When commenting on the figures in (a) you should take into account the situation of the company as described, and think in practical terms of the risks that it faces.
>
> In (b) remember the distinction between internal sources (generated by the company) and external sources (maintained by somebody else). Both types of source can provide useful information.

(a) **Expander Co: Aged receivables forecast as at 31 January 20X0**

Customer type	2 mths (Nov) $	1 mth (Dec) $	Current (Jan) $	Total $
Mobile phone shops			90,000	90,000
Specialist chain stores			200,000	200,000
Internet service providers			150,000	150,000
Total outstanding			440,000	440,000

Expander Co: Aged receivables forecast as at 29 February 20X0

Customer type	2 mths (Dec) $	1 mth (Jan) $	Current (Feb) $	Total $
Mobile phone shops			94,500	94,500
Specialist chain stores		200,000	210,000	410,000
Internet service providers		150,000	165,000	315,000
Total outstanding		350,000	469,500	819,500

Workings

	$ per unit	Units sold Jan	Growth rate %	Sales Jan $	Sales Feb $
Mobile phone shops	50	2,000	5	100,000	105,000
Cash sales				10,000	10,500
Credit sales				90,000	94,500
Month received				Feb	Mar
Outstanding at month end				90,000	94,500

ANSWERS

	$ per unit	Units sold Jan	Growth rate %	Sales Jan $	Feb $
Specialist chain stores	40	5,000	5	200,000	210,000
Month received				Apr	May
Outstanding at month end				200,000	410,000

	$ per unit	Units sold Jan	Growth rate %	Sales Jan $	Feb $
Internet service providers	30	5,000	10	150,000	165,000
Month received				Apr	May
Outstanding at month end				150,000	315,000

(b) **Factors to be considered when assessing creditworthiness of new customers**

Any two from:

(i) New customer should give **two good references**, including one from a bank, before being granted credit.

(ii) Credit ratings can be checked using a **credit rating agency**.

(iii) For large value customers, **a file** should be maintained of any available **financial information** about the customer, and its contents regularly reviewed.

(iv) The company could send a member of staff to **visit** the customer's premises, to get a first hand impression of the company and its prospects. This is particularly important in the case of prospective major customers.

103 Beff Co

Helping hand. (a) and (b) represent a hunt for worrying signs. What you are looking for is not just signs that a company is having problems paying suppliers, but signs of other problems that could in the fullness of time pull the company down. Does a high receivables level indicate poor management? Do increasing inventory levels indicate products that are no longer popular because they are perceived as out of date?

Marking scheme

		Marks
(a)	Cost now – current receivables (1 mark) × 5% (1 mark)	2
	Factor – new receivables (1 mark) split OFR 75:25 (1 mark) 75% × 8% (1 mark)	
	25% × 5% (1 mark) admin fee (1 mark)	5
	Credit controller – salary (1 mark) mew receivables (1 mark) × 5% (1 mark)	3
	Conclusion OFR	1
		11
(b)	Up to 2 marks per benefit	4
Total marks		15

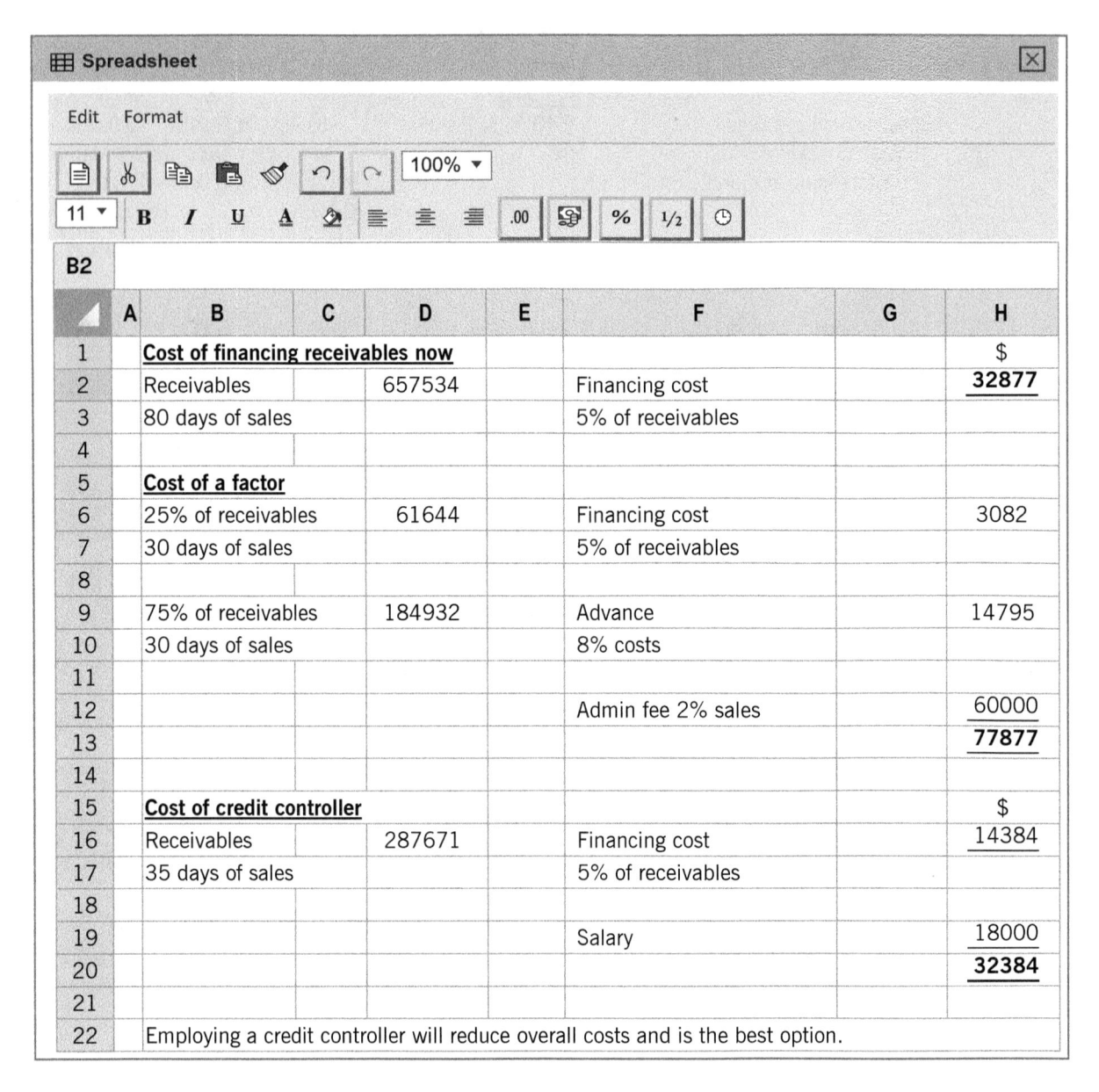

	A	B	C	D	E	F	G	H
1		**Cost of financing receivables now**						$
2		Receivables		657534		Financing cost		**32877**
3		80 days of sales				5% of receivables		
4								
5		**Cost of a factor**						
6		25% of receivables		61644		Financing cost		3082
7		30 days of sales				5% of receivables		
8								
9		75% of receivables		184932		Advance		14795
10		30 days of sales				8% costs		
11								
12						Admin fee 2% sales		60000
13								**77877**
14								
15		**Cost of credit controller**						$
16		Receivables		287671		Financing cost		14384
17		35 days of sales				5% of receivables		
18								
19						Salary		18000
20								**32384**
21								
22		Employing a credit controller will reduce overall costs and is the best option.						

Tutorial note. The workings here are simple enough to be embedded in the cells of the spreadsheet. The following table shows the formulae that have been used to generate these values and is shown here as a student aid, it would not be produced as a part of your answer.

ANSWERS

Spreadsheet

	A	B	C	D	E	F	G	H
1		**Cost of financing receivables now**						$
2		Receivables		=3000000*80/365		Financing cost		**=D2*0.05**
3		80 days of sales				5% of receivables		
4								
5		**Cost of a factor**						
6		25% of receivables		=3000000*30/365*0.25		Financing cost		=D6*0.05
7		30 days of sales				5% of receivables		
8								
9		75% of receivables		=3000000*30/365*0.75		Advance		=D9*0.08
10		30 days of sales				8% costs		
11								
12						Admin fee 2% sales		=3000000*0.02
13								**=H12+H9+H6**
14								
15		**Cost of credit controller**						$
16		Receivables		=3000000*35/365		Financing cost		=D16*0.05
17		35 days of sales				5% of receivables		
18								
19						Salary		18000
20								**=H16+H19**
21								

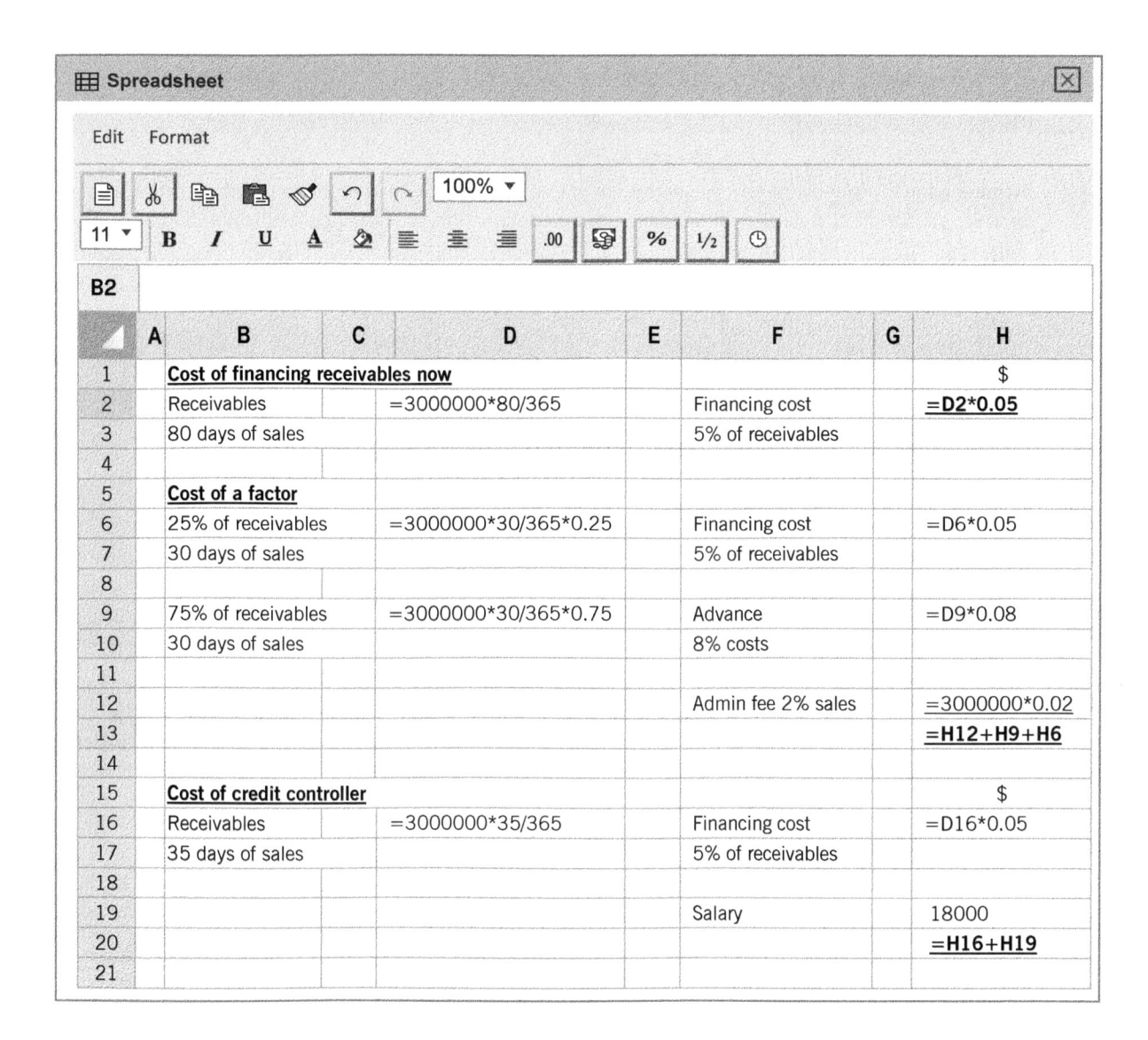

(b)

Benefits of using a factor

– A factor company is an outsourcing company which will take over the entire credit control function of a company. The main advantage of this is that it frees up the time of management to focus on the core products or services of a company.

– Factoring is a source of finance which grows along with the business. As the factor advances a proportion of the receivables balance, the extension in working capital is controlled.

– To small companies particularly, the non-recourse agreements which some factor companies provide can equate to a huge reduction in risk.

– In addition, the factor company is an expert in credit control and will often reply to customer queries and requests in a systematic and professional manner. This may mean that customers' perception of the company is enhanced.

Note. Only TWO benefits were required

104 Waste Co

> **Helping hand.** This question requires a considerable amount of explanation of text book knowledge so you must be clear in your mind of what debt factoring, invoice discounting and credit control is and how they work.
>
> Part (c) requires a straightforward comparison of costs under one option versus another. Always read the question carefully to ensure you pick everything up – it would be quite easy to miss the 25% increase in sales.

(a) **Debt factoring**

'Debt factoring' is a service provided by factors whereby the factor collects accounts receivable on behalf of their client and often invoices their client's customers as well. The factor also advances, to its client, a proportion of the money it is due to collect (typically about 80% is advanced).

Mr Trusty would find the service useful because he could both receive cash early and also delegate the administration of his invoicing, accounting and accounts receivable collection work.

There are two types of factoring agreements: 'with recourse' and 'without recourse' agreements. With the first of these agreements, although the factor advances monies, the risk of non-payment of accounts receivable balances stays with the client. If a balance is not recovered, the factor has 'recourse' to their client for the money. If the agreement is 'without recourse' the factor bears the risk of non-payment.

Debt factoring has to be paid for, usually as a percentage of the amounts advanced and as a percentage of turnover. Agreements without recourse to the client obviously cost more. Mr Trusty would have to compare the cost to those of employing an individual to do his invoicing and obtaining insurance against unpaid accounts receivable balances. In addition, there may be some stigma attached to debt factoring as clients sometimes assume that a business using a factor must be in financial difficulty.

(b) **Difference from invoice discounting**

Invoice discounting is a service whereby a provider (often a factoring company) purchases invoices from a client at a discount. In this case, they are merely advancing cash, rather than providing an accounts receivable collection service. For this reason, there is no administration fee payable (like there is for factoring), making invoice discounting a cheaper option.

(c) **Whether to factor accounts receivables**

Cost of factoring

New sales level = $2,550,000 × 125%	$3,187,500
Accounts receivable reduced to 35 days:	
$3,187,500 × 35/365	$305,651

	$
80% advanced by factor at 12%: $305,651 × 80% × 12%	29,342
20% still financed by overdraft: $305,651 × 20% × 10%	6,113
Admin fee: $3,187,500 × 1.3%	41,438
	76,893

Cost of not factoring but employing new staff

Accounts receivable reduced to 40 days:

$3,187,500 × 40/365	$349,315

	$
Overdraft cost $349,315 × 10%	34,932
Credit controller costs	47,000
	81,932

Waste Co should use the services of the factor since this will produce a saving, over the next year, of $5,039, compared to employing a credit controller.

ANSWERS

105 Jay Co

> **Helping hand.** To answer this question well you must know the receivables collection period and bad debt ratios and how to apply them. Remember to ignore any cash sales and therefore you should deduct them from the total sales figure to come to the credit sales figure.
>
> The other part of the question may require a brief explanation of facts. Be careful not to spend too long answering it by writing more than what is needed.

(a) **Current receivables collection period**

Credit sales = $1,581,743 − $14,250
= $1,567,493

Receivables days = receivables/credit sales × 365
= ($323,654 ÷ $1,567,493) × 365
= 75 days

(b) **Receivables needs to be reduced to:**

$1,567,493 × 45/365 = $193,253

Debts to be collected immediately = $323,654 − $193,253
= $130,401

(c) **Bad debt ratio**

Bad debt ratio = bad debts/credit sales × 100%
= $26,784 ÷ $1,567,493 × 100%
= 1.7%

(d) **Procedures for collecting debts**

(i) Telephone customers and request that they pay their debts as soon as possible, informing them if they have exceeded their credit period.

(ii) Write to customers, enclosing a copy of their most recent statement showing all their outstanding invoices.

(iii) Arrange a personal visit to customers' premises so that you can discuss the need for payment and any reasons for nonpayment.

(iv) Freeze customers' accounts so that they are forced to pay before they can order more goods.

(v) Send customers formal warnings or final demands, stating that if their debts are not paid, further action will be taken, and stating what that further action is.

(vi) Refer the debts to a debt collection agency who will pursue debts on the company's behalf.

(vii) Arrange for your solicitor to send your overdue customers a letter stating that if payment is not received within a certain period, legal proceedings will be commenced.

(viii) Commence legal proceedings ie issue a summons or a writ (depending on the amount of the debt).

Note. Only three were required.

106 Light Co

> **Helping hand.** Part (b) is straightforward if you remember that factoring is financially viable if it is cheaper than using the overdraft. Show all your workings as you will gain marks for method even if you get the numbers wrong.

(a) **Maximum discount**

To decide the **maximum discount** that Light Co should offer to its customers the company needs to consider the **cost** of the discount and the **benefit** of a reduced investment in receivables. At the very least the discount should not leave the company any worse off financially.

By offering a discount Light Co will save overdraft interest at 12% for a period of 23 days (the 30 day average payment period of customers reduced to a maximum of 7 to obtain the discount).

The maximum discount that should be offered is therefore:

$(1.12^{23/365} - 1) \times 100 = 0.717\%$

(b) **Whether to factor**

It will be **financially viable** for Light Co to factor its receivables if the cost of factoring is less than using the overdraft as finance.

Cost of finance using the overdraft

Sales	= $13,200,000 (current sales of $12m increased by 10%)
Receivables	= $2,531,507 (daily sales of $13.2m/365 = $36,164 × 70 days)
Cost of overdraft finance	= $2,531,507 × 0.12 = $303,781 (receivables' balance × 12% per year)

Cost of factoring

Sales	= $13,200,000
Receivables	= $1,012,603 (daily sales of $13.2m/365 × 28 days)
80% to be factored	= $810,082 ($1,012,603 × 0.8)
Balance to be financed by overdraft	= $202,521
Interest charge on advances	= $105,311 ($810,082 × 13%)
Overdraft interest on balance	= $24,303 ($202,521 × 12%)
Admin fee	= $198,000 ($13.2m × 1.5%)
Salary saved	= ($18,000)
Total cost	= $309,614

It is **not financially viable** to factor the receivables as it is more expensive than using the overdraft by $5,833.

107 Waste Co

> **Helping hand.** You can divide this into two distinct sections – defining debt factoring and then distinguishing between 'with recourse' and 'without recourse'. When distinguishing between the two, you will have to define each first.

Debt factoring is an arrangement to have debts collected by a factor company which advances a proportion of the money it is due to collect (typically about 80%). Mr Trusty is likely to find this service useful as it would help with liquidity and also enable him to delegate responsibility of debt collection to a third party.

There are two types of factoring arrangements – 'with recourse' and 'without recourse'.

'With recourse' means that the risk of non-payment by customers remains with the company rather than with the factor. The factor still advances money to the company but if a balance is not recovered the factor has 'recourse' to their client for the money.

'Without recourse' means that if the client's customers do not pay what they owe, the factor will not ask for the money back from the client.

A debt factoring service has to be paid for (usually a percentage of the amounts advanced and a percentage of turnover). The 'without recourse' arrangement will cost more than the 'with recourse' option. Mr Trusty will have to compare the cost of factoring and the insurance it brings with the unpaid accounts receivable balances. There may be some stigma attached to employing a factor as it may give the signal that the company is in financial difficulty.

ANSWERS

108 Mr Allan

> **Helping hand.** This question requires a comparison between the cost of factoring and the cost of not factoring. Don't forget to recommend whether Mr Allan should factor or not – there will be a mark for the recommendation.

With factoring:

		$
Interest on advance	80% × $75,000 × 30/365 × 8%	395
Administration fee	2% × $75,000	1,500
Wages		1,000
Overdraft interest	20% × $75,000 × 30/365 × 10%	123
		3,018

109 Mixed bank 1

109.1 The answer is Raw materials purchases

Raw material purchases will vary according to production requirements.

109.2 The answer is 30%

$$\text{Margin} = \frac{\text{Profit}}{\text{Selling price}}$$

Selling price = $35 + $15 = $50

$$\text{Margin} = \frac{\$15}{\$50}$$

= 30%

109.3 The answer is $\frac{\text{Average payables}}{\text{Purchases on credit terms}} \times 365 \text{ days}$

This is the accounts payable payment period ratio.

109.4 The answer is A measure of the value of work done under a contract

Quantum meruit is the measure of the value of work done under a contract.

109.5 The answer is A central bank

A central bank is the lender of last resort within an economy.

109.6 The answer is 17.7%

According to the Fisher effect, the required nominal rate of interest is:

(1 + real rate of return) × (1 + inflation rate)

= 1.07 × 1.10

= 1.177 or 17.7%

109.7 The answer is quantitative covenant

Setting limitations, such as total borrowings shall not exceed total shareholders' funds, is known as a quantitative covenant.

109.8 The answer is Variable costs

Over a sufficiently long enough period, all costs will eventually become variable costs.

FFM FOUNDATIONS IN FINANCIAL MANAGEMENT

109.9   The answer is $14 per kg

The relevant cost is $14 per kg. Since the material has no other use except as a substitute for material B, it would either be used in place of B or sold. As the company would only get $8 per kg from selling it, its best use is as a substitute, therefore saving $14 per kg.

109.10   The answer is $1,205

Year	$	Present value factor at 10%	Present value $
0	10,000	1.000	(10,000)
1	2,000	0.909	1,818
2	5,000	0.826	4,130
3	7,000	0.751	5,257
			1,205

110 Mixed bank 2

110.1   The answer is the cash book and cleared funds statement

Float causes the difference between what a company's cash book and cleared funds statement show as its cash position. Float is caused by timing differences, for example the delay in banking cheques, which are shown in the cash book once issued but do not affect cleared funds until the payment leaves the company's bank account.

110.2   The answer is All of them

They may all cause cash flow problems.

Trading losses mean the company takes in less cash than it pays out. Inflation causes the cost of raw materials and labour to rise and the company may not be able to pass these higher costs on to the customer. Growth requires investment in non-current assets and working capital - these must be paid for and the company may not feel the benefit of their cash generation for some time. Seasonal trends mean a company may have several 'quiet' months where little cash is received, but it may still have a level of costs that must be paid for.

110.3   The answer is It has a low proportion of debt to equity

Gearing is the measure of debt against equity within a company. Low geared companies have a low proportion of debt to equity.

110.4   The answer is (i), (iii) and (iv) only

General provisions for doubtful debt are not an allowable expense for tax purposes. Specific irrecoverable debts, however, are an allowable expense. Interest payments are generally allowed to be set off against tax.

110.5   The answer is Business and personal contacts

Business angel finance is usually obtained through business and personal contacts.

110.6   The answer is to purchase inventory

Long-term loans should be used to purchase assets that will benefit the company for a number of years rather than as a source of working capital.

110.7   The answer is 1.96%

$$\text{The real rate of interest} = \frac{\text{nominal rate of interest}}{1+\text{rate of inflation}} - 1$$

$$= \frac{1.04}{1.02} - 1 - 1$$

$$= 0.0196$$

$$= 1.96\%$$

110.8　　The answer is (ii), (iii) and (iv) only

Depreciation is not a cash flow and therefore is not a relevant cost. (ii) is an opportunity cost. (iii) and (iv) are avoidable costs and therefore also relevant.

110.9　　The answer is 7.27%

$$\text{IRR} = 5 + \left[\frac{2{,}500}{2{,}500 - -3{,}000} \times (10 - 5)\right]$$

IRR = 5 + 2.27 = 7.27%

110.10　　The answer is Profit and non-current assets both understated

If capital expenditure items were treated as revenue expenditure in a company's accounts, then profit on the statement of profit or loss and non-current assets on the statement of financial position would both be understated. This is because the debit for the asset would be posted as an expense on the statement of profit or loss rather than to the statement of financial position.

111 Mixed bank 3

111.1　　The answer is Statement 1 only

Only statement 1 is true

111.2　　The answer is 1.08

(216 + 42)/(180 + 60) = 1.08, to 2 dp

111.3　　The answer is 7.1%

$$\text{IRR} = 5\% + \left(\frac{20}{20+28} \times [10\% - 5\%]\right)$$

111.4　　The answer is (ii) and (iii) only

A decrease in the period of credit given by suppliers and an increase in the period of credit given to customers.

111.5　　The answer is (ii) and (iii) only

(i) is incorrect since holding costs decrease, not increase

111.6　　The answer is (i) and (ii) only

(iii) is wrong since time deposits don't have to be immediately available for withdrawal

111.7　　The answer is 17%

$$\text{IRR} = 10\% + \left(\frac{56}{56+28} \times [10\% - 20\%]\right)$$

= 16.67%

111.8　　The answer is 73 days

$$\frac{\text{work-in-progress}}{\text{COS} \times \text{degree of completion}} \times 365 = \frac{30{,}000}{300{,}000} \times 365 \times 365$$

= 73 days

111.9　　The answer is (ii) and (iii) only

(i) is wrong since most contracts don't have to be in a strict legal form

111.10　　The answer is All of the above

All of them are potential remedies.

112 Mixed Bank 4

112.1 The answer is $28,846

	$
Raw materials costs = $2.5m × 10%	250,000
Labour = $2.5m × 15%	375,000
Overheads = $2.5 × 5%	125,000
COS	750,000
Finished goods = $750,000 × 2/52	28,846

The other options are based on incorrect assumptions:

$250,000 × 2/52 =	9,615
$750,000 × 4/52 =	57,962
($250,000 + 375,000) × 2/52 =	24,038

112.2 The answer is $288,462

Receivables = $2.5m × 6/52	288,462

The other options could be calculated based on incorrect assumptions:

$2.5m × 8/52 =	384,615
$750,000 × 6/52 =	86,538
$750,000 × 8/52 =	115,385

112.3 The answer is Cash.

The others are all money market instruments.

112.4 The answer is **both** Assumption 1 and Assumption 2

Both of these are assumptions of the model.

112.5 The answer is Statement 2 is true and statement 1 is false

Only statement 2 is correct.

112.6 The answer is 20%

ARR = average annual profits (after depreciation)/average investment.
Annual depreciation = cost-residual value/10 = $100,000 per annum.
Profits after depreciation = $250,000 – $100,000 = $150,000 per annum
Average investment = $1,250,000 + 250,000/2 = $750,000
Therefore, ARR = $150,000/$750,000 = 20%.

The other options could be obtained through:

- Using average value of investment as $1,250,000 – 250,000 = $1,000,000
  150,000/1,000,000 = 15%.

- Erroneously ignoring depreciation = $250,000/$750,000 = 33%.

- Making both of those mistakes $250,000/$1,000,000 = 25%.

112.7 The answer is Neither X nor Y

Variable cost of producing X = $12 + $25 + $8 = $45.

Variable cost of producing Y = $13 + $27 + $7 = $47.

Since variable cost of producing both X & Y is less than buying them in, buy neither

If fixed costs are erroneously included, answer will be different.

112.8 The answer is $500

Relevant cost = Cost of best alternative = $500 (use as substitute)

ANSWERS

The other options are:

- Historic cost
- Proceeds of selling
- Net sale proceeds

112.9 The answer is Statement 2 only

Only statement 2 is true.

112.10 The answer is both statements are true.

113 Mixed bank 5

113.1 The answer is $80,000

	$
Non-current assets as at 31 December X6	250,000
Add back depreciation	30,000
Non-current assets as at 31 December X5	(200,000)
	80,000

The other options

- Ignore depreciation and look at the change in non-current assets only or
- Take closing assets as at 31 December X6.
- Or deduct rather than add back depreciation.

113.2 The answer is payback is 3.9 years   accounting rate of return is 11%

Time	Cash flow ($)	Cumulative cash flow ($)
0	(100,000)	(100,000)
2	35,000	(65,000)
3	35,000	(30,000)
4	35,000	5,000

Payback is therefore three years and (30,000/35,000) = 3.9 years.

Accounting rate of return = average annual accounting profit/initial investment Accounting rate of return = [(4 × 35,000 – 85,000)/5]/100,000 = 11%.

The other options arise if depreciation is excluded from the accounting rate of return or the timing of the cash flows is incorrect in the payback calculation.

113.3 The answer is (ii) only. Shareholders should benefit if a project is accepted which has a positive net present value.

113.4 The answer is Inventory

The others are all closer to cash.

113.5 The answer is 45%

Cost of not taking the discount = cost/benefit = 2/98 = 0.0204%

Convert to an annual percentage = $[\{1+0.0204\}^{365/20} - 1] = 45\%$

The other options can be arrived at by incorrectly using the following calculations:

- 2% × 12 = 24%
- $[\{1+2/98\}^{365/30} - 1] = 28\%$
- $[\{1+2/100\}^{365/30} - 1] = 27\%$

113.6 The answer is Quick ratio: Increase Accounts receivable payment period: No change

The transaction is for cash so accounts receivable are not affected. Inventory is not part of the quick ratio. Cash balances will improve, resulting in the quick ratio increasing.

113.7   The answer is A statutory demand for payment is issued

The other options come later in the process.

113.8   The answer is $20,000

50% × 25,000 + 30% × 15,000 + 15% × 20,000

The other options can be arrived at by incorrectly using the following calculations:

- Months incorrect and start with March (50% × 20,000 + 30% × 15,000 + 15% × 25,000 = 18,250)
- Accounting for bad debts within the original sales (50% × 25,000 x 0.95 + 30% × 15,000 + 15% × 20,000 = 19,375)
- May's sales

113.9   The answer is Unsystematic risk

By definition

113.10   The answer is $800

As the material is in frequent use by the company, the current purchase price is used as the relevant cost.

The other options can be arrived at by incorrectly using the following calculations:

- 50 × 7 + 50 × 8 = 750 ie NRV is used for the kgs in inventory
- 50 × 6 + 50 × 8 = 700 ie original cost is used for the kgs in inventory
- Using the original cost price of $6 to value the 100 kgs required

114 Mixed bank 6

114.1   The answer is 3.91%

Interest yield = (Coupon rate/Market price) × 100 = (4/102.25) × 100 = 3.91%

114.2   The answer is 17%

$$\left[\left(\frac{100}{100-d}\right)^{\frac{365}{t}} - 1\right]\% = [100/(100-1)]^{365/23} - 1 = 17.29\% \text{ (say 17\%)}$$

114.3   The answer is 1 and 2

Both retention of titles and period of free credit are optional terms and conditions that can be offered to a customer

114.4   The answer is both statements are true

Quantitative covenants are promises by the borrower to do something (for example, provide the bank with its annual financial statements). Quantitative covenants are promises by the borrower to keep within the specified financial limits.

114.5   The answer is Bill of exchange

A Bill of exchange is an unconditional offer in writing from one party to another regarding the party to whom it is addressed to pay a specified sum of money on demand (sight bill) or at a future date (term bill).

114.6 The answer is 20%

Depreciation = ($1.25 million − $250,000)/10 = $100,000

Profit per annum = $250,000 − $100,000 = $150,000

Average value of investment = ($1.25 million + $250,000)/2 = $750,000

ARR = $150,000/$750,000 = 20%

114.7 The answer is (i) and (ii) only

A customer's money does not have to be always available for immediate withdrawal.

114.8 The answer is $500

The relevant cost is the opportunity cost (the next best alternative use of the material) which is using it as a substitute for Material A. If the material was used in another contract, the company would have to buy Material A at a cost of $500. The other alternative is to sell the material for $490 which is of less value than the money saved by not having to purchase Material A.

114.9 The answer is (ii) and (iii) only

Holding costs will decrease as no inventory will actually be kept in store. Labour productivity will improve as there will be no down time waiting for material to arrive. Manufacturing lead times will decrease as there will be no time built in for waiting for delivery of inventory.

114.10 The answer is $90,000

	$
Non-current assets at end of 20X8	270,000
Add back depreciation	40,000
Less non-current assets at end of 20X7	(220,000)
Non-current assets purchased in 20X8	90,000

115 Mixed bank 7

115.1 The answer is (i) and (iii)

Reduction in credit rating and difficulty in obtaining credit from new suppliers.

115.2 The answer is 17%

$$\left(\frac{100}{100-1}\right)^{365/23} - 1 = 17.3\%$$

$$\left(1+\frac{1}{99}\right)^{365/23} - 1 = 17.3\%$$

115.3 The answer is 9,500.

Maximum inventory level = reorder level + reorder quantity − (min. usage × min. lead time).

Reorder level = max. usage × max. lead time = 1,000 × 10 = 10,000 kg.

Max. inventory level = 10,000 + 1,000 − (300 × 5) = 11,000 − 1,500 = 9,500.

The other options can be arrived at by incorrectly using the following calculations:
- 10 × 1,000
- 5 × 300
- 10 × 1,000 − 5 × 300

115.4 The answer is Bill of exchange

115.5 The answer is $17,124 cost

	$
Admin fee: $5,000,000 × 1%	50,000
Cost of financing receivables	
$5,000,000 × 30/365 × 8%	32,877
Total cost with factor	82,877
Less cost before factor	65,753
Net cost of factor	–17,124

115.6 The answer is the central bank.

The central bank is the government's banker. Investment and commercial banks may buy government debt but will not manage it. Debt factors work with commercial companies to help with credit control.

115.7 The answer is $209,350

The annuity factor at 10% per annum over a period of 5 years (3.791) is based on the same net cash flow arising at the end of each of the 5 years. It is multiplied by the figure of $64,000 to determine the present value (PV) of the net cash inflows. The resulting figure is $242,624. Because the net present value (NPV) of the investment project (ie PV of the net cash flows compared with the investment amount) is positive $33,274 then the investment amount will be less than the PV of the net cash inflows by that amount. Thus the investment amount is $209,350 ($242,624 - $33,274)

115.8 The answer is only statement 2 is true.

115.9 The answer is 1.71%

Interest yield = coupon rate/market price × 100% = 4/102.25 × 100% = 3.91%.

The other options can be arrived at by incorrectly using different concepts:

- Treating the interest yield as the same as coupon rate.
- Using the redemption yield not the interest yield.

Loss on redemption = $102.25 – $100 = $2.25.

$2.25/102.25 = 2.2%

Therefore, redemption yield = 3.91 – 2.2 = 1.71%

Showing the redemption LOSS as percentage (see above).

115.10 The answer is 8%

$$IRR = A + \left[\frac{a}{a-b} \times (B-A)\right]$$

Where A is the lower rate and B is the higher rate; a is the NPV at the lower rate and b is the NPV at the higher rate.

$$5\% + \frac{24,800}{37,200} \times (5\%) = \underline{approx.\ 8\%}$$

The other options could be calculated if the IRR formula was applied incorrectly.

116 Mixed bank 8 (December 2019 real exam)

116.1 The correct answer is borrowing can be arranged in bulk giving access to lower interest rate

116.2 The correct answer is the interest rate is normally lower than for long-term borrowing

116.3 The correct answer is Transactions, precautionary and speculative are the three motives identified by Keynes, therefore inflationary is the correct answer

116.4   The correct answer is $400,000/$0.25/3 × $5.00 × 0.9 = $2,400,000

116.5   The correct answer is to vote at company annual general meetings

There is no guaranteed dividend payment assurance that shares can be sold back to the company at the purchase price they paid and they rank after debt holders in the event of the company's liquidation.

116.6   The correct answer is 7.1 %

(1.05 × 1.02) – 1 = 7.1 %

116.7   The correct answer is $2.00

PAT and preference dividend/ordinary shares

($16m – $2m)/7m = $2.00

116.8   The correct answer is 1 and 2 only

Small young companies often suffer from a lack of assets to provide security for loans and trading track record. A lack of innovative ideas is rarely sited.

116.9   The correct answer is Bankruptcy

Bankruptcy is a term applied to individuals and not companies.

116.10   The correct answer is current ratio unchanged, acid test decreases

As the purchase of inventory for cash does not change the total value of current assets, the current ratio is unchanged. However, as inventory is excluded from the acid test ratio, the reduction in cash will cause the ratio to decrease.

116.11   The correct answer is 14.93%

14.93% $(1 + (2/98))^{365/(60-7)} - 1 = 14.93\%$

116.12   The correct answer is $51,200

$6.4m × 80% × (9% – 8%) = $51,200

116.13   The correct answer is An agreement by the borrower to obligations over and above repaying the loan

116.14   The correct answer is 2 only

A scrip (or bonus) issue of new equity shares will only dilute the value of the individual shares and redeemable preference shares are not equity. Therefore only a reduction in dividend paid can increase the equity finance available.

116.15   The correct answer is 1, 2 and 3

Credit control administration, finance provision and bad debt insurance are all services offered by factoring companies.

117 Mixed bank 9 (June 2020 real exam)

117.1   The correct answer is current assets less current liabilities

117.2   The correct answer is $5,559

Calculated by (($100 × 1,200 × 12 × 2/$0.2) 0.5 × $0.2) + $4,800

117.3   The correct answer is both supplier A and supplier B

Supplier A is more attractive as a 3% discount is better than a 2% discount when the number of days credit remains unchanged.

Supplier B is more attractive as the number of days free credit has increased from seven to ten.

117.4   The correct answer is ordinary shares, certificates of deposit, government stock

FFM FOUNDATIONS IN FINANCIAL MANAGEMENT

117.5 The correct answer is to enable companies to raise new finance

117.6 The correct answer is preparation of the company's annual report

Liquidity management, foreign exchange risk management and banking relationships are all mainstream areas of responsibility for the treasury function.

117.7 The correct answer is 1 and 3

Taxation does not form part of a government's monetary policy.

117.8 The correct answer is accountancy firms

Accountancy firms is the correct answer as they do not act as intermediaries on the capital markets.

117.9 The correct answer is $0.38

($12m – $4m – $0.4m)/$20m = $0.38

117.10 The correct answer is $2,226

$8,025/3.605 = $2,226

117.11 The correct answer is maximum usage (units per day) × maximum lead time (days)

With all other options, it is possible that a company would run out of inventory.

117.12 The correct answer is 1 and 3 only

If a company buys under a long-term fixed price contract, it will have safeguarded against the effects of inflation, and will not experience a decrease in wealth as a result of this.

117.13 The correct answer is $25

$25 is the correct answer as it represents the hourly rate + contribution lost.

117.14 The correct answer is 1 and 2 only

A rights issue is offered to existing shareholders.

117.15 The correct answer is 2 only

Low capital gearing means that the value of a company's equity is high compared to the value of its prior charge capital.

Appendix: Mathematical tables

Present Value Table

Present value of 1 i.e. $(1 + r)^{-n}$

Where   r = discount rate
              n = number of periods until payment

Discount rate (r)

Periods (n)	1%	2%	3%	4%	5%	6%	7%	8%	9%	10%	
1	0·990	0·980	0·971	0·962	0·952	0·943	0·935	0·926	0·917	0·909	1
2	0·980	0·961	0·943	0·925	0·907	0·890	0·873	0·857	0·842	0·826	2
3	0·971	0·942	0·915	0·889	0·864	0·840	0·816	0·794	0·772	0·751	3
4	0·961	0·924	0·888	0·855	0·823	0·792	0·763	0·735	0·708	0·683	4
5	0·951	0·906	0·863	0·822	0·784	0·747	0·713	0·681	0·650	0·621	5
6	0·942	0·888	0·837	0·790	0·746	0·705	0·666	0·630	0·596	0·564	6
7	0·933	0·871	0·813	0·760	0·711	0·665	0·623	0·583	0·547	0·513	7
8	0·923	0·853	0·789	0·731	0·677	0·627	0·582	0·540	0·502	0·467	8
9	0·914	0·837	0·766	0·703	0·645	0·592	0·544	0·500	0·460	0·424	9
10	0·905	0·820	0·744	0·676	0·614	0·558	0·508	0·463	0·422	0·386	10
11	0·896	0·804	0·722	0·650	0·585	0·527	0·475	0·429	0·388	0·350	11
12	0·887	0·788	0·701	0·625	0·557	0·497	0·444	0·397	0·356	0·319	12
13	0·879	0·773	0·681	0·601	0·530	0·469	0·415	0·368	0·326	0·290	13
14	0·870	0·758	0·661	0·577	0·505	0·442	0·388	0·340	0·299	0·263	14
15	0·861	0·743	0·642	0·555	0·481	0·417	0·362	0·315	0·275	0·239	15

(n)	11%	12%	13%	14%	15%	16%	17%	18%	19%	20%	
1	0·901	0·893	0·885	0·877	0·870	0·862	0·855	0·847	0·840	0·833	1
2	0·812	0·797	0·783	0·769	0·756	0·743	0·731	0·718	0·706	0·694	2
3	0·731	0·712	0·693	0·675	0·658	0·641	0·624	0·609	0·593	0·579	3
4	0·659	0·636	0·613	0·592	0·572	0·552	0·534	0·516	0·499	0·482	4
5	0·593	0·567	0·543	0·519	0·497	0·476	0·456	0·437	0·419	0·402	5
6	0·535	0·507	0·480	0·456	0·432	0·410	0·390	0·370	0·352	0·335	6
7	0·482	0·452	0·425	0·400	0·376	0·354	0·333	0·314	0·296	0·279	7
8	0·434	0·404	0·376	0·351	0·327	0·305	0·285	0·266	0·249	0·233	8
9	0·391	0·361	0·333	0·308	0·284	0·263	0·243	0·225	0·209	0·194	9
10	0·352	0·322	0·295	0·270	0·247	0·227	0·208	0·191	0·176	0·162	10
11	0·317	0·287	0·261	0·237	0·215	0·195	0·178	0·162	0·148	0·135	11
12	0·286	0·257	0·231	0·208	0·187	0·168	0·152	0·137	0·124	0·112	12
13	0·258	0·229	0·204	0·182	0·163	0·145	0·130	0·116	0·104	0·093	13
14	0·232	0·205	0·181	0·160	0·141	0·125	0·111	0·099	0·088	0·078	14
15	0·209	0·183	0·160	0·140	0·123	0·108	0·095	0·084	0·074	0·065	15

Annuity Table

Present value of an annuity of 1 i.e. $\dfrac{1-(1+r)^{-n}}{r}$

Where r = discount rate
       n = number of periods

Discount rate (r)

Periods (n)	1%	2%	3%	4%	5%	6%	7%	8%	9%	10%	
1	0·990	0·980	0·971	0·962	0·952	0·943	0·935	0·926	0·917	0·909	1
2	1·970	1·942	1·913	1·886	1·859	1·833	1·808	1·783	1·759	1·736	2
3	2·941	2·884	2·829	2·775	2·723	2·673	2·624	2·577	2·531	2·487	3
4	3·902	3·808	3·717	3·630	3·546	3·465	3·387	3·312	3·240	3·170	4
5	4·853	4·713	4·580	4·452	4·329	4·212	4·100	3·993	3·890	3·791	5
6	5·795	5·601	5·417	5·242	5·076	4·917	4·767	4·623	4·486	4·355	6
7	6·728	6·472	6·230	6·002	5·786	5·582	5·389	5·206	5·033	4·868	7
8	7·652	7·325	7·020	6·733	6·463	6·210	5·971	5·747	5·535	5·335	8
9	8·566	8·162	7·786	7·435	7·108	6·802	6·515	6·247	5·995	5·759	9
10	9·471	8·983	8·530	8·111	7·722	7·360	7·024	6·710	6·418	6·145	10
11	10·368	9·787	9·253	8·760	8·306	7·887	7·499	7·139	6·805	6·495	11
12	11·255	10·575	9·954	9·385	8·863	8·384	7·943	7·536	7·161	6·814	12
13	12·134	11·348	10·635	9·986	9·394	8·853	8·358	7·904	7·487	7·103	13
14	13·004	12·106	11·296	10·563	9·899	9·295	8·745	8·244	7·786	7·367	14
15	13·865	12·849	11·938	11·118	10·380	9·712	9·108	8·559	8·061	7·606	15

(n)	11%	12%	13%	14%	15%	16%	17%	18%	19%	20%	
1	0·901	0·893	0·885	0·877	0·870	0·862	0·855	0·847	0·840	0·833	1
2	1·713	1·690	1·668	1·647	1·626	1·605	1·585	1·566	1·547	1·528	2
3	2·444	2·402	2·361	2·322	2·283	2·246	2·210	2·174	2·140	2·106	3
4	3·102	3·037	2·974	2·914	2·855	2·798	2·743	2·690	2·639	2·589	4
5	3·696	3·605	3·517	3·433	3·352	3·274	3·199	3·127	3·058	2·991	5
6	4·231	4·111	3·998	3·889	3·784	3·685	3·589	3·498	3·410	3·326	6
7	4·712	4·564	4·423	4·288	4·160	4·039	3·922	3·812	3·706	3·605	7
8	5·146	4·968	4·799	4·639	4·487	4·344	4·207	4·078	3·954	3·837	8
9	5·537	5·328	5·132	4·946	4·772	4·607	4·451	4·303	4·163	4·031	9
10	5·889	5·650	5·426	5·216	5·019	4·833	4·659	4·494	4·339	4·192	10
11	6·207	5·938	5·687	5·453	5·234	5·029	4·836	4·656	4·486	4·327	11
12	6·492	6·194	5·918	5·660	5·421	5·197	4·988	4·793	4·611	4·439	12
13	6·750	6·424	6·122	5·842	5·583	5·342	5·118	4·910	4·715	4·533	13
14	6·982	6·628	6·302	6·002	5·724	5·468	5·229	5·008	4·802	4·611	14
15	7·191	6·811	6·462	6·142	5·847	5·575	5·324	5·092	4·876	4·675	15

Mock Exam 1
(Specimen Exam)

Foundations In Accountancy
FFM
Foundations in Financial Management

Mock Exam 1

Specimen exam

Questions	
Time allowed	2 hours
This exam is divided into two sections:	
Section A: ALL 15 questions are compulsory and MUST be attempted	
Section B: ALL 7 questions are compulsory and MUST be attempted	

DO NOT OPEN THIS EXAM UNTIL YOU ARE READY TO START UNDER EXAMINATION CONDITIONS

Section A

1 **Which of the following statements about rights issues is/are true?**

Statement 1: They are more expensive to organise than an offer for sale of shares to the general public.

Statement 2: If all shareholders fully exercise their rights their percentage share of the ownership of the company will be unchanged.

- ○ Both the statements are true
- ○ Only statement 1 is true
- ○ Only statement 2 is true
- ○ Neither statement 1 nor 2 is true

2 **Which is the correct ranking of investments in order of risk to the investor?** (Highest risk first)

- ○ Loan stock, preference share, equity share
- ○ Preference share, loan stock, equity share
- ○ Equity share, loan stock, preference share
- ○ Equity share, preference share, loan stock

3 An airline needs to expand its capacity and is considering leasing a new aeroplane for a period of five years. The economic life of the aeroplane is 25 years.

Which of the statements made about the lease is/are true?

Statement 1: It will protect the lessor against changes in technology

Statement 2: It will give the lessee use, but not legal title, of the aeroplane

- ○ Both statements 1 and 2
- ○ Neither statement 1 nor 2
- ○ Statement 1 only
- ○ Statement 2 only

4 **Which of the following will a venture capitalist usually require in order to invest in a business?**

(1) A future exit route
(2) A current stock market quotation
(3) An equity stake in the business

- ○ 1 and 2
- ○ 1 and 3
- ○ 2 and 3
- ○ 3 only

5 Inflation is forecast to be 6.40 % in the coming year and an investor requires a real return of 2.00 % per year.

What nominal rate of return does the investor need to earn on the investment?

- ○ 2.00%
- ○ 4.40%
- ○ 8.40%
- ○ 8.53%

6   A company is negotiating a contract with a customer for ongoing supply of goods on credit.

   Which of the following are optional terms and conditions that might be included in the contract from the outset?

   (1) A retention of title clause
   (2) Offer
   (3) The period of free credit

   O   1 and 2
   O   1 and 3
   O   2 and 3
   O   2 only

7   **Which of the following statements is/are an advantage of financial intermediation?**

   Statement 1: Financial intermediation helps retain the liquidity of the investor

   Statement 2: Risk to the investor is reduced as the monies are not directly linked with one borrower

   O   Statement 1 only
   O   Statement 2 only
   O   Both statements 1 and 2
   O   Neither statements 1 nor 2

8   **Are the following statements true or false?**

   Statement 1: Monetary policy is concerned with taxation and government expenditure

   Statement 2: Quantitative controls are designed to restrict how much the clearing banks lend

	Statement 1	Statement 2
O	True	False
O	False	True
O	False	False
O	True	True

9   The cost of ordering a batch of raw material has increased.

   How is the economic order quantity and average inventory level affected?

	Economic order quantity	Average inventory level
O	Higher	Higher
O	Higher	Lower
O	Lower	Higher
O	Lower	Lower

10 **Which of the following statements is/are true?**

   Statement 1: An advantage of centralised cash management is that the level of funds held for precautionary purposes will be higher than in a decentralised treasury

   Statement 2: The cost of negotiating an overdraft will be considered as a variable cost under Baumol's cash management model

   O   Statement 1 only
   O   Statement 2 only
   O   Both statements 1 and 2
   O   Neither statement 1 nor 2

FFM FOUNDATIONS IN FINANCIAL MANAGEMENT

11 All of C Co's sales and purchases are on credit. The following forecast information for 2017 is available for C Co:

	$
Sales	210,000
Purchases	175,000
Inventory	14,000
Receivables	23,000
Payables	16,000

Assuming there are 365 days in a year, what is C Co's cash operating cycle?

- ○ 22 days
- ○ 36 days
- ○ 31 days
- ○ 44 days

12 **Which of the following statements is/are true?**

Statement 1: With-recourse factoring means that any bad debts are suffered by the factor

Statement 2: An invoice discounter will not take over the administration of the client's receivables

- ○ Statement 1 only
- ○ Statement 2 only
- ○ Both statements 1 and 2
- ○ Neither statement 1 or 2

13 Blot Co has the following budgeted information for March:

	$'000
Accounting profit	90
Increase in receivables	15
Increase in inventory	10
Increase in payables	12
Depreciation	8

What is the budgeted increase in the cash balance for March?

- ○ $85,000
- ○ $69,000
- ○ $61,000
- ○ $95,000

14 A company has equity shareholders' funds of $20m and a profit before interest of $4m. Its capital gearing ratio (long term debt to equity) is 56% and it has an interest cover of 3.2 times. It has a short-term overdraft which costs 5% per year.

If it uses its overdraft to repay a $4m long-term bank loan, which costs 6% per year, what will be its new capital gearing and interest cover ratios?

- ○ 36% and 3.3 times
- ○ 56% and 3.3 times
- ○ 36% and 4.0 times
- ○ 56% and 4.0 times

15 The following statements have been made about a bank's rights in relation to its customers:

   (i) The bank has the right to be repaid overdrawn balances on demand, except where the overdraft terms require a period of notice.

   (ii) The bank can use the customers' money in any legally or morally acceptable way that it chooses.

   (iii) A customers' money must always be available for immediate withdrawal, irrespective of the terms of the deposit.

   Which of the above statements are true?

   ○ (i) and (ii) only
   ○ (i), (ii) and (iii)
   ○ (i) and (iii) only
   ○ (ii) and (iii) only

Section B

1 BN Co

BN Co manufactures virtual reality game consoles. The market has grown significantly over the past few years and is expected to continue to grow. BN Co is planning to launch a new console, the VR King. The introduction of the VR King will have no impact on sales of existing consoles as it is expected to appeal to a different segment of the market.

Investment

Marketing costs already incurred to promote the VR King amount to $1m. BN Co will need to make a further investment of $16m in production equipment at the start of the project if the VR King is introduced. The VR King will have a four year life, at the end of which the equipment will have a residual value of $4m. Depreciation is calculated using the straight line method.

Sales and production

Sales and production of the VR King over its lifecycle are expected to be:

Year 1	20,000 units
Year 2	40,000 units
Year 3	60,000 units
Year 4	20,000 units

The selling price in Year 1 and Year 2 will be $700 per unit. The selling price will be reduced to $500 in Year 3 and will remain at this level for the remainder of the project.

Costs

(i) The total variable cost of the VR King, including labour, materials and variable overhead costs is estimated to be $300 per unit and this is expected to remain constant throughout the life of the project.

(ii) The additional fixed overhead expected to be incurred directly as a result of increasing the production capacity is $8m each year including depreciation charges.

(iii) In addition to the fixed overhead above, there will be an apportioned head office charge of $0.2m each year.

Other information

A cost of capital of 10% is used to evaluate projects of this type. The finance director is concerned that the cost of capital could increase during the life of the project.

Required

(a) Calculate the net present value (NPV) of the VR King project and conclude whether BN Co should introduce the VR King. Show all calculations. **(11 marks)**

(b) Calculate the internal rate of return (IRR) for the VR King project and comment on the results. **(5 marks)**

(c) Explain TWO advantages which the NPV method of investment appraisal has compared to the payback method. **(4 marks)**

(Total = 20 marks)

2 Lyp Co

Over the last year, Lyp Co purchased $50,000 worth of goods from Supp Co.

Lyp Co always takes the 50 days credit Supp Co offers. Supp Co has now offered Lyp Co a 1.5% discount if they pay within 15 days. If Lyp Co pay after 15 days, they will have to perform a special BACS run at an annual cost of $200. Lyp Co has a short-term cost of finance of 8% and has no surplus cash.

Assume that there are 365 days in a year.

Required

Calculate the net loss or gain to Lyp Co from accepting the discount.

Note. Perform all calculations to the nearest $. (5 marks)

3 Functions of a central bank

List FIVE functions of a central bank. (5 marks)

4 Stock exchange listing

Briefly explain THREE reasons why a company would seek a stock exchange listing. (5 marks)

5 JIT Inventory

Briefly explain THREE conditions for a JIT inventory system to operate successfully. (5 marks)

6 Drab Co

Drab Co's turnover is $1,105,528 and receivables are $106,010.

Irrecoverable debts are 1% of sales and a credit controller is employed costing $11,000 per year.

Drab Co has approached a factoring company, Fact Co, who has put forward the following proposed terms:

- Receivable days will be reduced to 25 days.
- Fact Co will suffer the irrecoverable debts.
- 80% of the new receivables balance would be advanced at an interest rate of 5%.
- Fact Co would charge 1.5% as sales insurance against irrecoverable debts.

In addition, Drab Co would no longer employ a credit controller and it is believed sales would drop by 0.5%.

Other information:

- Annual cash profits are 75% of sales value.
- Working capital is funded by an overdraft costing 7% per year and this is expected to continue into the future.
- Assume 365 days in a year.

Required

(a) **Prepare calculations which show whether or not the services of Fact Co should be employed and state your conclusion.**

  Note. Prepare all calculations to the nearest $. (11 marks)

(b) **Briefly explain how invoice discounting differs from debt factoring.** (4 marks)

(Total = 15 marks)

7 Mr Forest

Mr Forest has won a contract to clear a large area of scrubland and replant it with new trees.

The contract is due to take four months, starting on 1 March 20X9. The following information is available:

- Mr Forest is going to sell an old machine and buy a new one. The sale of the old machine on 1 March 20X9 will generate a profit of $800.

- The new machine will cost $60,000, five times the expected net book value brought forward of his old machine as at 1 January 20X9, on which depreciation of $300 per month is charged.

- The cost of the new machine will be paid in two instalments, 25% on 1 March and the remaining 75% six months later. The first payment will be due on delivery of the new machine at the beginning of the contract.

- The monthly depreciation on the new machine will be calculated over ten years on a straight line basis.

- The price for the contract is $125,000, which is due to be received:

  March 4%
  April 12%
  May 30%
  June 54%

- Mr Forest's current workforce will be able to complete the work in March and April at a cost of $7,500 per month.

- Additional labour will be hired in May and June and this will increase the labour cost by 50%. Labour is paid in the month incurred.

- The new trees will cost $50,000, and this will be paid in two equal instalments in May and June.

The business is expected to have an overdraft of $10,000 on 1 March 20X9. The bank charges interest of 1% per month on overdrawn balances. The interest is calculated on the closing bank balance each month and is payable the following month. No interest is paid by the bank on positive balances.

Required

Prepare a monthly cash budget for each of the months March, April, May and June 20X9, showing clearly any workings. (15 marks)

Answers to Mock Exam 1
(Specimen exam)

MOCK EXAM 1 (SPECIMEN EXAM) // ANSWERS

Section A

1. Only statement 2 is true.

   Statement 1 is untrue as advertising shares to the general public involves additional costs

2. Equity share, preference share, loan stock

   The lower risk comes from the improved security and priority that the investments offer.

3. Statement 2 only

   Statement 1 is false as the underlying asset is the same.

4. 1 and 3

   Venture capitalists will require equity stake and an exit route, but this does not have to be via a current stock market listing.

5. 8.53%   8.53% (1.064 × 1.002) – 1

6. 1 and 3

   An offer is required in order to create a contract but it is not a term in the contract.

7. Both statements 1 and 2

   The functions of financial intermediation include liquidity transformation and pooling of risk.

8. False   True

   Statement 1 is false as monetary policy is related to interest rates and money supply.

   Statement 2 is the definition of quantative controls.

9. Higher   Higher

   The higher the cost of ordering a batch the more infrequently it should be done and therefore the higher both the order quantity and the average inventory held will be.

10. Neither statement 1 nor 2

    The level of precautionary funds will be lower as risk can be pooled and the cost of negotiating an overdraft is a fixed cost.

11. 36 days

    Inventory days = $14,000/$175,000 × 365 = 29 days
    Receivables = $23,000/$210,000 × 365 = 40 days
    Payables = $16,000/$175,000 × 365 = 33 days
    Operating cycle = 29 + 40 – 33 = 36 days

12. Statement 2 only

    Statement 1 is false as this is the definition of without recourse.

13. $85,000

	$'000
Profit	90
Increase in receivables	(15)
Increase in inventory	(10)
Increase in payables	12
Depreciation	8
Increase in cash	85

14. 36% and 3.3 times

    36% and 3.3x ($20m × 0.56) – $4m / $20m and $4m / (($4m / 3.2) – $0.04m)

15. (i) and (ii) only

    Statement (iii) is false as depending on the terms of deposit the bank may require notice.

Section B

1 BN Co

(a)

	T0 $(000)	T1 $(000)	T2 $(000)	T3 $(000)	T4 $(000)
Marketing costs					
Production equipment	(16,000)				4,000
Apportioned head office charge					
Contribution (W1)		8,000	16,000	12,000	4,000
Fixed costs (W2)		(5,000)	(5,000)	(5,000)	(5,000)
Net cash flow	(16,000)	3,000	11,000	7,000	3,000
Discount factor at 10%	1	0.909	0.826	0.751	0.683
Present value	(16,000)	2,727	9,086	5,257	2,049

Net present value = $3,119,000

The NPV can also be calculated using the =NPV function.

If the cash flows are in a spreadsheet as follows:

	A	B	C	D	E	F
1		T0	T1	T2	T3	T4
2		$(000)	$(000)	$(000)	$(000)	$(000)
3	Net cash flow	-16,000	3,000	11,000	7,000	3,000
4						

The =NPV function is calculated as = NPV(0.1,C3:F3), this gives the present value of the cash flows in years 1 to 4 as $19,126.

The outlay of $16,000 is then deducted to give a project NPV of $3,126 (000).

This is slightly more accurate than the previous method, but either are acceptable in the exam.

As the net present value is positive, BN Co should launch the new VR King.

Marketing costs are not relevant as they are sunk. The apportioned head office charge is not relevant as it is not a cash flow.

Workings

1

	T1	T2	T3	T4
Sales volume	20,000 units	40,000 units	60,000 units	20,000 units
Selling price per unit	$700	$700	$500	$500
Variable cost per unit	$300	$300	$300	$300
Contribution per unit	$400	$400	$200	$200
Total contribution	$8,000,000	$16,000,000	$12,000,000	$4,000,000

2 Depreciation per year = ($16 million − $4 million)/4 years = $3 million

Incremental fixed costs per year	$8 million
Less depreciation per year	$3 million
Incremental cash fixed cost	$5 million

(b)

	T0 $(000)	T1 $(000)	T2 $(000)	T3 $(000)	T4 $(000)
Net cash flow	(16,000)	3,000	11,000	7,000	3,000
Discount factor at 20%	1	0.833	0.694	0.579	0.482
Present value	(16,000)	2,499	7,634	4,053	1,446

Net present value = $(368,000)

IRR = A + (a/ (a − b)) × (B − A)
    = 10 + (3,119/ (3,119 + 368)) × (20 − 10)
    = 18.94%

Alternatively, using the =IRR function, if the net cash flows are in cells as follows:

	A	B	C	D	E	F
1		T0	T1	T2	T3	T4
2		$(000)	$(000)	$(000)	$(000)	$(000)
3	Net cash flow	-16,000	3,000	11,000	7,000	3,000
4						

=IRR(B3:F3) gives the IRR as 18.8%. This is slightly more accurate than the previous method, but either is acceptable in the exam.

The IRR helps to identify the point where the project's NPV changes from positive to negative as a result of a change in the cost of capital. Although the finance director is concerned that the cost of capital could rise during the lifetime of the project, this project is still viable with a cost of capital which is almost double.

(c) The NPV method of investment appraisal has the following advantages over the payback method:

- It takes into account the time value of money. Money received or paid in the present is worth more than the same amount in the future due to its potential earning capacity.

- It considers all cash flows which occur during the life of a project and not simply the cash flows which occur up to the payback point in time. A project which generates excellent cash flows after the payback can be rejected in favour of one which generates poor cash flow if the payback is marginally longer than the target payback period.

- A project with a positive NPV is expected to lead to an increase in shareholder wealth whereas the cut off point for deciding what an acceptable payback period is arbitrary.

Note. Only two advantages were required.

2 Lyp Co

Payables discount

Current payables = 50/365 × $50,000 = $6,849
New payables if discount is taken = 0.985 × $50,000 × 15/365 = $2,024
Reduction in payables $4,825
Interest cost = 0.08 × $4,825 = $386
Discount gained = $50,000 × 0.015 = $750
Cost of BACS run = $200
Benefit of discount = $750 − $386 − $200 = $164

3 Functions of a central bank

Functions of a central bank

- Banker to the banks. It provides a system for transactions between banks.

- Banker to the government. It disburses government expenditure.

- Issuing currency. It prints and issues notes and coins for the government.

- Lender of last resort to the banking system.

- Monetary policy. It executes monetary policy on behalf of the government.

- Reserve management. It manages the foreign exchange reserves of the country and may buy or sell them to influence the exchange rate.
- Maintain financial stability. It supervises the other banks.

(**Note.** Only FIVE functions were required.)

4 Stock exchange listing

- Access to a wider pool of finance. The amount of finance available to a private, unlisted company is limited. If a company needs more finance than is currently available to it, it may seek a stock exchange listing. A listing may also improve a company's credit rating, and more investors may then be willing to invest.

- Enhancement of the company image. A listed company is perceived as being more financially stable. This may result in, for example, increased buying power.

- Increased marketability of shares. It is difficult for the shareholders in a private, unlisted company to sell their shares as there is no market to sell the shares on easily. If a company is listed, there is a market on which the shares can be sold easily, the shares are more marketable making them more attractive.

- Facilitation of growth by acquisition. Should a listed company wish to make a takeover offer on another company, the terms of the offer could include an exchange of shares.

- Realisation of capital by the owners. A stock exchange listing gives the founder members the ability to sell their shareholding, or part of it, allowing them to use the cash how they wish, for example, to invest in other projects.

(**Note.** Only THREE reasons were required)

5 JIT Inventory

- The company has to have a reliable supplier, with whom they have a good working relationship, who is preferably close by. This will allow the company to order materials and know that the goods will arrive promptly. Many companies will try to have one supplier for a particular component of raw material, to try to strengthen the supplier relationship.

- Quality must be a priority because:
  - As so little inventory is held, there are no 'spares', therefore the raw material must be good enough to take straight into the production process, as if it is faulty production will cease.
  - The quality of the work in progress must be consistently high. If partially completed units have to be thrown away due to shoddy workmanship, this will lead to delays in fulfilling customer demands.

- The workforce need to be flexible. Depending on customer demand, the workforce may need to increase or decrease their working hours, or be skilled enough and willing to work on different parts of the production process.

- The premises should be laid out in such a way that the time taken to transfer goods from raw material stock holding to the production process and into finished goods stock holding is minimised. This should result in reduced lead times.

(**Note.** Only THREE conditions were required)

6 Drab co

(a) Current situation

		$
Irrecoverable debts	0.01 × $1,105,528	11,055
Financing receivables	0.07 × 106,010	7,421
Credit controller		11,000
		29,476

With the factor

New sales = $1,105,528 × 0·995 = $1,100,000
New receivables = 25/365 × $1,100,000 = $75,342

		$
Financing remaining receivables	20% × $75,342 × 0.07	1,055
Credit insurance	0.015 × $1,100,000	16,500
Cost of advance	80% × $75, 342 × 5%	3,014
Lost profit	$5,528 x 0.75	4,146
		24,715

Drab Co should employ the services of Fact Co.

(b)
- With invoice discounting, a selection of invoices are purchased, rather than the whole sales ledger.
- Invoice discounters do not take over the running of the sales ledger.
- Invoice discounting is usually used in the short term, factoring is a longer term decision.
- Bad debts remain a cost to the company, and not a cost to the invoice discounter, but a factor will bear the cost of bad debts in a non-recourse agreement.

7 Mr Forest

	March $	April $	May $	June $
Income	5,000	15,000	37,500	67,500
Old machine (W1)	12,200			
New machine ($60,000/4)	(15,000)			
Labour (increase by 50% May and June)	(7,500)	(7,500)	(11,250)	(11,250)
Trees			(25,000)	(25,000)
Net cash flow for the month	(5,300)	7,500	1,250	31,250
Balance b/fwd	(10,000)	(15,400)	(8,054)	(6,885)
Interest (1% of the bal b/fwd)	(100)	(154)	(81)	(69)
Balance c/fwd	(15,400)	(8,054)	(6,885)	24,296

Working

	$
NBV 1 January 20X9 ($60,000/5)	12,000
Depreciation for January and February	(600)
NBV at date of disposal	11,400
Profit on disposal	800
Cash received 1 March 20X9	12,200

Marking scheme

Item No.	Part	Sub Part	Marking Item (MI)	Marks	No. of Items Required
1	a		Marketing	1	
1	a		Production equipment	1	
1	a		Apportioned HO charges	1	
1	a		Contribution	3	
1	a		Fixed costs	2	
1	a		Discount factor	1	
1	a		NPV	1	
1	a		Conclusion	1	
1	b		Discount factor	1	
1	b		NPV	1	
1	b		IRR	1	
1	b		Comment IRR result	2	
1	c		Up to 2 marks per adv	4	
2			Reduction in payables	2	
2			Interest cost	1	
2			BACS	0.5	
2			Discount gained	1	
2			Benefit of discount	0.5	
3			Function list 1 each	5	
4			Reasons expl 2 each	5	
5			Reasons expl 2 each	5	
6	a		Irrecoverable debt	1	
6	a		Financing receivables	1	
6	a		Credit controller	1	
6	a		20% financing receivables	2	
6	a		80% financing receivables	2	
6	a		Lost profit	2	
6	a		Insurance	1	
6	a		Conclusion	1	
6	b		Differences	4	
7			Income	2	
7			Cash from old machine	3	
7			Ignore profit on old machine	1	
7			New machine	2	
7			Labour	2	
7			Trees	1	
7			Ignore depreciation	1	
7			Balance b/fwd	1	
7			Interest	2	

Mock Exam 2

Foundations In Accountancy

FFM

Foundations in Financial Management

Mock Exam 2

Questions	
Time allowed	2 hours
This exam is divided into two sections:	
Section A: ALL 15 questions are compulsory and MUST be attempted	
Section B: ALL 7 questions are compulsory and MUST be attempted	

DO NOT OPEN THIS EXAM UNTIL YOU ARE READY TO START UNDER EXAMINATION CONDITIONS

Section A – ALL FIFTEEN questions are compulsory and MUST be attempted

1. A deposit account offers interest of 2% per quarter.

    What is the equivalent annual compound rate of interest to one decimal place?

    - ○ 26.8%
    - ○ 24.0%
    - ○ 8.2%
    - ○ 8.0%

    (2 marks)

2. Which of the following statements are true?

    1. An individual can petition the court to declare themselves bankrupt
    2. A creditor can petition the court to declare an individual bankrupt

    - ○ Statement 1
    - ○ Statement 2
    - ○ Both statements are true
    - ○ Neither statement is true

    (2 marks)

3. A company's current ratio is 2 and quick (acid test) ratio is 1. Inventory is bought and paid for immediately by increasing the overdraft.

    What will the values of the current ratio and quick ratio be after the above transaction has taken place?

	Current Ratio	Current Ratio
○	Greater than 2	Greater than 1
○	Greater than 2	Less than 1
○	Less than 2	Greater than 1
○	Less than 2	Less than 1

    (2 marks)

4. What is the quick (acid test) ratio?

    - ○ Current assets – current liabilities
    - ○ Current assets – inventory – current liabilities
    - ○ Assets – liabilities
    - ○ Assets – inventory – liabilities

    (2 marks)

5. Which of the following statements are true/false?

    Statement 1: Warrants can be sold separately to the loan notes they are attached to.

    Statement 2: The owner of a preference share will **always** receive the associated preference dividend

	Statement 1	Statement 2
○	True	False
○	False	True
○	True	True
○	False	False

    (2 marks)

6   The following information is available for a company:

	Expected Total Sales
	$
June	10,000
July	12,000
August	15,000

All sales are on credit. Receivables pay 20% in the month of sale, 50% in the month following sale, 25% two months after sale and 5% never pay.

What are the expected cash receipts in August?

- O $11,500
- O $11,750
- O $11,350
- O $10,750

(2 marks)

7   If capital expenditure is treated as revenue expenditure in the financial statements, what is the impact on profit in the period of purchase?

- O It will be overstated
- O It will be understated
- O There will be no impact
- O It is impossible to say without further information

(2 mark)

8   A company has the following information for non-current assets:

	20X1	20X2
Non-current assets at closing net book value at the year end	$350,000	$400,000

Depreciation included in the 20X2 statement of profit or loss is $35,000.

What is the value of non-current assets acquired during 20X2, assuming no disposals were made in the period?

- O $50,000
- O $15,000
- O $85,000
- O $400,000

(2 marks)

9   Which of the following statements is/are true?

1   A certificate of deposit is a negotiable instrument
2   A certificate of deposit cannot be traded

- O Statement 1 only
- O Statement 2 only
- O Both statements are true
- O Neither statement is true

(2 marks)

10 A project requires an initial investment of $100,000 and will produce a contribution of $50,000 each year for five years, after which time the scrap value will be $5,000. Fixed costs excluding depreciation are $17,000 per year.

What is the accounting rate of return, on an average investment basis, to the nearest percentage point?

- O 63%
- O 14%
- O 29%
- O 27%

(3 marks)

11 Which of the following statements is/are true?

Statement 1: Monetary policy can be tightened through an increase in interest rates.
Statement 2: In a period of high inflation, a company will need to review its selling prices regularly.

- ○ Statement 1 only
- ○ Statement 2 only
- ○ Both statements 1 and 2
- ○ Neither statement 1 nor statement 2

(2 marks)

12 The following information about E Co is available:

	$
Operating profit	100,000
Finance charges	(20,000)
Profit before tax	80,000
Taxation	(24,000)
Profit for the period	56,000

E Co has 20,000 ordinary shares.

What is the earnings per share in $?

- ○ $2.80
- ○ $5.00
- ○ $0.25
- ○ $0.36

(2 marks)

13 The following information is available:

	$
Cash	30,000
Receivables	40,000
Inventory	25,000
	95,000
Payables	(10,000)
Working Capital	85,000

What is the quick (acid test) ratio?

- ○ 6.5 times
- ○ 8.5 times
- ○ 9.5 times
- ○ 7 times

(2 marks)

14 Dis Co is considering offering a discount of 2% to its customers if they pay within ten days rather than the current 25 days. There are 365 days in the year.

What is the annual cost to Dis Co of offering such a discount?

- ○ 34.3%
- ○ 61.9%
- ○ 63.5%
- ○ 33.5%

(2 marks)

15 Which of the following statements are true/false?

Statement 1: The Alternative Investment Market is regulated by the London Stock Exchange.

Statement 2: The higher the level of gearing an organisation has, the higher the risk to the business if sales fall.

	Statement 1	Statement 2
○	False	False
○	True	False
○	False	True
○	True	True

(2 marks)

(Total = 30 marks)

Section B – ALL SEVEN questions are compulsory and MUST be attempted

1 Frame Co

Frame Co buys frames for spectacles from fashion houses, makes the plastic lenses to order and then fits them into the frame.

The business is going through financially difficult times. Frame Co therefore needs to forecast its working capital requirement for next year, so that it can accurately budget its cash requirement.

The following forecast figures are available:

	$ per unit
Sales price	100
Cost of a frame from the fashion house	40
Cost of plastic for the lens	20
Labour	15

Overheads are semi-variable and experience has shown that when the output is 20,000 units, overheads are $300,000, and when output is 28,000 units, overheads are $400,000.

Output next year is expected to be 25,000 units.

Inventories
Raw material inventory is held for five weeks. Work-in-progress includes direct materials, labour and variable overheads. Goods are held in work-in-progress for two weeks and are 100% complete with respect to frames, 50% complete with respect to plastic lenses and 40% complete with respect to labour and variable overheads. The spectacles are made to order and so finished goods inventory is zero.

Accounts payable

Credit taken:	
Frames	3 weeks
Plastic lenses	7 weeks
Labour and variable overheads	4 weeks

Accounts payable
All customers are credit customers and pay after eight weeks.

Required

(a) Calculate the working capital requirement for Frame Co for the next year. Assume that there are 52 working weeks in a year. Work to the nearest $. **(15 marks)**

(b) Frame Co is keen to reduce the time raw materials are held in inventory and the company is considering using the just in time (JIT) approach to managing their inventory.

Briefly explain the JIT approach to inventory management and the conditions required for a JIT approach to work. **(5 marks)**

(Total = 20 marks)

2 Tent Co

Tent Co makes tents and is considering making a different design of tent.

This would require an initial investment of $65,000 and thereafter cash flows are predicted to be as follows:

Time	Net cash flow
	$
1	18,000
2	19,000
3	20,050
4	20,050

Required

Calculate the Internal Rate of Return of the investment over a four year time period. Assume that the investment has no scrap value. **(5 marks)**

3 Treasury

Describe TWO of the functions undertaken by a treasury department. **(5 marks)**

4 Credit

Define the terms invoice discounting and debt factoring, clearly distinguishing between with and without recourse factoring. **(5 marks)**

5 Business angels

Define the term 'business angel' and state FOUR disadvantages of this type of financing **(5 marks)**

6 Mr Home

Mr Home modifies vans and makes them into motor homes. He modifies the vans to a customer's specific requirements. He recently completed the modification of a van for Mr Travel, but Mr Travel can no longer afford to pay for the work due to the collapse of his own business. Mr Travel had paid a non-returnable deposit of $2,000. Mr Home has met another customer, Mr Away, who is considering buying the van if certain further modifications are made. The work is expected to take two weeks to complete.

Mr Home has prepared the following information on the work to be completed for Mr Away:

		$
Fabric	20 metres at $50 per metre	1,000
Wood	15 metres at $30 per metre	450
Labour	55 hours at $10 per hour	550
Overheads		1,815
Hire of machine		400
Cost of preparing the information		90
Profit required		215
Price to be charged		4,520

The following information has been collected:

Fabric

The fabric is used to make the cushions and is customer specific. Mr Home has 11 metres of the specific material required by Mr Away in inventory. The inventory of this fabric has arisen as too much was purchased at a cost of $70 per metre for a previous contract. If not used in the contract for Mr Away, the fabric could be sold for $30 per metre. The current purchase price is $50 per metre.

Wood

There are 12 metres of wood held in inventory which originally cost $28 per metre. The cost now is $30 per metre, but it could be sold for $29 per metre. If it is not used on this project, the wood could be heat treated at a total cost of $60, used in normal production and so save the business $400.

Labour

Mr Home has enough work currently scheduled to keep his employees fully employed. In order to complete the modifications for Mr Away, employees will have to be removed from another job on which they earn a contribution of $5 per hour.

Overheads

The variable overhead rate is $8 per labour hour and covers costs such as electricity. It is considered to be the best available estimate of the true variable overhead cost. The fixed overheads are charged as 250% of the labour costs. The charge covers depreciation of $500 per week and general business overheads.

Hire of machine

A special machine will be required to cut the wood. The machine is needed for the whole of the time the van is being refurbished. The machine costs $200 per week with a minimum hiring fee of $450.

Cost of preparing the statement

Mr Home has spent three hours preparing the figures and he charges his time at $30 per hour.

Profit

5% is the mark-up normally required by Mr Home.

Required

Prepare a schedule of relevant costs for Mr Home, stating clearly the minimum price that he should charge Mr Away for the modifications. Explain your treatment of each item detailed in the question, including those you consider irrelevant. **(15 marks)**

7 Fineed Co

(a) Explain the term gearing in relation to a company's capital structure. **(2 marks)**

(b) Explain the importance of gearing to:

    (i) A company looking to raise extra loan finance; **(2 marks)**
    (ii) A credit controller seeking information to set a credit limit for a new customer. **(2 marks)**

(c) The following financial information is available for Fineed Co for period ending 30 September 2012:

Extract from the Statement of profit or loss

	$
Operating profit	36,000
Interest charges	(15,000)
Profit before tax	21,000
Taxation	(5,800)
Profit for the period	15,200

Extracts from the Statement of Financial Position

	$
Equity and reserves	
Total equity and reserves	400,000
Non-current liabilities	
Loan	100,000
5% preference shares	50,000
Current liabilities	
Payables	50,000

Required

Calculate the gearing ratio for Fineed Co, showing clearly the formula used. Comment on the level of gearing in the company. **(4 marks)**

(d) Define the term interest cover and explain the importance of this ratio to a bank when deciding whether or not to grant a loan. **(5 marks)**

(Total = 15 marks)

Answers to Mock Exam 2

Section A

1 The correct answer is: 8.2%

$1.02^4 - 1 = 8.2\%$

2 Both statements are true.

An individual can petition the court to declare themselves bankrupt.

A creditor can also petition the court to declare an individual bankrupt

3 The correct answer is: Current ratio: Less than 2. Quick ratio: Less than 1.

By calculating the ratios using sample numbers the impact of the changes can be seen.

Current ratio = $\dfrac{\text{current assets}}{\text{current liabilities}} = \dfrac{10}{5} = 2$. If current assets and current liabilities are increased by the same amount $\dfrac{11}{6} = 1.83$

Quick ratio = $\dfrac{\text{current assets - inventories}}{\text{current liabilities}} = \dfrac{5}{5} = 1$

If current liabilities are increased $\dfrac{5}{6} = 0.83$

4 The correct answer is: Current assets – inventory – current liabilities

5 The correct answer is: Statement 1 – True. Statement 2 – False

Warrants are usually issued as part of a package with unsecured loan notes, but, once issued, they are detachable from the notes. A preference dividend can only be paid if sufficient distributable profits are available.

6 The correct answer is: $11,500

0.2 × $15,000 + 0.5 × $12,000 + 0.25 × $10,000 = $11,500

7 The correct answer is It will be understated

If capital expenditure is treated as revenue expenditure, that means that revenue expenditure is overstated. So profit will then be understated in the financial statements.

8 The correct answer is: $85,000

Without any acquisitions the 20X2 NBV would be $350,000 – $35,000 = $315,000

The difference between this and the actual is the acquisitions in the year, $400,000 – $315,000 = $85,000

9 The correct answer is statement 1 only

A certificate of deposit is a negotiable instrument in bearer form, in other words, they can be bought and sold and the title belongs to the holder. A certificate of deposit can be traded.

10 The correct answer is: 27%

$\text{ARR} = \dfrac{\text{Estimated average profits}}{\text{Estimated average investment}} \times 100\%$

$\dfrac{\left[(\$50{,}000 \times 5 - \$17{,}000 \times 5 - \$95{,}000)/5\right]}{\left[(\$100{,}000 + \$5{,}000)/2\right]} \times 100\% = 27\%$

11 The correct answer is: Both statements 1 and 2

Statement 1 is true – An increase in interest rates by the central bank eventually has the effect of reducing borrowing, and so reducing spending in the economy.

Statement 2 is true – In times of high inflation, a company should review its prices regularly to cover rising costs and prevent a fall in its profit margins.

12 The correct answer is: $2.80
EPS = PAT/number of shares. EPS = $56,000/20,000 = $2.80

13 The correct answer is: 7 times
Quick ratio = Current assets excluding inventory/Current liabilities

= ($30,000+$40,000) /$10,000 = 7

14 The correct answer is: 63.5%
The discount reduces the period of credit by 25 – 10 = 15 days. The cost for receiving the money 15 days earlier is 2% of the amount owed. The annualised cost is therefore:

$$\left(\frac{100}{100-2}\right)^{365/15} - 1 = 63.5\%$$

15 The correct answer is: Both statements are true.

Statement 1: In the UK, the principal capital markets are the Stock Exchange '**main market**' (for companies with a full Stock Exchange listing) and the more loosely regulated 'second tier' **Alternative Investment Market (AIM),** which is also regulated by the Stock Exchange.

Statement 2: Higher gearing means a higher proportion of debt capital in the capital structure of the organisation. If sales fall, both operating profits and profits after tax will also fall. However, the percentage fall in profits after tax and in earnings per share is greater in a high-geared company than in a lower-geared company. This means that the risk for a higher-geared company is greater.

Section B

1 Frame Co

> **Helping hand.** There is a fair amount of information to process in order to produce the working capital requirement forecast. It is not particularly difficult, so set up a proforma and work through it methodically, slotting numbers in as you go. In part (b), you are asked to 'explain' which means that you have to do more than just provide the definition.

Marking scheme

		Marks
(a)	High low method and variable cost	1
	Raw materials	1
	WIP 1 mark for frames, 2 marks each of the other elements	5
	Accounts receivable	1
	Accounts payable 2 marks each element	6
	Working capital requirement	1
(b)	Definition	2
	Conditions: 1 mark each	3
		20

(a) Variable overhead per unit = ($400,000 − $300,000)/(28,000 − 20,000) = $12.50 per unit.

Working capital requirement

Current Assets

		$	$
Current assets			
Raw materials	(5/52 × 40 × 25,000)		144,231
Work-in-progress			
Frames	(2/52 × 40 × 25,000)	38,462	
Lenses	(2/52 × 20 × 25,000 × 0.5)	9,615	
Labour and variable overhead	(2/52 × (15 + 12.5) × 25,000 × 0.4)	10,577	
			58,654
Accounts receivable	8/52 × 100 × 25,000		384,615
Total current assets			587,500
Current liabilities			
Accounts payable			
Frames	3/52 × 40 × 25,000	57,692	
Lenses	7/52 × 20 × 25,000	67,308	
Labour and variable overhead	4/52 × (15 + 12.5) × 25,000	52,885	
Total current liabilities			(177,885)
Working capital requirement			409,615

(b) **Just in time (JIT)**

JIT considers raw material inventory, work-in-progress and finished goods. The idea is that there is a continuous flow from raw materials warehousing, through the production process, into finished goods and straight out to the customer. Levels of all inventories and holding costs kept to a minimum.

For the system to operate efficiently, certain conditions must apply:

- The company must have a reliable supplier, with whom they have a good working relationship, who is preferably close by. The company can then order materials and know that the goods will arrive when expected. Many companies will try to have one supplier for a particular component of raw material, to try to strengthen the supplier relationship.
- In a JIT system, quality is a priority for the following reasons;
  - Little, or no, inventory is held, so there is no excess material. This means that raw materials must all be taken straight into the production process – if the raw materials are sub-standard or faulty, then production will have to stop.
  - The quality of the work-in-progress must be consistently high. If partially completed units have to be thrown away due to, for example, poor workmanship, this will lead to delays in fulfilling customer demands. Ensuring the quality of work-in-progress should result in reduced wastage costs.
- The workforce need to be flexible. Depending on customer demand, the workforce may need to increase or decrease their working hours, or be skilled enough and willing to work on different parts of the production process. A flexible workforce should lead to increased labour productivity.
- The premises should be laid out in such a way that the time taken to transfer goods from raw material inventory holding to the production.

2 Tent Co

Helping hand. If you used different discount rates then you may have a slightly different answer, but it should be similar to the answer below.

Marking scheme

	Marks
NPV at different discount factors	3
IRR	2
	5

Calculate the NPV of the cash flows at two different discount factors.

Time	Net cash flow $	Discount factor at 10% $	Present value $	Discount factor at 5% $	Present value $
0	(65,000)	1	(65,000)	1	(65,000)
1	18,000	0.909	16,362	0.952	17,136
2	19,000	0.826	15,694	0.907	17,233
3	20,050	0.751	15,058	0.864	17,323
4	20,050	0.683	13,694	0.823	16,501
			(4,192)		3,193

NPV is positive at 5% and negative at 10%

If we assume that NPV falls at a constant rate between $3,193 at 5% and $(4,192) at 10%, this is a fall of $7,385 between 5% and 10%, an average fall of $7,385/5% = $1,477 in NPV for each 1% increase in the discount rate.

IRR is where the NPV = 0

$3,193/$1,477 = 2.16% above 5%

IRR = 7.16%

3 Treasury

> **Helping hand.** You should have found this a relatively straightforward recitation of book learning. Note that the suggested answer contains more than you would need for full marks.

Marking scheme

	Marks
1–3 marks per function	5
	5

Functions of the Treasury Department

- Corporate Financial objectives, financial aims and strategies, financial and treasury policies, financial and treasury systems.
- Liquidity management, making sure the organisation has the liquid funds it needs and invests surplus funds, including the management of banking relationships and money management.
- Funding management, the treasurer needs to know what sources of funds could be used to finance the organisation and the terms of the financing. The aim is to ensure that an organisation can borrow funds at the best terms possible.
- Currency management, for a company that is involved with international transactions with an exposure to foreign exchange risk, the treasurer should ensure that the risk from any foreign currency transactions is at an acceptable level.
- Corporate finance, including raising share capital and dividend policy.

Note. Only two were required.

4 Credit

> **Helping hand.** You are asked to define discounting and debt factoring with particular reference to difference recourse factoring makes, so ensure that you do clearly explain this.

Marking scheme

	Marks
Invoice discounting	Up to 2
Debt factoring	Up to 2
With and without recourse	Up to 2
Maximum	5

Invoice discounting is a service where a discounter purchases trade debts at a lower price than their face value. This enables the company from which the debts are purchased to raise working capital, while still extending credit to its customers. The administration of a client's receivables ledger is not taken over by the invoice discounter.

Debt factoring is related to discounting. It is an outsourcing arrangement in which the factor takes on responsibility of the credit control function on behalf of a client. The factor advances a proportion of the money it is due to collect to the client.

With recourse factoring, means that the factor can ask for their money back from the client if the customer does not pay their debt. The client bears the risk of irrecoverable debts.

Without recourse factoring means that the factor cannot ask for their money back from the client if the customer does not pay their debt. The factor bears the risk of irrecoverable debts.

5 Business angels

Marking scheme

	Marks
Define business angel	1
Disadvantages	1 mark each
Maximum	5

Business angels

Definition

Business angels are wealthy individuals or groups of individuals, who invest directly in smaller businesses.

Disadvantages

- This form of financing can be difficult to set up due to the informal nature of the finance (there is no formal marketplace for business angels).
- The money available from a Business angel may be limited, and large sums may only be available from a consortium of business angels.
- Business angels generally require a high return on their investment due to the high risk taken.
- Business angels may require a seat on the board, or another way to control the actions of the company.
- Business angels will require an exit route to realise their investment, such as flotation.

6 Mr Home

Helping hand. In relevant costing questions you will generally be asked to explain why you have assesed costs as being irrelevant, so make sure you include these in your answer. You will be throwing away marks if you neglect to do this!

Marking scheme

	Marks
1 mark per entry in the schedule, except for wood inventory, fixed overhead and labour which have 2 marks each.	14
Presentation	1
	15

Relevant costs

		$
Non-returnable deposit	This is a past/sunk cost, so not relevant	–
Fabric	Amount in inventory: relevant cost is sales proceeds forgone (11m × $30)	330
	Amount to be purchased : relevant cost is purchase price (9m × $50)	450
Wood	Amount in inventory: Relevant cost is sales proceeds forgone (12m × $29), as they are greater than the amount that could be saved ($400 – $60)	348
	Amount to be purchased: Relevant cost is purchase price (3m × $30)	90
Labour	Already fully utilised (55hrs × ($10 + $5)), is the contribution foregone before the cost of labour	825
Variable overhead	$8 × 55 hours: the future incremental cost	440
Fixed overhead	Ignore depreciation as it is not cash	–
	Ignore general business overheads as they are not incremental	–
Hire of machine	Required for 2 weeks $200 × 2 = $400. However the minimum hire charge is $450	450
Cost of preparing the statement	This is a past/sunk cost, so not relevant	–
Profit	Not a cash flow, so ignore	–
Minimum price		2,933

7 Fineed Co

Helping hand. This was primarily a narrative question with a simple calculation. If you have studied your text book, you should have found this quite straightforward. In part (c) make sure that you relate your answers to the specifics mentioned in the question. There were a lot of parts to the questions, with each part only scoring a few marks, so make sure you don't get carried away and spend too much time on any one part.

Marking scheme

			Marks
(a)	Gearing		
	Explanation		2
(b)	(i)	Raising extra finance 1 mark per point	2
	(ii)	Credit controlled 1 mark per point	2
(c)	Gearing calculation		
	Formula		1
	Calculation of ratio		2
	Comment		1
(d)	Interest cover		
	Definition		2
	Importance		3
			15

(a) **Gearing**

Companies are financed by different types of capital and each type expects a return in the form of interest or divident. Gearing is a method of comparing how much of the long-term capital of a business is provided by equity (ordinary shares and reserves, and prior charge capital (loan creditors and/or preference shares) In other words, it is a measure of the extent to which the net assets of a business are financed by long-term borrowing.

(b) (i) High gearing is where there is more debt finance than equity finance in the company. If the gearing of a company is considered too high, a company may find it difficult to raise finance through a finance provider as the risk of default could be thought too high.

(ii) Trade debts generally take a lower priority in a company's planning than interest payments on other types of debt, and if a company becomes insolvent secured loans would be paid first. If the gearing of new customer is considered too high, a credit controller may decide to refuse credit or set a lower credit limit.

(c) **Gearing**

There are two ways in which this can be calculated. Either:

Prior charge capital/Equity = $150,000/$400,000 = 0.375

or Prior charge capital/Total long-term capital = $150,000/($150,000 + $400,000) = 0.27

The calculations show that Fineed would generally be considered as having low gearing.

(d) **Interest cover**

Interest cover is a measure of financial risk which is designed to show the risks in terms of profit rather than in terms of capital values. It shows the number of times that **interest payments** are **'covered' by profits**.It is important to a bank when deciding whether or not to grant a loan, as it considers the ability of the borrower to pay the interest. A low level of interest cover would indicate a higher risk of default by an organisation.

Tell us what you think

Got comments or feedback on this book? Let us know.
Use your QR code reader:

Or, visit:

https://bppgroup.fra1.qualtrics.com/jfe/form/SV_3I4HcTxq3uoISCa

Need to get in touch with customer service?
www.bpp.com/request-support

Spotted an error?
www.bpp.com/learningmedia/Errata